Ayyubid Cairo

Ayyubid Cairo
A Topographical Study

Neil D. MacKenzie

The American University in Cairo Press

Dar el Kutub No. 7058/91
ISBN 977 424 275 0

Printed in Egypt by the American University in Cairo Press

Contents

Preface

Unless otherwise noted, dates are given in both their Hijra and Christian year, the Hijra first. A glossary of Arabic terms is contained in Appendix A. The letters *'ayn* and *hamza* are indicated by ' and ' respectively.

A table of Fatimid and Ayyubid rulers is given in Appendix B. Three maps are contained in the rear flap: 1) al-Qahira; 2) al-Qahira and its environs; and 3) al-Fustat. Site numbers for these are noted in the text, as well as in the list of numbered sites (Appendix C).

Introduction

The purpose of this study is to determine the physical changes brought about in the city of Cairo during the Ayyubid dynasty. Topographically this area encompasses the Fatimid enclosure of al-Qahira and all divisions of the Egyptian capital developed by the Ayyubids, viz:

a) the walled city of al-Qahira

b) al-Fustat

c) all land between al-Fustat and al-Qahira, especially that enclosed by Saladin's enceinte

d) new land created by the westward shift of the Nile

e) areas to the north and northwest of al-Qahira including al-Maqs and al-Husayniya

f) al-Qarafa (cemetery area east and northeast of al-Fustat)

g) the island of al-Roda

h) such aspects of Giza as had relevance to the building of Cairo, especially the arches (*qanatir*) of Qaraqush and the boat-bridges (*jusur*).

Chapter One

Cairo at the End of the Fatimid Dynasty

Al-Fustat, the first Islamic capital of Egypt, was founded in 20/640 by Arab forces besieging the Byzantine fortress of Babylon, now Qasr al-Sham'. Extending from the Nile to the Muqattam hills, al-Fustat was divided into quarters (*khitat*) for the various Arab tribes, radiating from the mosque of 'Amr ibn al-'As. With the Abbasid takeover of the caliphate in 132/750, the provincial capital shifted to al-'Askar, to the north of al-Fustat in the area of the present Midan Sayyida Zaynab. This in turn was eclipsed by the establishment of al-Qata'i' (literally, 'sections', for various regiments) by Ahmad ibn Tulun in 254/868. Al-Qata'i', located to the east of al-'Askar, was centered on Ibn Tulun's (extant) mosque, and extended to the present citadel. Following the overthrow of the Tulunid dynasty in 292/905, much of al-Qata'i' was destroyed and the combined area of the three cities became amalgamated under the common name of al-Fustat.

The Fatimid city of al-Qahira, founded by Jawhar al-Siqilli in 358/969 and completed in 361/971, was the fourth Islamic capital of Egypt. This walled city was established also to the north of al-Fustat, in a sparsely populated area occupied only by a convent, a small palace, the garden of the Ikhshidid ruler Kafur, and, on the bank of the Nile, the village of Umm Dunayn (later known as al-Maqs).[1] The western enceinte of al-Qahira overlooked the Khalij, a seasonal Nile-fed canal emanating from al-Fustat and proceeding to the north and northeast.

Al-Qahira was founded as a royal/religious quarter with its necessary support facilities, both military and logistic. The focal

2

point of the city was Bayn al-Qasrayn, an open parade ground between the two Fatimid palaces (eastern and western). Around the palaces were various markets, arsenals, kitchens, and other facilities for the royal family, its supporting staff, and military contingents. Specific quarters (*harat*) were assigned to divisions of the Fatimid army, both within the enceinte and immediately to its north and south. South of the palaces were the mosque of al-Azhar, center of Fatimid religious propaganda, the Dar al-'Ilm ('palace of sciences'), and various administrative and support facilities.[2]

The walled city of al-Qahira, as founded by Jawhar, contained buildings fulfilling five different functions:

a) living quarters—both royal and secular, often combined with administration

b) defense needs and quartering of troops

c) markets and arsenals for the provisioning of the above

d) religious centers

e) cemetery areas.

Living quarters and administration centers

The positions of the Fatimid palaces, based upon Maqrizi's description, have been adequately traced by Ravaisse. These palaces, while serving as the residences of the royal family and the harem, were also the main centers of pageant and ceremony for the Fatimid caliphate.[3] They were surrounded by smaller palaces and pavilions belonging to the royal family and various dignitaries. Other palaces and pavilions were constructed throughout al-Qahira, especially overlooking the Khalij (e.g. the pavilion of Lu'lu', founded by al-'Aziz).[4]

Defense needs and quartering of troops

The original enceinte of al-Qahira was built of mud brick, and a trench (*khandaq*) was dug on its northern side as further protection against Qarmatian incursions. Within these walls, exclusive of the royal/administrative complex in the central area, the city was divided into *harat* assigned to specific divisions of the Fatimid army. Military *harat* were established to the north and south of the city as well. According to the Persian traveler Nasir-i Khusraw the original walls were effectively eclipsed by 438/1046–47 as a result of extensive building both within and without.[5] To the west, at al-Maqs, a naval shipyard and arsenal were established early in the Fatimid period.

Markets and arsenals

The primary storehouses and arsenals for the Fatimid palaces were located to the south and east of the great eastern palace. Actual markets for the day-to-day provisioning of the caliphate and its entourage—royal, religious, administrative, and military—were centered on Bayn al-Qasrayn. The primary marketing and manufacturing area catering to the needs of the common people remained, however, al-Fustat.[6] Without specific authority the people of al-Fustat were denied entrance to the royal city, and contented themselves with their own still thriving commercial capital. Water, with the exception of certain wells of questionable capacity, was brought into the city on camel and donkeyback.[7]

Religious centers

The mosque of al-Azhar, to the south of the eastern palace, was the focal point of Fatimid religious policy and propaganda. Completed in 361/971–72, this was the first congregational mosque (*jami'*) in al-Qahira, followed by the al-Hakim mosque (just outside Bab al-Futuh) founded by the caliph al-'Aziz in 380/990–91.[8] Smaller mosques and chapels were located both within the city and without.

Cemetery areas

With the exception of Turbat al-Za'faran, the mausoleum of the Fatimid caliphs in the eastern palace, there were probably no tombs of any importance within the Fatimid enceinte during the early years of the caliphate. The cemetery area of this time was a continuation and extension of al-Qarafa at the east of al-Fustat. It was bounded (approximately) by al-Rasad and Basatin on the south, the Muqattam on the east, and the shrine (*mashhad*) of Sayyida Nafisa on the north. Al-Qarafa had been the primary burying ground of al-Fustat since the Islamic conquest, and included the tombs of such notables as 'Amr ibn al-'As, 'Uqba ibn Nafi', and the Imam al-Shafi'i.[9]

Suburbs and Extensions to the Early Fatimid City (exclusive of al-Fustat)

North and northwest of al-Qahira

The early Fatimids established several military *harat* to the north of al-Qahira. The most important was Harat al-Husayniya, which was itself divided into several quarters for various military units. Maqrizi divides al-Husayniya into two sections: the first was outside Bab al-Futuh and stretched to al-Khandaq, housing the army in Fatimid times; the second extended from Bab al-Nasr north to al-Ridaniya. Under the Fatimid caliphate, the latter area included nothing but Musalla al-'Id, an oratory founded by Jawhar.[10] According to Ibn 'Abd al-Zahir, al-Husayniya was inhabited by about seven thousand Armenians and included a number of markets (*aswaq*).[11] He gives no date for this settlement, but it may well be contemporary with the vizierate of Badr al-Jamali (466–87/1073–94).

Al-Maqs became a shipyard and arsenal for the Fatimid navy under the reign of al-Mu'izz (341–65/953–75). Located near the site of Bab al-Hadid (and the modern Ramses railway station), al-Maqs remained the port of al-Qahira for over two hundred years. Clerget has pointed out that the construction of a *jami'* at al-Maqs, the building of pavilions and palaces to the west of the Khalij, the restoration of the Khalij itself, the use of recent alluvial lands by the people of al-Qahira as recreation areas, and the necessity of maintaining contact with the port and arsenal all contributed to the development of this northwest suburb of al-Qahira. How 'soon,' however, the city 'included' al-Maqs, is questionable based upon the evidence Clerget presents.[12]

West, south, and southwest of al-Qahira

The west bank of the Khalij, south of al-Maqs and north of al-Hamra' al-Quswa (the northwestern boundary of al-Fustat), was primarily occupied by gardens and pavilions, including several ponds, e.g. Birkat Batn al-Baqara (later al-Azbakiya) and Birkat al-Farayin (in the present area of Bab al-Luq). As the alluvial lands extended farther to the west, other ponds were formed and gardens added. Overlooking the Khalij on both banks were pavilions, such as Manzarat al-Lu'lu' and Dar al-Dhahab. Much of this area served as promenades and recreation grounds for the people of al-Qahira, despite heavy flooding following the annual opening of the Khalij.[13]

To the south of Bab Zuwayla, the first Fatimid structure of note was Bab al-Jadid, built by al-Hakim (386–411/996–1021). Between Bab Zuwayla and the northern and northeastern banks of Birkat al-Fil, the Fatimids founded eight military *harat*. Some of these, such as Harat al-Yanisiya, were established by the early caliphs. Others, such as Harat al-Masamida, were granted to military contingents as late as the reign of al-Amir (495–524/1101–1131). According to Maqrizi, the buildings stretched from Bab al-Jadid to the empty spaces near the *mashhad* of Sayyida Nafisa during the Fatimid period, although he does not give any precise dates. Gardens were established along the east bank of Birkat al-Fil under the early Fatimids, and the shores of this pond—later surrounded by gardens—were effectively free of population until ca. 600/1203–1204.[14]

To the southeast of Bab Zuwayla, in the area of the present Darb al-Ahmar, was a cemetery dating from the foundation of the *harat* between Bab al-Jadid and Birkat al-Fil. This cemetery extended to the outcrop now occupied by the citadel of Cairo.[15] This outcrop was previously the site of Qubbat al-Hawa', a pavilion built in 194–95/809–811 by Hatim, Abbasid governor (*wali*) of Egypt. Qubbat al-Hawa' was supplanted by a number of mosques and tombs under the Fatimids.[16]

Al-Fustat and its Environs under the Early Fatimids

For the purpose of this study, we will consider al-Fustat in relationship with three of its neighboring areas, viz: the island of al-Roda immediately to its west; Birkat al-Habash and Basatin to its south; and al-Qarafa, the cemetery area to its east. These areas, with the possible exception of al-Qarafa, were historically and geographically associated with al-Fustat, rather than with al-Qahira, throughout the mediaeval period.

Despite the foundation of al-Qahira, al-Fustat, as the center of commerce, supply, and manufacturing, remained the economic mainstay of the capital. The texts of Ibn Hawqal, Nasir-i Khusraw, and al-Muqaddasi, supplemented by those of Maqrizi, Yaqut, Ibn Duqmaq, and Qalqashandi, give us physical descriptions of al-Fustat and its environs which, despite blatant contradictions even within the same narratives, probably present a reasonable picture of al-Fustat during the first half of the Fatimid period in Egypt.

The religious, commercial, and administrative center of al-Fustat was, from the time of its foundation in 20/641, the mosque of 'Amr. A center of scholarship and jurisprudence, this *jami'* was intensely restored and embellished under al-Hakim. Surrounding the mosque, except on the *qibla* (Mecca-facing) side, were the markets, the most famous of which was Suq al-Qanadil, immediately to the north. These markets were noted—especially by al-Muqaddasi and Nasir-i

Khusraw—for the quality of their wares, the variety of foreign merchandise, and the abundance and variety of fruits and vegetables indigenous to Egypt. Noted also were the number of merchant ships in the port, both indigenous and foreign, and travelers—presumably mostly merchants—from other Islamic countries and from Christian states as well. Local manufacturers produced ceramics, glass, metalwork, leather, and paper products of high quality; the artistic excellence of the pottery and glass is attested by numerous archaeological excavations over the last sixty years.[17]

Ibn Hawqal (ca. 367/978) describes al-Fustat as one third the size of Baghdad. In length about a parasang (four miles), al-Fustat was heavily populated and included vast empty spaces, enormous markets, imposing centers of commerce, large private terrains, flower gardens, and green parks, although the soil was generally saline. The majority of the houses were constructed in baked brick, often five to seven stories, with their ground floors usually unoccupied. Some of these houses were occupied by up to two hundred persons. There were two Friday mosques (*jawami'*), those of 'Amr and Ibn Tulun. Surrounding the mosque of Ibn Tulun were the ruins of al-Qata'i'.[18]

Al-Muqaddasi, who visited al-Fustat in 453/1061–62, gives us a description similar to that of Ibn Hawqal. However, while lauding the virtues of the commercial facilities and religious centers (he again lists two Friday mosques, 'Amr and Ibn Tulun), he embarks on a series of the city's shortcomings, including the narrowness of the streets, dirtiness of the houses and water, the excessive number of dogs, the presence of fleas, bedbugs, and mange, and the constant fear of famine.[19] Ibn Ridwan, physician to the caliph al-Hakim, describes al-Fustat as one of the most unhealthy cities imaginable. Its situation, in a basin with the river on the west and the Muqattam hills to the east, blocked easterly winds and subjected the city to the disadvantages, as well as the benefits, of a low-lying, semi-enclosed river port. While the higher levels of al-Fustat—'Amal Fawq and the area of the mosque of Ibn Tulun to the north, al-Qarafa to the east, and al-Sharaf to the south—admittedly were more hygienically situated, the conditions of the central section (that bordering the river) were highly unsanitary indeed. Not only were the houses high and the streets narrow, but the inhabitants were accustomed to throwing their dead animals into the streets to rot, as well as into the river itself. Latrines drained directly into the Nile, the direct source of almost all water supply. The fumes from the chimneys attached to the numerous baths of the city spread smoke throughout the area.

Dust, especially during the summer, was severe. Despite some immunity to these conditions, the people of al-Fustat were the most prone to disease of all Egyptians. During the winter and early spring, fish from the Mediterranean swimming upstream arrived at al-Fustat, where they putrefied, although they were apparently eaten nonetheless by the people of al-Fustat and al-Qahira. The Nile between al-Roda and al-Fustat was often dry during the late spring and early summer, and various waste materials were thrown into it to rot.[20] Clearly, Ibn Ridwan's al-Fustat is hardly a paragon of hygiene.

The description of al-Fustat by Nasir-i Khusraw, who visited it in 438/1047, while most informative, is nonetheless an exaggerated panegyric. His description of the port and market facilities has been briefly noted above. Al-Fustat, according to this Persian traveler, was built on elevated terrain, with the mosque of Ibn Tulun built on an eminence on the edge of the city. This suggests that the contemporary al-Fustat included the former capitals of al-'Askar and al-Qata'i', at least as far as the mosque of Ibn Tulun. Houses rose from seven to fourteen stories with up to 350 persons per house—in both cases obvious exaggerations. There were seven *jawami'* in the city, that of 'Amr being the central and most important. This stands opposed to the descriptions of al-Muqaddasi and Ibn Hawqal; perhaps Nasir-i Khusraw included certain mosques to the east such as Masjid al-Qarafa. The distinction between *masjid* and *masjid al-jami'* is in any case often blurred, in both mediaeval and modern definitions.

Along the Nile bank were many pavilions and kiosks. Water was raised and transported by means of water scoops (*sawaqi*) and camels, and channeled even to gardens atop houses within the city. Access to the island of al-Roda was facilitated by a bridge of thirty-six boats, although no bridge continued to Giza. There were more boats available along the Fustat riverbank than at either Basra or Baghdad.[21]

Nasir-i Khusraw, then, describes al-Fustat in glaring hyperbole. The manifold shortcomings discussed by Ibn Ridwan and al-Muqaddasi are not even hinted at. This, too, in the period immediately before the horrendous 'time of troubles' of al-Mustansir (v.i.). Nasir's description of al-Qahira is again, although eminently useful, greatly exaggerated. It is highly unlikely that the hygienic conditions prevailing in 438/1047 had changed significantly for the better since Ibn Ridwan's account; on the contrary, the successive narratives of Ibn Ridwan and al-Muqaddasi suggest deterioration.

Perhaps Nasir-i Khusraw's personal Shiite leanings partly blinded him to al-Fustat's deficiencies. In any case, one point is clear. Whatever al-Fustat's hygienic shortfalls, Nasir's extensive inventory of commercial products and local manufacturing shows that trade was flourishing at mid-fifth/eleventh century. This was immediately before the internal unrest and famines of al-Mustansir's reign brought catastrophic ruin and disorder. The people of al-Fustat enjoyed a security and prosperity that the traveler hardly saw equaled elsewhere.

The shipyards and dockyards built at al-Roda in 54/673–74 and 263/876–77 were, according to one account, supplanted by a third constructed at al-Fustat in 325/936–37 by Muhammad ibn Tughj al-Ikhshid. This dockyard was built at Bustan al-Jurf, near the entrance to the Khalij (to the east of the extant intake tower of the al-Ghuri acqueduct).[22]

Muhammad ibn Tughj, Maqrizi relates in his description of al-Roda, removed the Roda dockyard to al-Fustat and replaced it with the garden of al-Mukhtar. Elsewhere, however, he mentions the two dockyards existing simultaneously from the time of Muhammad ibn Tughj onward. During the reign of the caliph al-Amir, the vizier al-Ma'mun ibn al-Bata'ihi ordered that warships (*shuwani*) and Nile boats (*marakib niliya*) be built at the Fustat dockyard, which he enlarged, while the construction of warships (*harbiyat*) and decked warships (*shalandiyat*) was to be concentrated at al-Roda. The Fustat dockyard, Maqrizi further notes, lasted until shortly before 700/1300–1301 when it became a garden, Bustan Ibn Kisan. (This, no doubt, was the result of the alluviation of the Nile on its eastern shore.)[23]

The island (*jazira*) of al-Roda, beyond its military associations, was, under the early Fatimids, a populated city (*madina*) with a *wali* and a judge (*qadi*). During the reign of al-'Aziz one spoke of "al-Qahira, Misr, and al-Jazira."[24] A *jami'*, many elaborate houses, pavilions, and gardens adorned al-Roda at the time Nasir-i Khusraw saw it. He states, however, that there was *formerly* a town here, suggesting that the island had by then become an exclusive area of retreat. Giza, on the other hand, was a major commercial center and the point of departure for Maghribi caravans, as well as a much sought-after locale for pavilions and villas, well away from the less sanitary conditions of al-Fustat.[25]

Birkat al-Habash, to the south of al-Fustat, was the largest of the alluvial ponds in the Cairo area. It was at least partially supplied by Nile water through Khalij Bani Wa'il and two smaller intermediary ponds. Birkat al-Habash was the site of several pavilions of the Fatimid nobility.[26] To the north was al-Qarafa (later al-Qarafa al-Kubra), a cemetery containing burials of early religious and political figures, a center of pilgrimage with important—often monumental—mosques, shrines (mashahid), and tombs. Al-Qarafa, during the Fatimid period, was also the site of numerous palaces and other secular retreats (qusur, jawasiq) for the nobility of Cairo; it had already become a 'city of the dead.' While Clerget considers al-Qarafa at this time "un exemplaire typique de la cité funéraire musulmane," there was not, to my knowledge, a similar phenomenon on the same scale anywhere else in the Islamic world.[27]

Al-Qahira at Mid-Fifth Century

The sources on al-Qahira, in the middle of the fifth/eleventh century, are, as for al-Fustat, primarily Nasir-i Khusraw, Maqrizi, and Ibn Ridwan. Ibn Hawqal, in a brief description of al-Qahira ca. 367/978, noted that the walls of Jawhar enclosed an open area three times more vast than that actually built upon. These free spaces were intended as animal reserves in case of attack. Seventy years later the city still apparently maintained much free space. According to Nasir-i Khusraw, the houses were separated by orchards and gardens, so that the trees of one did not touch the walls of another, and one house could be destroyed without damaging the next. The palaces, described in great detail (although not approaching the detail of Maqrizi), were of great height, with no adjoining construction. As previously mentioned, Nasir-i Khusraw states that the city was not enclosed in a fortified wall, but that the buildings and houses themselves were higher than a rampart, some of them five to six stories. The houses of al-Qahira were built of precious marble, not of plaster, brick, or ordinary stone. In the city were twenty thousand shops, many of which were leased, along with innumerable caravanserais (khanat), and other public edifices. Nasir mentions four jawami' in al-Qahira: al-Azhar, al-Nur, al-Hakim, and al-Mu'izz (al-Maqs).[28]

Nasir-i Khusraw notes that wells dug near the Nile furnished al-Qahira with sweet water, while those farther removed became brackish. Potable water was carried from the Nile by camels, while individual water-carriers circulated in those streets where camels could not pass. Within the city, wells—sometimes equipped with hydraulic lifts—serviced orchards and gardens. The space between al-Qahira and Misr (al-Fustat) was filled with gardens and some houses; "during the summer, this entire plain resembles an ocean, with the garden of the sultan, which, situated on an eminence, is not inundated." The site of this garden is not certain.[29]

Ibn Ridwan, writing, perhaps, at mid-fifth/eleventh century, finds al-Qahira considerably more hygienic than al-Fustat. More open to the air, with lower houses and better streets, al-Qahira was generally less infected and further from decay, especially as most waste materials were dumped outside the city. Al-Qahira was not without its imperfections, however. Most of its water came from wells with little capacity and so shallow that they were infiltrated by latrines. The depressions between al-Fustat and al-Qahira were filled by ground leakage (*rashsh al-ard*) during the days of inundation. Some of the drains of al-Qahira emptied into these depressions, resulting in contaminated water, and oppressive vapors emanated towards both al-Qahira and al-Fustat. A southerly wind brought the foul air of both al-Fustat and these depressions to al-Qahira, especially to its southern quarters. In addition, during flood seasons, the people of al-Qahira drank the water of the Khalij, which had already passed through the contamination of the Fustat shore. Indeed, Ibn Ridwan places the blame for most of al-Qahira's hygienic short-comings on its proximity to al-Fustat. In terms of hygiene the physician rates the following localities best to worst: al-Qarafa, al-Qahira, al-Sharaf (the heights immediately south of al-Fustat), 'Amal Fawq and al-Hamra', Giza, with al-Fustat the worst, especially around the mosque of 'Amr. He describes al-Maqs (situated on the Nile bank) as humid, and al-Khandaq as low and swampy.[30]

The descriptions of al-Qahira by both Nasir-i Khusraw and Ibn Ridwan—even given Nasir's hyperbole and Ibn Ridwan's somewhat severe, although probably not unrealistic, criticism of health conditions—portray al-Qahira as considerably more attractive than al-Fustat. The depressions (*bata'ih*) between al-Qahira and al-Fustat probably refer to Birkat al-Fil, Birkat Qarun, and Birkat Farayin.[31] The gardens and few houses in the area of these alluvial ponds, while perhaps presenting a welcome respite to the residents of the two cities, were nonetheless subject to the discomforts and diseases found throughout the area. There is, however, one salient point. Despite Nasir-i Khusraw's exaggerations and Ibn Ridwan's negative portrayals, al-Qahira and al-Fustat were still thriving communities in

438/1047. The catastrophic crises of al-Mustansir's reign, although imminent, had yet to descend upon the Egyptian capital.

The Crises of the Reign of al-Mustansir
(ca. 450–66/1058–74)

The political crises of this period are well documented and will be dealt with only briefly here. Beginning in 446/1054–55, a combination of Turkish and Berber soldiers vied for supremacy over the Sudanese slave troops, and the resulting conflict, in conjunction with a series of low Niles, brought twenty years of anarchy, famine, and epidemic not only to the Egyptian capital but throughout the entire country as well. One vizier, al-Yazuri, managed to maintain a degree of control over the warring factions, but after his assassination in 450/1058, chaos reigned supreme. Until the appointment of Badr al-Jamali in 466/1074, the caliphate remained without an effective vizier, and al-Mustansir became essentially a pawn in the hands of the Turkish soldiery. With the black troops driven to Upper Egypt and the Berbers (former allies of the Turks) chased into the Delta, the Turks were left in control of the capital. While provinces were subjected to brigandage, al-Qahira and al-Fustat suffered from looting and despoliation by the Turks.[32]

The most severe period of this crisis was that of the great famine of 457–64/1064–72. Beside the vicissitudes of the river, the anarchy of the countryside was a major factor. The incessant raiding and counterraiding of Turks, Berbers, and Sudanese throughout the provinces greatly damaged—if not destroyed—the irrigation systems throughout Egypt. According to the genealogist al-Jawwani, "The Nile continued to rise and fall, but none could be found who would sow the land. Fear of the soldiers and the brigandage of the slaves reigned throughout." The ensuing famine and epidemic in al-Qahira and al-Fustat with its concurrent high prices, starvation to the point of cannibalism, and a soaring mortality rate, resulted in the abandonment, looting, and eventual destruction of innumerable buildings—residences and otherwise—throughout the area.[33]

According to Maqrizi,

Because of this famine, al-Fustat was destroyed; the emplacements of al-'Askar and al-Qata'i' were abandoned, as well as the region adjoining al-Fustat from al-Qarafa (where the rubble mounds [akwam] are today) to Birkat al-Habash. When the Amir al-Juyush Badr al-Jamali arrived and became head of the government, the rubble was removed from the region adjoining Misr near al-Qahira where al-'Askar and al-Qata'i' formerly had been; there was only an empty space and *akwam* between Misr and al-Qahira and between Misr and al-Qarafa. The state of affairs [prosperity] of al-Fustat returned almost to that reached before the crisis.[34]

This passage warrants both elucidation and expansion. It was indeed the appointment of Badr al-Jamali that, in addition to an adequate harvest in 465/1072–73, raised the capital and the country as a whole from the depth of anarchy and ruin. The warring factions were suppressed, if not eliminated; the economy was restored. Permanent changes had, however, befallen al-Qahira and al-Fustat. Whereas depopulation and abandonment had occurred throughout, the revitalization of al-Qahira as the actual capital was of the most immediate importance. The reuse of building materials within the city apparently stripped much, but not all, of the building remnants of the former areas of al-Qata'i' and al-'Askar. Earlier on the vizier al-Bazuri had ordered the building of a wall to hide the ruins of al-Qata'i' and al-'Askar. This wall was constructed between the ruins and the road upon which the caliph traveled to al-Fustat. In addition, al-Bazuri built a second wall (probably for the same purpose) near the mosque of Ibn Tulun. That many of these ruins remained, however, is evident from Maqrizi's later narrative of events during the reign of the caliph al-Amir (495–524/1101–1131).[35]

The most significant construction under Badr was the rebuilding and extension of the walls and gates of al-Qahira itself. As mentioned earlier, the mud brick walls of Jawhar were effectively eclipsed at the time of Nasir-i Khusraw's visit (although occasional remnants were visible and recorded by Maqrizi as late as the ninth century of the Hijra). While the relative positioning of the gates remained effectively unchanged, the walls themselves were extended. On the western side, the wall was extended somewhat closer to the edge of the Khalij, enough to enclose a new north-south street, then and now known as Shari' Bayn al-Surayn. The new eastern wall enclosed slightly more territory, particularly in the area of Harat al-Bataliya. The northern wall—much of which is still extant—now encompassed Harat al-Rihaniya and the mosque of al-Hakim, while the southern enceinte now reached the present Bab Zuwayla. As one can see from the plans of Ravaisse and Creswell, the amount of new territory enclosed is not significant. This is, perhaps, due to the amount of devastation within and the necessity for the restoration of the original area.[36]

The salient point is this. What had been greater Fustat (the combined areas of al-Fustat, al-'Askar, and al-Qata'i') was now reduced to an area whose eastern boundary ran, approximately, from the western point of Birkat al-Habash to the neighborhood of the mosque of Ibn Tulun. The farthest delimitation of al-Fustat came a century later.[37]

The Reigns of the Caliphs al-Amir and al-Hafiz (495–544/1101–1149)

The vizierate of Badr al-Jamali, followed by that of his son al-Afdal (d.515/1121), resulted in a period of relative stability and prosperity for al-Qahira. During this period, and the remainder of al-Amir's reign, several changes occurred in the suburban areas of the capital.

Northern section

To the north of Bab al-Nasr were unused spaces, with the exception of the garden of al-Ridan (Ridaniya) and Musalla al-'Id. The tomb of Badr al-Jamali (d. 487/1094) was the progenitor of Bab al-Nasr cemetery; this area remained a burial ground until after 700/1300–1301. To the north of Bab al-Futuh were gardens and a pavilion. After 500/1106–1107 a band (ta'ifa) of Husayniya built a number of houses outside Bab al-Futuh, stretching to al-Khandaq.[38]

Western section

The area between the Khalij and the eastern bank of the Nile was extended by alluvial deposits around 500/1106–1107; according to Maqrizi, the Nile retreated to expose Minsha'at al-Fadil (later Minsha'at al-Mahrani), together with Bustan al-Khashshab. These areas were within the modern districts of Fam al-Khalij and Sayyida Zaynab; they will be discussed in detail below. This was also the time of the formation of Jazirat al-Fil, opposite Ard al-Ba'l (north of al-Maqs). This former island is now included in the modern district of Shubra. With those two exceptions, the Nile bank between Minsha'at al-Mahrani and Ard al-Ba'l remained relatively stable throughout the Fatimid period; the alluviation, according to Maqrizi, increased gradually between 500/1106–1107 and 700/1300–1301. These 'new lands' added to earlier districts such as al-Luq were, by and large, composed of gardens interspersed with alluvial ponds. They remained, as in the earlier years of the Fatimid dynasty, favorite locales for promenades and for the construction of pavilions to escape the crowded and unhygienic conditions of al-Qahira and al-Fustat.[39]

Southern and southeastern areas

To the south of al-Qahira the ruined areas of al-Qata'i', al-'Askar, and al-Fustat remained effectively as they had been during the vizierate of Badr al-Jamali. While substantial amounts of building material were removed by Badr for reconstruction within al-Qahira, there were apparently enough building remnants to warrant the order for redevelopment issued by the vizier al-Bata'ihi, probably shortly after 515/1121–22. His edict declared that, for a period of three days, anyone owning a house or property in the ruined areas of al-Qahira or Misr (al-Fustat) must either reoccupy it or rebuild upon it. Those who could not afford rebuilding must either sell or lease such property or forfeit their rights of ownership. In addition a wall was built to hide the ruins of al-'Askar and al-Qata'i' (whether this wall was indeed secondary to that of al-Bazuri is questionable.)[40]

Such rebuilding and rejuvenation as occurred appears to have been located within the immediate vicinity of Shari' al-A'zam, the main thoroughfare even to the present day, between Bab Zuwayla and the *mashhad* of Sayyida Nafisa.[41] In the Fatimid period, this artery divided into two main branches at the *saliba*, or cross street, still extant to the northeast of the mosque of Ibn Tulun. These branches were the principal roads between al-Qata'i' and al-Fustat. The eastern road continued the line of Shari' al-A'zam to the *mashhad* of Sayyida Nafisa, where it turned to the southwest and ran directly to Bab al-Safa', the eastern gateway to al-Fustat. The western road, a continuation of the *saliba*, crossed the Jisr al-A'zam, or grand dike, between Birkat al-Fil and Birkat Qarun. It then proceeded southwest to Fam al-Khalij and Bab al-Sahil, and followed the al-Fustat shore to Qasr al-Sham' and the mosque of 'Amr.[42]

The latter, or western, route was the road followed by the caliph when he officiated at the annual opening of the Khalij. The eastern route was, according to Salmon, that used by the caliph on his processions to al-Fustat to pray at the mosque of 'Amr. Although Salmon's source for this assertion is uncertain, as the most direct route from al-Qahira to al-Fustat it is highly plausible. The walls constructed to hide the ruinous areas of al-Qata'i' and al-'Askar were probably built along one or both of these thoroughfares.[43]

As mentioned above, the first structure built outside Bab Zuwayla was Bab al-Jadid, constructed by the caliph al-Hakim. This was followed by the establishment of several military *harat*, including Harat al-Yanisiya and Harat al-Hilaliya.[44] These foundations were established on both sides of Shari' al-A'zam, which developed simultaneously as the principal route from al-Qahira to al-Fustat and as an artery serving the military *harat* themselves. One of the larger *harat*, that of al-Masamida, was founded under al-Amir by the vizier al-Bata'ihi after 515/1121–22. As well as accommodating the military faction under the leadership of 'Abd Allah al-Masmudi, this *hara* also enhanced al-Bata'ihi's plan for redevelopment of the area.[45] The reconstruction effort, it appears, was largely concentrated on the Shari' al-A'zam artery and its eastern continuation to al-Fustat. Ibn 'Abd al-Zahir states:

> [The people] built until no ruins came between the two cities [al-Qahira and Misr]. They built in the street [i.e. outside Bab Zuwayla] from Bab al-Jadid to the *jabal* [mountain] in width. The *jabal* is the present location of the citadel. . . . They built to such an extent that workers and officials performed the last evening prayer in al-Qahira and returned to their homes in Misr with light, lamps, and illuminated markets extending to Bab al-Safa'. . . . Thus, one who goes out from Bab al-Jadid al-Hakimi [has] on the right Birkat al-Fil extending to Bustan Sayf al-Islam and a number of gardens. In front of those places were inhabited shops extending to Misr. The activity continued both day and night.[46]

Further building activity occurred under the reign of al-Hafiz (524–44/1130–49), on the same line as Harat al-Masamida and to its south; the southern limit is uncertain, but Maqrizi believes it to have reached the area of the *mashhad* of Sayyida Nafisa, i.e., following roughly the same course as Shari' al-A'zam. These buildings were, according to Ibn 'Abd al-Zahir, houses with shops on their ground floors.[47]

In describing the outskirts (*zuwahir*) of Fatimid Cairo, Maqrizi states that the plain between Shari' al-A'zam and the *jabal* (site of the present citadel) was, with the exception of the military *harat* (al-Yanasiya, al-Hilaliya, and later, al-Masamida) empty of buildings until after 500/1106–1107. When the vizier al-Salih Tala'i' constructed his mosque just to the southeast of Bab Zuwayla (555/1160), the area behind this mosque, extending to the former region of al-Qata'i' (i.e.

the present Rumayla beneath the citadel), became a cemetery for the people of al-Qahira until the end of the Fatimid dynasty.[48] While this does not categorically rule out Maqrizi's earlier statement that the reconstruction under al-Bata'ihi extended to the above-mentioned *jabal*, it is highly unlikely that a major building development (ca. 515/1121–22) made way for a cemetery area forty years later in an area described as empty. The evidence would suggest, then, that Maqrizi's former statement is an exaggeration.[49] Al-Bata'ihi's redevelopment probably followed, almost strictly, Shari' al-A'zam and its eastern extension to al-Fustat.

The 564/1168 Fire

Al-Fustat was burned to prevent the Crusaders under Amalric from using it as a vantage point from which to attack the walled city of al-Qahira. The point in question is the extent of the burning vis-a-vis the areas ruined previous to the fire. This question is particularly relevant to that part of al-Fustat, principally around the mosque of 'Amr and Qasr al-Sham', which remained relatively intact and which was restored and repopulated under Saladin. There is, to date, no undisturbed archaeological evidence of Ayyubid occupation at al-Fustat. Such evidence might suggest either a period of continuous occupation or Fatimid remains with evidence of Ayyubid rebuilding; it has yet to be found. Excavations by George Scanlon on Kawm al-Jarih and to the east of the mosque of 'Amr have shown undisturbed deposits that generally suggest an abandonment of the area during the late fifth/eleventh century.[50] The more extensive excavations of 'Ali Bahgat, to the east of Qasr al-Sham', were, unfortunately, not systematically controlled, and stratigraphic evidence is lacking. They did expose part of the enclosure wall of Saladin (572/1176–77, v.i.), which was built over previous ruins. The date of the ruin of the underlying structures, however, remains uncertain. Post-fire looting, removal of building materials, and incessant dumping have precluded an ash layer; while there may be occasional signs of burning on building remnants, it would be impossible to prove that they resulted from a specific fire.

Given the preservation of the 'Amr mosque, Qasr al-Sham', and the areas of al-Fustat which were later restored (v.i.), it is unlikely that the 564/1168 fire spread much farther to the west than the eastern boundary of al-Fustat in Mamluk, and, indeed, present times. This is corroborated by Abu Salih's description of the local churches, which will be examined in the discussion of Ayyubid Fustat in Chapter Three.

Summary

Immediately following the 564/1168 fire, the general topography of greater Cairo was as follows. Al-Qahira, ravaged by the vicissitudes of the previous century and overcrowded with the refugees of al-Fustat, remained roughly within the limits of the walls of Badr al-Jamali. Major extensions took place in al-Husayniya to the north and in the *barat* to the south of Bab Zuwayla. Recent cemetery areas included that of Bab al-Nasr and that between Bab Zuwayla and al-Rumayla. The lands between al-Qahira and the Nile were occupied by gardens and the occasional pavilion, as was the vicinity of Birkat al-Fil and Birkat Qarun to the southeast. The former areas of al-'Askar, al-Qata'i', and the lion's share of al-Fustat were ruinous; al-Qarafa probably remained relatively stable. The island of al-Roda, like the area of Birkat al-Fil, remained largely an area of gardens, promenades, and pavilions.

Chapter Two

The Ayyubids of Egypt: An Historical Summary

By the middle of the sixth/twelfth century, the Fatimid caliphate had experienced irreversible decline. The caliphs, stripped of real power, had become pawns of largely unscrupulous and frequently changing viziers. Internal rivalries between palace factions, conflicts between military elements (Turks, Sudanese), and internecine strife further weakened the administration. Truncated in area, the Fatimid domain included little more than Egypt itself and its northeastern approaches from Palestine. Anarchy, famine, plague, the non-collection of taxes, and the debasement of coinage sapped the economy, although the agricultural, manufacturing, and commercial activities of Egypt remained relatively unscathed. It was, rather, political turmoil which had brought the caliphate to its breaking point.[1]

The nadir and extinction of the Fatimid caliphate were directly associated with the aggressive and mutually hostile policies of two dynamic personalities: Amalric, Crusader king of Jerusalem; and Nur al-Din, Zangid ruler of Mosul, Aleppo, and Damascus. Nur al-Din's designs on Egypt were fostered by three factors. Firstly, the weakened condition of the Fatimid caliphate rendered Egypt vulnerable to the Crusaders, against whom Nur al-Din had declared religious war (*jihad*). Secondly, he hoped to use Egypt's economic resources to finance his campaigns. And thirdly, he wished to restore orthodox Islam to Egypt. The Crusaders, on the other hand, stymied by the Zangids to their north and northeast, naturally looked towards Egypt to further their aggressive policies. The Fatimid vizier Shawar, attempting to maintain his precarious hold on the government, played the Zangids off against the Crusaders by a combination of skillful diplomacy and outright deceit. Between 558/1162–63 and 564/1168, the Crusaders and Zangids each invaded Egypt three times, culminating in Amalric's abortive siege of al-Qahira and his final retreat to Palestine before the imminent approach of Nur al-Din's forces.

Among the mainstays of Nur al-Din's regime—both militarily and politically—were Ayyub ibn Shadhi and his brother Shirkuh. Of Kurdish origin, they had risen through numerous vicissitudes to be governor of Damascus and commander of the Zangid armies respectively. It was Shirkuh, accompanied by his nephew Salah al-Din ibn Ayyub (Saladin), who led the successive Egyptian expeditions culminating in the execution of Shawar and his own assumption of the vizierate of the now moribund Fatimid caliphate. Saladin, a seasoned commander at the age of thirty, had already established his military prowess in the reinforcement of Bilbays and the defense of Alexandria against Amalric. On the death of Shirkuh only weeks after he had acquired the Fatimid vizierate, Saladin succeeded him in that post and as commander of the Syrian expeditionary force in Egypt.

Between 564/1169 and 567/1171, Saladin—despite a Crusader attack on Damietta and a major rebellion in al-Qahira—attained undisputed leadership of Egypt, thanks to his reorganization and refinancing of the Fatimid armies and the grudging support of Nur al-Din. His final suppression of the Fatimid caliphate and the official restoration of Egypt to Sunni Islam was followed shortly by the death of the caliph al-'Adid (567/1171). The remaining members of the Fatimid family were placed under permanent house arrest. Saladin then became de facto ruler of Egypt, and we may consider this the effective beginning of the Ayyubid regime. Saladin still professed subservience to Nur al-Din, but relations became strained to the breaking point because of Saladin's inability and/or unwillingness to render substantial financial and military support in the effort against the Crusaders. The opportune death of Nur al-Din in 569/1174 prevented an almost certain outbreak of hostilities.

Nur al-Din's successors being relatively weak and ineffective, a vacuum was established in the Near East which was rapidly filled by Saladin and immediate members of his family. Egypt, Muslim Syria, the Yemen, and several districts of Mesopotamia came under Ayyubid control, and expeditionary conquests established the regime—at least temporarily—in Nubia and Tripolitania. Under the suzerainty of Saladin, the Ayyubid family—assisted by a largely Kurdo–Turkish military cadre—founded a Near Eastern empire which lasted for some eighty years, with Cairo as its capital. Undergoing many changes of fortune, generally for the worse, the Ayyubid regime in Egypt can be effectively divided into three periods: its apogee under Saladin and his son al-'Aziz; a period of holding and consolidation under al-Malik al-'Adil and al-Malik al-Kamil; and a rapid decline under al-Malik al-Salih.

Saladin's policy of aggrandizement had as its ostensible theme the liquidation of the Crusader kingdoms and the restoration of Sunni Islam. As Ehrenkreutz suggests, a more realistic appraisal might place considerable emphasis on simple personal ambition. However, Saladin did indeed repress the major Shiite concentrations in Egypt and the Yemen, and considerably truncated the Crusader realm, capturing Jerusalem in 583/1187.[2] The Third Crusade, however, and the surrender of Acre to the Franks (587/1191), curtailed Saladin's advances. With some of its territory restored, the kingdom of the Crusaders survived for yet another century. Following Saladin's death at Damascus (589/1193), his son al-'Aziz succeeded him in Egypt, while other family members acquired provinces of varying importance. Al-'Aziz's death in 595/1198–99 resulted in an interfamiliar civil war, in which al-Malik al-'Adil, Saladin's brother, ultimately established himself and his family as the dominant power within the Ayyubid empire.

The regime of al-'Adil and his son, al-Malik al-Kamil, was one of stabilization and detente with the Crusaders. Al-'Adil, the senior member of the Ayyubid family, had continuously proven himself a faithful ally of his elder brother; the consistent wrangling between the sons of Saladin necessitated the interposition of a strong hand. Having proclaimed himself sultan at Cairo in 597/1200, al-'Adil

> distributed the governments of Damascus and Djazira among his sons, and after the last hostilities in [A.D.] 1201, of the other former princes, he only permitted those of Aleppo, Hims, and Hama, who were forced to do homage to him, to continue to exist.[3]

Negotiations with the Crusaders resulted, under al-Malik al-Kamil, in the restoration of Jerusalem, Bethlehem, and Nazareth to the Franks. As Cahen points out, the 'Adili line followed a policy of detente, firstly in order to improve its trading relations with Europe, and secondly "to avoid giving pretext for further Crusades. Further

Crusades did in fact take place, but their immediate initiative came entirely from Europe, rather than from the Franks of the east."[4]

Since Egypt was the economic and military mainstay of the Ayyubid empire, such unity and cohesion as existed within that empire were generally based on Cairo, usually in association with Damascus. Later Crusader activity—emanating from Europe—thus concentrated on Damietta while (at least through the reign of al-Malik al-Kamil) relative peace was maintained with the Franks of the Levant. Although occasionally at pains to maintain family unity, al-Kamil generally managed to control the Ayyubid domains. This was due, firstly, to the force of his personality, and secondly, to his victory in the Fifth Crusade (615–18/1218–21). A major civil war following his death, however, resulted in the accession to the sultanate of al-Malik al-Salih, al-Kamil's eldest son, who had been entrusted with the government of Hisn Kayfa (now in southeastern Turkey). It was raw power which ultimately rendered al-Salih suzerain of Egypt and Ayyubid Syria, and his choice of allies—as well as foes—sowed the seeds of the imminent dissolution of the Ayyubid domain. His use of Khwarazmian troops in wars against his relatives in Syria and the Jazira created widespread devastation and resentment. This resulted in an alliance of al-Nasir Da'ud and al-Salih Isma'il (Ayyubid rulers of Karak and Damascus) with the Franks, and ultimately in the crusade of St. Louis of 647/1249. In addition, al-Salih's massive procurement and utilization of Turkish slave–soldiers (*mamalik*, singular *mamluk*) as the mainstay of the Egyptian army fostered the overthrow of his dynasty shortly after his death (647/1249) and the establishment of the Mamluk kingdom in Egypt and, ultimately, Syria.[5]

The dynamics of the Ayyubid establishment—political aggrandizement and the *jihad*—were supported by five basic elements: the military, the religious establishment, foreign trade, the internal economic and social developments of Egypt, and the bureaucratic structure of the administration.

The Military

The armies of Saladin, as previously stated, were based on Kurdo–Turkish troops. They were augmented, in the initial period, by residual Fatimid contingents and Arab tribal forces.[6] Undoubtedly, *mamalik* were used throughout Ayyubid rule, but they became the core of the military forces only under al-Malik al-Salih. Because of an almost consistent cash shortage, amirs were often assigned the income from specific industries (*iqta'*) in return for the maintenance of a certain amount of armed men, usually cavalry. Various family members and powerful amirs (when not warring among themselves) supplied military contingents for the Egyptian administration from their own appanages. This was especially true at such times as the Cairo–Damascus liaison remained intact. A major weakness in this system was that individual regiments frequently were attached only to a specific leader, and the disappearance of the leader

> did not entail that of the body or bodies of troops formed by him, within which there prevailed a vigilant solidarity, arising out of fear of the new bodies of troops. The rivalries between Asadiyya (from Asad al-Din Shirkuh), Salahiyya, 'Adiliyya, Kamiliyya, Ashrafiyya etc. play a great part in the quarrels between Ayyubid pretenders.[7]

Major external enemies included the Rum Seljuks, the Artukids, the Georgians, and, of course, the Crusaders. The Egyptian navy, reequipped by Saladin, scored considerable success against the Crusaders, but was almost irreparably destroyed during the siege of Acre (585–87/1189–91).[8] Egypt was thenceforth secured by the elimination of fortified places (including Ascalon) which could be used by the Crusaders to attack the Delta; by the construction of new fortifications (e.g. Damietta); by the land army; and by espionage.[9] In addition, citadels (both urban and rural), and city walls were constructed or refurbished throughout the realm.

The Religious Establishment

As the champion of Sunni Islam, Saladin vigorously pursued the suppression of the heterodox regimes in Egypt and the Yemen, in addition to his campaigns against the Crusaders. While his altruism may be open to question, considerable territory was indeed restored to the spiritual sovereignty of the Abbasid caliphate at Baghdad. The Egyptian religious establishment (*'ulama'*), predominantly Shafi'i, were often directly involved with the secular administration of the government. Orthodoxy was encouraged by the introduction of the religious school (*madrasa*) to Egypt, an institution already well established in Zangid territories. By founding a monastery for dervishes (*khanqah*) at Cairo, Saladin promoted the arrival of Sufism.[10]

Christians and Jews were reasonably well treated under the Ayyubids, and Christians were frequently employed within the Egyptian bureaucracy. Such anti-Christian sentiment as emerged was generally a counter-effect of the Crusades, and was sporadic at worst. As Cahen points out, "The Ayyubid period in Egypt was one of vitality for the Coptic church."[11]

Foreign Trade

The Ayyubids almost consistently supported trade with Europe. Saladin encouraged commercial intercourse with the merchants of Pisa, Genoa, and Venice, who flocked to Alexandria to take advantage of the transit trade between Egypt and the Red Sea. However, non-Muslim traders were barred from the Red Sea area. The trade with Italy supplied, in addition to customs revenues, necessary raw materials for both the navy and the army. Later Ayyubids, particularly al-'Adil and al-Kamil, fostered improved trading relations with the Europeans, except during the periods of major Crusader attacks.

> A normal and intended consequence of the peace policy adopted towards the Franks was the resumption and intensification of commercial relations with the Italians (and now, to a lesser extent the Southern French and the Catalans). Even before formal treaties had been concluded once more, as is shown by the private documents in the Venetian and Genoan archives, Genoan, Pisan, and Venetian ships, after the Third Crusade, were once again going to Alexandria, and to a lesser extent, Damietta. Under al-'Adil, a series of agreements confirmed their rights, a reduction in customs dues, and administrative and judicial facilities. . . . Egypt sold to Europe, besides the products of the Indian Ocean which passed through its territory in transit, native resources, the chief of which at this time seems to have been alum. Naturally the Crusades, or the fear of surprise attacks, were liable to provoke crises, as for instance the day in [A.D.] 1215 when three thousand merchants assembled at Alexandria were temporarily arrested. But even after the Damietta crusade, relations were resumed . . . and lasted in the main without undue interruption until the middle of the century.[12]

Internal Economic and Social Developments

Egypt was the economic mainstay for the rest of the Ayyubid regime. The internal stability enjoyed by Egypt (and at certain times by Ayyubid Syria) fostered almost ideal conditions for agriculture, foreign and domestic commerce, and manufacturing. Under Saladin, most of the non-canonical taxes (*mukus*) were eliminated, and the collection of canonical taxes vastly improved. On the other hand, the coinage was seriously debased.[13] Later Ayyubids, especially al-'Adil and al-Kamil, coupled expedient foreign policy with a sound internal administration. This was particularly true under the ministry of Ibn Shukr, who served as vizier (although not consistently) to both these rulers. Al-Kamil's special interests included

> maintenance of forests, irrigation works, state cultivation of sugar cane, etc. In general Egypt, in contradistinction to the other Ayyubid states, remained, as always, the country par excellence with a partially nationalized economy, especially for mining and forest production, trade in metals and wood, certain means of transport, and tools, arms, etc.[14]

Careful financial administration also included close supervision of the *iqta'* system.

Administrative/Bureaucratic Structure

The Ayyubid establishment was a loosely federated structure, which, under the best conditions, was centrally controlled by the suzerain at Cairo and/or Damascus. The individual territories were ruled—almost autonomously—by various members of the Ayyubid family, often with lesser relatives and important amirs ruling smaller segments within these territories. This system lacked cohesion and only worked under the authority of a firm central rule. The alternative (often the case) was interfamiliar alliances and outright warfare. While the term *sultan* was only occasionally employed, the basic concept of the sultanate was firmly established in Egypt, to be developed by the following regime of the Bahri Mamluks. Viziers were only occasionally employed by the ruler at Cairo, although they frequently served the lesser princes in the appanages. Often a deputy (*na'ib*) was assigned to replace the sultan on his absences from Egypt. Under the later Ayyubids such deputies were frequently assigned to the Asiatic provinces to replace recalcitrant princes. The central administration was divided into four major divisions (*dawawin*, singular *diwan*), those of the army, the treasury, the chancelry, and religious endowments. Various posts, especially in the chancelry, were occupied by members of the *'ulama'*, and a generally constructive alliance prevailed between cleric and lay members of the bureaucracy.[15]

Summary

The major lasting effects of the Ayyubids in Egypt were the suppression of the Fatimid caliphate and Isma'ilism (albeit a veneer), and the introduction of the concept of the sultanate which was adopted by the Mamluks. The *jihad* prosecuted by Saladin, while restoring Jerusalem and other territories to Islam, received a definitive setback from the Third Crusade. It was followed with a policy of detente by Saladin's successors, especially al-'Adil and al-Kamil. This policy of detente, while a definite boon to Egyptian–European trade, was marred by Crusader attacks (originating from Europe) on Egypt, specifically Damietta. These attacks caused the return to bellicose policies of al-Salih which resulted in the crusade of St. Louis, and provided—almost immediately—the reason for the already overpowerful *mamalik* to seize the Egyptian domain.

While trade was almost consistently supported, this support was undermined by several factors: the debasement of coinage, the ban on non-Muslims from the Red Sea trade zone, the resumption of the *mukus*, and, probably, the destruction of the Ayyubid navy. The administrative policy, the sultanate, vizierate, *dawawin*, and *iqta'* system were products of a combination of Fatimid and Zangid–Seljuk traditions, and were inherited by the Mamluk regime.

In the final analysis, the mainstay of the Ayyubids was their family solidarity—their willingness to rally around a central ruler (normally based in Egypt) in times of external crisis. Three major sovereigns (Saladin, al-'Adil, and al-Kamil) succeeded in maintaining this federation despite intermittent succession challenges and/or civil wars. The last Ayyubid, al-Salih, rendered the confederation inviable through his resumption of hostilities with the Crusaders; his inability to unite family members about him except through sheer force; and his massive recruitment of *mamalik* as the core of his army. Egypt then succumbed to over two and a half centuries of rule by the Turkish slave–soldiers.

Chapter Three

Basic Topographical Changes under the Ayyubids

The most obvious achievement of the Ayyubid rulers of Cairo was their attempt to enclose the cities of al-Qahira and al-Fustat within one massive wall based on Qal'at al-Jabal (the 'citadel'). The citadel, begun by Saladin and first occupied by his nephew al-Malik al-Kamil, was constructed on Qubbat al-Hawa' (a small spur of the Muqattam, formerly the site of an Abbasid pavilion). During the Fatimid period this spur was the site of several mosques and tombs, all of which were removed for the citadel's construction.[1] The enceinte of this new 'greater Cairo' was constructed by Saladin's deputy Baha' al-Din Qaraqush, who also supervised the construction of the citadel and other defense works. The area enclosed by the wall was roughly triangular in shape: on the north it followed the same line as the wall of Badr al-Jamali but extended to al-Maqs; on the east, it ran south from Burj al-Zafir to Bab al-Wazir (just north of the citadel); and from the citadel southeast to Bab al-Qantara at al-Fustat, just south of Qasr al-Sham'. While a western wall from Bab al-Qantara to Bab al-Hadid at al-Maqs was planned, specific construction at various intervals was never completed.[2]

The salient point here is that while following an established pattern of successive Islamic dynasties in establishing new centers of administration and defense (viz. the citadel), Saladin also chose to surround the four earlier capitals—al-Fustat, al-'Askar, al-Qata'i', and al-Qahira—with a wall. This wall, while excluding some areas which were (and still remain) totally ruinous, would both protect this expanded city from further invasions and serve as a guideline for restoration within. The walled enclosure set the basic plan for the development of Cairo until well after the French occupation six hundred years later.

On Saladin's assumption of the Fatimid vizierate in 564/1171, al-Qahira had been subject to a population change which had begun with the appointment of Badr al-Jamali in 466/1074. Badr al-Jamali opened the city for settlement by "soldiers, archers, Armenians, and all who possessed the ability to build there."[3] However, whether many non-military and/or non-administrative personnel actually moved in is doubtful. Maqrizi's description of the individual *harat* tends to center on their establishment rather than their vicissitudes throughout two centuries of Fatimid rule.[4] If the al-Qahira of al-Mu'izz included only the caliph's family, retinue, administrators, and troops, those who took advantage of the edict of Badr al-Jamali may well have been simply another group of support troops, probably Armenians. Whatever the case, the administration of Saladin was the second and final step in this 'popularization' process.

Here Badr and Saladin have several points in common. Both were called in to preserve the Fatimid dynasty from anarchy and/or external attack. Both were strong viziers who succeeded in establishing their own families as the mainstays of Egyptian rule. Both assumed their administrations when al-Qahira was physically in acute disarray and beset with ruins. In Badr's case this resulted from the 'time of troubles' of al-Mustansir. Saladin faced a combination of the general decadence and anarchy prevailing within the Fatimid caliphate, the probable overcrowding as a result of the 564/1168 al-Fustat fire, and the slave revolt of 564/1168 with the ensuing burning and destruction in the southern quarters of the city. Finally, both Saladin and Badr contributed to the decline and ultimate abolition of the sanctity and exclusiveness of the Fatimid city by opening it to settlement by their own soldiers and followers and such other members of the populace who could afford it.

Developments in al-Qahira

The revolt of the Sudanese slave–soldiers in 564/1168 caused considerable damage within the Fatimid city. The assault of Shams al-Dawla on the fleeing Sudanese soldiers and Armenian archers resulted in the burning not only of the Armenian quarter, but also in the conflagration of many houses in which the slaves took refuge in their flight towards Bab Zuwayla. The Armenian quarter was "close to Bayn al-Qasrayn," probably to its south, the direction in which the slaves were fleeing toward their barracks in al-Mansuriya, outside Bab

Zuwayla. Most of the destruction within the walled city, then, would appear to have been concentrated in the southern section, between the Fatimid palaces and Bab Zuwayla.[5]

In discussing the changes in al-Qahira following the Ayyubid takeover, Maqrizi states that after the accession to power of Saladin in 567/1171–72,

He [Saladin] gave to the city its character of a defended place and he opened it up for the housing of the common people and the throng. The palaces of the caliph were reduced in extent, and he allocated some of them as living quarters and some of them were torn down. . . . They became *khitat, harat, shawari'* [main streets], *masalik* [roads], and *aziqqa* [alleys]. The sultan settled in the great Dar al-Wizara until the citadel was built, and Saladin returned to it [occasionally] and stayed in it, as did his son al-'Aziz and his brother al-'Adil, but when al-Malik al-Nasir Muhammad [al-Kamil] . . . took power, he moved from Dar al-Wizara to the citadel, and lived in it. The market of horses, camels, and donkeys was removed to al-Rumayla beneath the citadel.[6]

In another passage Maqrizi states:

Saladin assumed control of the palace and its contents in the storages, *dawawin,* etc. in both wealth [*amwal*] and precious things. . . . He inspected the servants and slaves in [the eastern palace] and he let go those who were free and employed the remainder of them. He let for sale all old and new. He continued the sale of what he found in the palace for ten years. He emptied the inhabitants from the palaces and bolted the doors. Then his amirs took possession of them. He boarded up the buildings and residences of the caliphs and their following. He assigned some of them to his leading men, and he sold some of them. Then he divided the palaces. He gave the great palace to the amirs, and they lived in it. His father Najm al-Din Ayyub ibn Shadhi was assigned Qasr al-Lu'lu' on the Khalij as his residence. His [Saladin's] companions took over buildings connected to the Fatimid dynasty, and if a man [i.e. one of these men] wanted a house, he threw out its inhabitants and settled in it. Al-Qadi al-Fadil said that in . . . [5]67/1171–72 the contents of the special storehouses in the palace were exposed. There were a hundred boxes of magnificent clothing, valuables, etc. The inspector was Baha' al-Din Qaraqush. The western palace was emptied. The amirs Musik and Abu al-Hija' al-Samini and others from the Ghuzz lived there.[7]

Al-Qadi al-Fadil further mentions that the pavilions and promenades, formerly exclusive, were now filled as well.[8]

The palaces and royal properties, then, were partitioned and allotted, and the city opened to the general populace. One apparent contradiction concerns the disposition of the western palace. In his descriptions of the palaces, Maqrizi notes that the western palace was turned over to al-Malik al-'Adil, and it was there that al-Kamil was born. This is at variance with al-Qadi al-Fadil's description, above, unless the "Ghuzz," etc., occupied the palace only for a very short time. The Fatimid family was interned in Dar al-Muzaffar in Harat Barjawan, north of the western palace. Although the sexes were allegedly separated to prevent procreation, the Fatimids were removed to the citadel under the reign of al-Kamil and, as Casanova points out, still survived during the reign of Baybars almost a century later.[9]

Three travelers (Ibn Jubayr, 'Abd al-Latif al-Baghdadi, and Ibn Sa'id al-Maghribi) leave us descriptions of al-Qahira during the Ayyubid dynasty. That of the Spanish pilgrim Ibn Jubayr (578/1183) concentrates on religious institutions and will be dealt with in its proper chapter. 'Abd al-Latif, the Baghdad physician, lived in Egypt during the famine years of 596–98/1200–1202. The famine began in Muharram, ensuant upon a low Nile. Refugees from the provinces, who sought a haven in al-Qahira and al-Fustat, found the Egyptian capitals themselves rife with bad air, famine, and disease, to the point that cannibalism was endemic. A great number of the poor had retreated to the island of al-Roda, where they lived in mud huts. Despite the provincial exodus, the capital area became further and further depopulated. The largest part of al-Fustat was abandoned. Houses on the Khalij and Birkat al-Habash, as well as those at al-Maqs, Harat al-Halab (south of Bab Zuwayla), and their neighborhoods were absolutely deserted. In al-Qahira itself, collective residences (*rubu'*), houses, and shops in the heart of the city were for the most part deserted, "to the point that in the most frequented place of the city, there is a collective residence [*rab'*] composed of fifty apartments which were all empty except for four guards." The nilometer (on al-Roda) was above water.[10]

In 598/1201–1202, 'Abd al-Latif states that Harat al-Hilaliya (outside Bab Zuwayla), the major part of the *shari'* (which his translator DeSacy interprets as Shari' al-A'zam), the palaces on the Khalij, Harat al-Yanisiya, al-Maqs, and their neighboring areas contained no living people; one saw, rather, collapsed dwellings, and most of their inhabitants dead within. Al-Qahira, was, nonetheless, considerably more populated than al-Fustat, where the markets and streets were empty.[11]

Another Spanish traveler, Ibn Sa'id al-Maghribi, lived in Egypt between 637 and 639 (1239–40 and 1241–42), i.e. during the early years of the reign of al-Malik al-Salih. His description of al-Qahira, which concentrated on matters of sanitation and health, is probably the best obtainable for the later Ayyubid period. That some parts of the Fatimid palaces still stood was evident from his visit to a large audience hall (*iwan*), in which the caliphs used to sit. This *iwan* was allegedly patterned after the Taq-i Khusraw at Ctesiphon. In referring to Bayn al-Qasrayn, Ibn Sa'id states:

> If al-Qahira were only this it would be considerable, because of the extent and perfection of the ideas of its rulers. But this is only a small area. From it one enters a narrow area and then a dusty passage encroached upon by shops, with horses pushing against the pedestrians. This place oppresses the hearts and burns the eyes. . . . Most of the lanes [*durub*] of al-Qahira are dark and narrow, full of dirt and refuse. The buildings on them are [constructed] of reeds and earth, very high, restraining the path of air and light between them. I never saw in all the cities of the Maghrib such bad conditions as this. When I walked there my chest tightened and I was in great apprehension until I reached Bayn al-Qasrayn.[12]

Ibn Sa'id continues:

> Among the disadvantages of al-Qahira is that although it is in the country of the great Nile, people die in it of thirst because of its distance from the river, so that [the river] did not oppress [the city] and erode its houses. When the inhabitants sought the pleasures of the river, they walked a long distance outside of it, between the buildings outside its wall, to the place called al-Maqs. Al-Qahira's air remains turbid from the black dirt kicked up by walking. . . . When a traveler approaches it, he sees a wall black and dirty, and filthy air. He becomes dejected, and his spirit sinks.[13]

In a comparison of al-Fustat with al-Qahira, Ibn Sa'id maintains that

> al-Fustat is richer in commodities and cheaper in prices than al-Qahira, because of its proximity to the Nile. The boats which arrive with merchandise unload there, and this merchandise is sold nearby. This is not in keeping with the shore of al-Qahira, too far removed from the city. However, al-Qahira is richer in prosperity, esteem, and decorum [*hishma*] than al-Fustat because it [has] the better religious schools [*madaris*], larger *khanat*, and more important houses, because of the amirs living there. It is, in effect, associated with the sultanate because of its nearness to the citadel. All the affairs of the sultanate are [there] more numerous and more prosperous. There are the embroideries and other decorative materials for both men and women. However, in our time, the sultan has devoted himself to building Qal'at al-Jazira [al-Roda] which is facing al-Fustat and made it the seat of his sultanate; the building at al-

Fustat increased, many of the amirs moved there, and its markets expanded. In front of the bridge to the island, the sultan had built a great roofed marketplace [*qaysariya*], to which the soldiers' market was transferred from al-Qahira, and where furs, broadcloth, and similar things were sold.[14]

Al-Qahira, then, at mid-seventh/thirteenth century, appears to have been a crowded, unhealthy area. This was mitigated by the presence of important religious and commercial institutions, along with important residences, fostered by their proximity to the center of power and by the relatively open area of Bayn al-Qasrayn. These mitigations are somewhat questionable because of two factors. Firstly, the political centers progressively shifted to the citadel and the island of al-Roda; secondly, the Fatimid palaces gradually decayed and were destroyed, while Bayn al-Qasrayn became filled with such institutions as the Dar al-Hadith of al-Kamil and the *madrasa* of al-Salih (v.i.).

Suburbs to the North and Northwest of al-Qahira

Al-Husayniya

According to Ibn 'Abd al-Zahir, during the reign of al-Malik al-Kamil, the Ashraf al-Husayniyin (*ashraf* = descendants of the Prophet) arrived from the Hijaz and settled outside Bab al-Nasr. There they built tanneries, manufacturing leather products similar to those of al-Ta'if. Troops quartered here after the Husaynis built great buildings. While Ibn 'Abd al-Zahir maintains that the quarter took its name from these Husaynis, Maqrizi calls this an error, as the *hara* was known from the Husayni regiment who were quartered there during the reign of al-Hakim. This error, however, does not negate the later settlement of the Hijazi contingent.

Maqrizi notes that many easterners, driven to Egypt by the Mongols, populated al-Husayniya during the period 610–56 (1213–58). Other Ayyubid establishments included a square (*midan*) and caravanserai and public fountain (*khan sabil*), both established outside Bab al-Futuh by Qaraqush. A part of the outskirts of Bab al-Nasr remained a cemetery until after 700/1300–1301, when it was populated. Eventually buildings stretched from Bab al-Nasr to al-Ridaniya. Ibn 'Abd al-Zahir adds that Husayniya was the largest of the soldiers' *harat*; however, the soldiers who settled the district following the Hijazis may well not have arrived until the Mamluk dynasty.[15]

Al-Maqs

During the Fatimid period al-Maqs was known primarily for its arsenal and dockyard, which appear to have been exclusively of a military nature, and will be discussed in Chapter Four. It also had a *jami'*, and there were several pavilions in the immediate area. When the north wall of al-Qahira was extended to al-Maqs by Qaraqush, and the terminal tower constructed, the building (*'imara*) stretched from there to the city (*balad*).[16] One might assume that this building stretched within the wall, but it may have connected al-Maqs with Husayniya as well.

As to the port facilities, how many remained at this time is questionable. Among the *mukus* abolished by Saladin in 567/1171 were a half (of a percentage?) on goods arriving at al-Maqs and a duty for the protection of storage of grains and cheese. This suggests that al-Maqs served at least as an entrepot and/or customs station for goods.[17] However, the sands of the islands of Bulaq and Jazirat al-Fil (v.i.) were rapidly encroaching on al-Maqs, Ard al-Tabala, and Ard al-Ba'l to the north. Al-Qadi al-Fadil, cited by Maqrizi, states that

> in 577/1181–82 Saladin rode to inspect the shore of the Nile at al-Maqs. Indeed it had expanded. He set to work on the shoreline at al-Maqs and what followed it which had been extended [by silting] far beyond the new wall and *qasr* [i.e. tower at al-Maqs]. Chosen nobles were present and he consulted them. They advised him to raise the banks by the removal of the sands, the islands of which had turned away the water channel. [The sands] had blocked it and stopped it.[18]

Such conditions would hardly depict an active naval dockyard at this time, or perhaps even the continuation of the customs and storage facilities previously mentioned. It is safe to consider al-Maqs from this date simply as a suburb of al-Qahira. It was protected on the north by Saladin's extended wall, while its western flank was gradually extended by alluviation, and its southern boundaries reached the northern outskirts of the similarly alluvial territories of Bab al-Luq (v.i.). Its use as a naval dockyard (barring further evidence) was terminated.

Ard al-Tabala

The gardening areas of Ard al-Tabala lay immediately north of al-Maqs, on the site of the present Fajjala. Ibn Sa'id (ca. 637/1239–40) notes that the best vista in the outskirts of al-Qahira was Ard al-Tabala, especially in the days of clover and flax.[19]

Hubs al-Juyushi

Hubs al-Juyushi consisted of lands in two areas: those on the west bank of the Khalij known as al-Minya and al-Amiriya, now in the general location of Minyat al-Siraj (immediately north of present-day Shubra); and certain areas of Giza. These lands were inalienably endowed on the heirs of Badr al-Jamali. In 587/1191–92 Saladin placed his brother al-'Adil in charge of the navy. Among other properties and revenues, part of Hubs al-Juyushi was devoted to the fleet. Saladin then alienated the remainder of the legacy of Badr al-Jamali, other than the endowment (*hubs*) already reserved for the navy. Then the legists (*fuqaha'*) declared the invalidity of the *hubs*, and it became land tax (*kharaj*) property, known as Bilad al-Mulk. In Maqrizi's time these areas were divided between religious endowment (*waqf*) and the royal *diwan*, and were largely planted with flax.[20]

Bulaq and Jazirat al-Fil

The alluvial islands of Bulaq and Jazirat al-Fil developed into the modern quarters of Bulaq and Shubra respectively. Bulaq encroached upon and gradually eliminated the port of al-Maqs, while Jazirat al-Fil, almost immediately to the north, eventually coalesced with the Nile shore at Ard al-Tabala, Ard al-Ba'l, and Minyat al-Siraj. These areas were relatively clear of silting until the end of the Fatimid dynasty. At that time a large boat, known as al-Fil, broke up and sands built up against it, forming the island of the same name. In his description of Bulaq, Maqrizi gives the date of the formation of Jazirat al-Fil as after 570/1174–75. At this time, the water receded from the wall of al-Qahira which ended at al-Maqs (v.s.), where sands and islands grew up until there was no water passing except during flood season. "Through the length of the year reeds and alfalfa grew there, and the *mamalik* of the sultan shot arrows into these hills of sand."[21] That the sands and islands of Bulaq coalesced as a result of the earlier formation of Jazirat al-Fil to its north is most probable; in any case, Jazirat al-Fil was cultivated during the reign of Saladin, who endowed the island in *waqf* on his *madrasa* in al-Qarafa. The definitive attachment of Bulaq and Jazirat al-Fil probably took place toward the end of the third reign of al-Nasir

Muhammad ibn Qalaun, when extensive building and agricultural activities occurred at both sites and the former islands amalgamated with the more southern alluvial lands of al-Luq, already considerably developed under the Ayyubid dynasty.[22]

Al-Luq and the West Bank of the Khalij

The west bank of the Khalij, stretching from al-Maqs to Fam al-Khalij (the present site of the intake tower of the al-Ghuri acqueduct) was, during the Fatimid period, occupied primarily by pavilions, promenades, and gardens, together with alluvial ponds such as Birkat Fir'awn and Birkat Batn al-Baqara (later al-Azbakiya). A gradual resurgence of the Nile after 600/1203–1204 created new lands which were rapidly monopolized, planted, and, in some cases, settled upon. The southern section, al-Minsha'a, included Minsha'at al-Fadil (later Minsha'at al-Mahrani) in the present district of Fam al-Khalij and stretched northeast toward Sayyida Zaynab. To the north lay al-Luq, a blanket term for a district which stretched from Bustan al-Zahri (just north of Qanatir al-Siba' ('the Bridges of Lions') near the current Midan Sayyida Zaynab) north to al-Maqs near the present Bab al-Hadid. Its western and eastern boundaries were the Nile and the Khalij respectively. Within this area were subdivisions: al-Khawr and al-Dikka, roughly between Bab al-Hadid and al-Azbakiya; al-Dhikr; the general district of Bab al-Luq; and several monopolized areas to be discussed below.

The name al-Luq existed under the Fatimids. It apparently referred to the area around the present Midan Bab al-Luq and its environs along the Nile shore, which ran roughly upon the line of the present street of Muhammad Bey Farid. Upon the withdrawal of the Nile from these lands, the alluvial territories became known as Zahir ('outskirts') al-Luq, and were subdivided into gardens and squares (*mayadin*) under the Ayyubids and Mamluks.[23] The same applied to areas to the south at the former Bustan al-Khashshab. Here, in an area roughly between the former Qantarat al-Sadd and the present Fam al-Khalij, al-Qadi al-Fadil established an immense garden variously known as Bustan al-Fadil, Minsha'at al-Fadil, and, during Mamluk times, Minsha'at al-Mahrani. This garden provided grapes and dates for the people of al-Fustat. In addition, al-Qadi al-Fadil built a mosque on the garden's edge, and buildings were constructed around it. "The constructions increased, and Muwaffaq al-Din al-Dabbaji established a garden there during the reign of Baybars, on which Dabbaji spent one thousand dinars." Shortly thereafter a reversal of the Nile destroyed both the mosque and the garden of al-Fadil, although the mosque was soon reconstructed by the amir Baha' al-Din ibn Huna.[24]

The new lands (Zahir al-Luq) north of Minsha'at al-Fadil were divided into monopolies (ahkar, singular hikr) which were granted or sold to amirs and other dignitaries under the Ayyubids and early Mamluks, apparently directly by the Treasury (Bayt al-Mal). These properties in turn could be sold, increased, or endowed by their owners. Maqrizi gives an extended listing; here we will examine those of Ayyubid date to determine their topographical significance and changes of ownership.[25]

Qit'a of al-Qadi al-Fadil

According to Maqrizi, al-Qadi al-Fadil bought a large section of land (qit'a) in the area of al-Luq. He bought this property from Bayt al-Mal and others, and spent a large sum of money on his purchase. This hikr became known as Bustan Ibn Quraysh and, as some of it penetrated Midan al-Zahri, the garden was probably in the general vicinity of Bab al-Luq, partly overlooking the Nile. It was endowed on the spring of al-'Ayn al-Ruzqa at al-Madina, and the revenue from this waqf was annually transferred to al-Madina for the cleaning of this spring and its environs.[26]

Bustan Ibn Tha'lib

This garden of seventy-five feddans (seventy-eight acres) extended from Minsha'at Ibn Tha'lib near Bab al-Luq to al-Dikka (just south of al-Maqs, near the present Azbakiya), and included Birkat Qarmut and al-Khawwar. Maqrizi provides an extensive description of the fruits and vegetables produced here, and notes that it was provided with spring wells and included a great pavilion and a number of houses. The garden was surrounded by a wall and had a great gate "facing the place today known as Bab al-Luq." Fakhr al-Din ibn Tha'lib, one of the amirs of al-Malik al-'Adil, was leader (sahib) of al-Madrasa al-Sharifiya in al-Qahira. His son, Husn al-Din ibn Tha'lib, sold the garden to al-Malik al-Salih in 643/1245–46 for three thousand Egyptian dinars. It was here that al-Salih founded his midan (Midan al-Salih) and constructed the gate, Bab al-Luq, for which the area is still named, possibly on the same site as the entrance to Bustan Ibn

Tha'lib. This *midan*, the site of the present Midan Bab al-Luq, was approached from the east by a road leading directly from Qantarat al-Kharq (a bridge over the Khalij at the site of the present Midan Ahmad Maher, popularly known as Midan Bab al-Khalq). Earlier, this point on the Khalij had been a quay for the water carriers of al-Qahira. Qantarat al-Kharq was constructed by al-Malik al-Salih for access to his new *midan*.[27]

The exact extent of the area known as Bab al-Luq is difficult to ascertain. However, its southern perimeter reached Bustan al-Zahri; its eastern the Khalij at Qantarat al-Kharq; the western boundary was the Nile itself. The quarter included Jami' al-Tabbakh (a mosque probably constructed by an early Mamluk), and bordered upon Birkat al-Shiqaf. Maqrizi notes that in former times there were a number of pavilions on this pond, in "the days when the lands of al-Luq were the places of outings before they were divided into *ahkar* and houses were built. That was after the year 600/1203–1204".[28]

Maqrizi's description of Midan al-Salih states that its location extended from Jami' al-Tabbakh to Qantarat Qadadar on Khalij al-Nasri. Khalij al-Nasri was the western canal dug by al-Nasir Muhammad ibn Qalaun which followed the approximate line of the modern Shari' Muhammad Bey Farid. The location, according to the French expeditionary map, of Bab al-Luq (here referring to a quarter) was effectively abutting this canal. The precise location of Jami' al-Tabbakh cannot be determined. One can only safely assume that the Ayyubid *midan* occupied the present site of Midan Bab al-Luq; its minimal area can be determined only by function. Maqrizi states that al-Salih made the garden of Ibn Tha'lib into a *midan*; it is highly unlikely, however, that this *midan* extended as far north as al-Dikka. While *mayadin* were often established for military exercises and display, Midan al-Salih appears to have been founded largely for recreational purposes.

> He [al-Malik al-Salih] founded there splendid pavilions overlooking the great Nile. He would ride to it, and play ball in it. . . . The kings continued to play ball in this *midan* after al-Salih until the water of the Nile withdrew from its neighborhood.[29]

Ball playing (presumably polo) and the construction of pavilions require a considerable area. Therefore it might be assumed that the term *midan* refers to a large field or open area in a southern portion of Bustan Ibn Tha'lib, possibly with a smaller square or epicenter at Bab al-Luq as well. The gate of Bab al-Luq, constructed by al-Salih as the entrance to his *midan*, was described as a great gate, which, having suffered extensive damage through warfare, finally disappeared after 740/1339–40.[30]

Hikr al-Baghdadiya

One of the largest gardens of the Fatimid dynasty, this *hikr* was near Khalij al-Dhikr, to the west of the pavilion of Lu'lu'. According to al-Qadi al-Fadil, in 594/1197–98 al-Malik al-'Aziz ordered the cutting of the date palms in this garden and the establishment of a *midan* in its place. "He plowed its soil and he removed what was in it from its origins."[31] Maqrizi continues: "Then the people monopolized what was in this garden and built upon it. It [the area in general] is now neglected, occupied by hills and dirt."[32] No further information is given on the activities of this *midan*. One can only assume that its function was relatively short-lived and that it was partitioned in the later Ayyubid or early Mamluk dynasty.

Al-Dikka, al-Khawr

One of the largest gardens of Cairo, al-Dikka, according to Maqrizi, was situated between the lands of al-Luq and al-Maqs. In modern terms, this area would be roughly between al-Azbakiya and Midan Bab al-Hadid. During the Fatimid period the caliphs maintained a pavilion there.

> Its windows overlooked the Nile; nothing intervened between it and the Giza shore. At the end of the Fatimid dynasty this garden became derelict and it was divided into monopolies [*hukara*]; people built in it, and it became a large district due to its fine location. An important market was established here; scribes and others lived in the area. It became populous, [but] after 806/1403–1404 it fell into ruins.[33]

Al-Khawr (literally, water drain), designating the area between Khalij al-Nasri and Khalij Fam al-Khawr, comprised a section of Bustan Ibn Tha'lib. This area was also known as Bustan al-Khawr al-Sa'bi, after the pavilions of al-Sa'bi, a shaykh who died in 603/1206–1207.[34]

Hikr Khaza'in al-Silah

Formerly known as Hikr al-Awsiya, this *hikr* was located between al-Dikka and Qantarat al-Muski (a bridge on the Khalij). In 614/1217–18, al-Malik al-'Adil endowed (*waqafa*) the income of this property on

Khaza'in al-Silah (the 'arsenal'), along with a number of places at al-Fustat and Qalyub.[35]

Hikr Ibn Munqidh

Located outside Bab al-Qantara on the bank of Khalij al-Dhikr, this garden was first named after (and presumably owned by) al-Sharif al-Jalis, also known as al-Bata'ihi. It was later acquired by the amir Sayf al-Dawla ibn Munqidh, a deputy of Sayf al-Islam Tughtakin (Ayyubid ruler of the Yemen 577–93/1181–96). The property was then transferred to Shaykh 'Abd al-Muhussin al-Makhzumi, surnamed Ibn al-Sirfi.

> He endowed it on the authorities [*jihat*] [and it] reverted finally to the poor staying at the *mashhad* of Sayyida Nafisa and to the poor contained in the prisons of al-Qahira; this was in the year 643/1245–46. Then the garden was done away with and its lands divided.[36]

Other Ayyubid *ahkar*

Four other *ahkar* of the Ayyubid period are noted on the west bank of the Khalij. These are of relatively minor importance, and will be noted only briefly here. The *ahkar* of Jawhar al-Nubi, Ibn al-Asad Jafril, and Khatlaba were properties of amirs of al-Kamil. Finally that of al-Buwashqi belonged to the amir Azdan al-Buwashqi, one of the amirs of al-Malik al-Salih.[37]

Recreations, abominations, and prohibitions

From the reign of al-'Aziz onward, several instances of excessive drinking, carousing, and ribaldry were noted in the Cairo area, especially on the Khalij and the Nile shore. Although al-Malik al-'Aziz was especially zealous in the discouragement of such activities, they continued throughout the Ayyubid period. Maqrizi, in his *Kitab al-suluk*, states that in 590/1193–94 al-'Aziz, while riding to Giza, passed by Bab Zuwayla and disapproved of the prominence of the benches of wine-sellers in the markets; he ordered them destroyed. In addition, "the sultan passed Sana'at al-'Ama'ir, a dockyard occupying the site of Sana'at Misr [the Fatimid dockyard established at Bustan al-Jurf, near Fam al-Khalij, v.s.]. [There] he ordered the blocking of the windows of the houses adjoining the Nile. They were blocked."[38] During the same year, the *muhtasib* of al-Qahira demolished the cabarets and stables erected by Sadr al-Din Darbas in front of the mosque of al-Azhar, near his house.[39] In 594/1197–98, al-'Aziz forbade his amirs to build along the Nile shore (although Maqrizi does not further specify the area). Cavalry were assigned to prevent further building and to destroy such foundations as were already established. "This order was rigorously carried out . . . ."[40]

In the *Mutajaddadat* of 594/1197–98, al-Qadi al-Fadil states:

[Al-'Aziz] forbade the travel of observers in boats on the Khalij, the exhibition of abominations, and the transportation of women with men; and he hung a group of boat captains by their hands. [Al-Qadi al-Fadil] said on Wednesday the nineteenth of Ramadan reprehensible actions took place—unknown in Egypt from any times past—and atrocities which went out from the houses into the streets. The water in the Khalij flowed by the grace of God—after the despondencies and the rise of the Nile to the sixteenth cubit. The people engaged in activities of depravity and idleness in boats on a day of the month of Ramadan and with them were whores who played upon lutes. One heard their voices, their lewdness, and their customers with them in their boats. These men kept neither their hands nor their looks from these women nor did they fear retribution from any amir or civil officer. The people [in general] dreaded the censorship which followed this event.[41]

It would appear that the presence of water attracted dissipation. Some fifty years later, Ibn Sa'id describes the Khalij—"[that section] which is between al-Qahira and al-Fustat and principally frequented nearer al-Qahira"—as encroached upon from both sides "by numerous pavilions full of people engaged in riotous living, to the extent that respectable men would not pass in a boat." As might be expected, the exertions of al-Malik al-'Aziz had only temporary effect.[42]

Summary

Under the Fatimids, the area of al-Luq and the west bank of the Khalij was largely occupied by pavilions, promenades, and some gardens. When alluviation created new lands under the Ayyubids and early Mamluks, this territory was sold or assigned as *ahkar* to political and/or religious magnates; these *ahkar* in turn could be subdivided, sold, transferred, or bequeathed. Housing, and in one case a market, existed from the beginnings of the Ayyubid dynasty if not before. Such buildings, however, were probably small clusters or individual structures for the care of gardens; this was generally the case even at the time of the Napoleonic conquest. The income from these gardens, whether directly or by endowment, was assigned to individual proprietors, religious and charitable institutions, and government agencies.

Secondary to its agricultural associations, the west bank of the Khalij under the Ayyubids was utilized as a place of recreation by the sultans with their *mayadin* and associated pavilions, by amirs, and, perhaps, by certain lower-class people in the construction and/or reuse of pavilions and other buildings on the Khalij and on the Nile shore.

Area between al-Qahira and al-Fustat

This area can be defined within the following boundaries: on the north Bab Zuwayla and the southern wall of al-Qahira; on the west, the eastern bank of the Khalij; on the south, the northern boundaries of al-Fustat (from al-Hamra' al-Quswa extending east to the *mashhad* of Sayyida Nafisa and the beginnings of the southern Qarafa); and on the east, the present Darb al-Ahmar and the citadel. Within the enceinte (or the projected enceinte) of Saladin, this area included most of the former capitals of al-'Askar and al-Qata'i', Birkat al-Fil and Birkat Qarun, and Darb al-Ahmar and the citadel with its associated areas. The settlement patterns and land use of this district during the Ayyubid period are somewhat dubious. Maqrizi's testimony runs somewhat at variance with that of 'Abd al-Latif al-Baghdadi and Ibn Sa'id al-Maghribi and, on more than one occasion, contradicts itself. After its burning in the suppression of the Sudanese slave revolt of 564/1168, Harat al-Mansuriya (outside Bab Zuwayla to the west of Shari' al-A'zam) was ploughed over and planted as a garden. This presumably applied to neighboring *harat* as well, as Maqrizi states that the area outside Bab Zuwayla became gardens as far as the *mashhad* of Sayyida Nafisa. Neighboring these gardens was a road going from them to the citadel, a reference to either Darb al-Ahmar or the *saliba* of Ibn Tulun.[43]

The citadel, which will be discussed in detail in Chapter Four, was a focal point for new building, both in its immediate surroundings and on the two arteries connecting it with a) the Khalij and al-Fustat (the *saliba*) and b) Bab Zuwayla and al-Qahira (Darb al-Ahmar). The market of horses, camels, and donkeys was transferred to al-Rumayla (present Midan Salah al-Din) when al-Malik al-Kamil definitively moved to the citadel from Dar al-Wizara. Adjacent to al-Rumayla was the probable site of the royal stables, and to the south, the

Qaramidan (Maqrizi's Midan al-Qal'a), formerly the site of the *midan* of Ahmad ibn Tulun. This *midan* was reconstructed by al-Malik al-Kamil, who built three ponds on its periphery which contained drinking water apparently supplied directly from the Nile. The *midan* then became inactive for a period of time until the succession of al-'Adil II (635–37/1238–40) who revitalized it. Al-Malik al-Salih added another waterwheel (*saqiya*) and planted trees on its sides. Following the death of al-Salih, the condition of the *midan* gradually deteriorated until it was destroyed by al-Malik al-Mu'izz Aybak in 651/1253–54.[44]

Although Darb al-Ahmar (the thoroughfare from Bab Zuwayla to the citadel) certainly developed during this period, the extent of building under the Ayyubids is questionable. Maqrizi states, in referring to the outskirts of Bab Zuwayla, that the first to build between this gate and the *jabal* (i.e. site of the citadel) was the vizier al-Salih Tala'i' when he founded his mosque in 555/1160. Between this mosque (immediately outside and to the left of Bab Zuwayla) and the escarpment, a cemetery was established "from the time when the *harat* were founded outside Bab Zuwayla."[45] As earlier noted, these *harat* were founded both in the earlier years of the Fatimid dynasty and later in the early sixth/twelfth century. They would, in any case, predate the founding of the mosque, and it is thus safe to assume that the cemetery was well established by 545/1150–51. According to Maqrizi, the construction of the citadel attracted people to Darb al-Ahmar, who gradually built in the area, removing the graves in the process of construction.[46] Elsewhere, however, Maqrizi reports:

> All of what was in the road from the left of Bab Zuwayla was empty of buildings until after 500/1106-1107. When the vizier al-Salih Tala'i' . . . built his mosque outside Bab Zuwayla, what was outside of it towards al-Qata'i' of Ibn Tulun became a cemetery for the people of al-Qahira until the end of the Fatimid dynasty and Saladin founded the citadel . . . [and one walked to the citadel on the left between the tombs and the *jabal*]. Then, after the time of hardships [*mihan*], the buildings now present grew up little by little after 700/1300–1301.[47]

The date of the hardships noted above is questionable. Maqrizi may allude to the famines and plagues of 597–98/1201–1202, but this is doubtful as al-Kamil did not move permanently to the citadel until 604/1207–1208. He may, also, refer to any of several natural or political disturbances which occurred during the seventh/thirteenth century. Lacking further evidence, we can only assume that the building activity on Darb al-Ahmar, supplanting the Fatimid cemetery between Bab Zuwayla and the citadel, took place between ca. 604 and 700 (1207 and 1301), as the needs for goods and services of the resident Ayyubid and Mamluk sultans increased.

With the exception of gardens, probably related to the military *harat* outside Bab Zuwayla, the surroundings of Birkat al-Fil were unoccupied under the Fatimid dynasty. During the early Ayyubid period the pond was bordered by two gardens of note: on the north Bustan al-Habanniya, dating from Fatimid times; and on the east Bustan Sayf al-Islam Tughtakin ibn Ayyub (brother of Saladin and viceroy of the Yemen). The latter garden dominated the pond; it boasted spacious galleries (*dahaliz*) and was surmounted by kiosks (*jawasiq*) facing the four cardinal points. Maqrizi states that it was not until ca. 600/1203–1204 that the shores of Birkat al-Fil became populated; prior to this time it was surrounded by a vast plain stretching north to the *harat* of the Sudanese and Yanisiya. The houses there were some of the finest in Egypt. Maqrizi further notes that many easterners, driven to Egypt before the onslaught of Genghis Khan, settled around Birkat al-Fil and on both sides of the Khalij between 610 and 656 (1213–14 and 1258). This assertion is seconded by Ibn Laqlaq, who states (ca. 637/1239–40) that a massive building boom occurred outside the city because of refugees from Syria and the east in many places and ways (*turuqat*).[48]

However, the degree of devastation and/or lack of rebuilding as a result of Saladin's burning of the slave quarters is open to question. 'Abd al-Latif, in his description of the events of the famine years 597–98/1201–1202, notes in 597/1201 that the houses on the Khalij and in Harat al-Halab were absolutely deserted. In 598/1201–1202 he further notes that Harat al-Hilaliya, the major part of the main street outside Bab Zuwayla, the palaces on the canal, and Harat al-Yanisiya, along with neighboring districts, were abandoned and in ruins. Since 'Abd al-Latif had lived in Cairo since 591/1194–95, it is likely that he had seen these areas populated before the famine years, thus either negating Maqrizi's statement that following the destruction of Harat al-Mansuriya only gardens existed between Bab Zuwayla and the *mashhad* of Sayyida Nafisa, or suggesting considerable building activity in this area during the twenty-five years following the slave revolt.[49]

When al-Malik al-Salih began construction of his pavilions on Jabal Yashkur (the heights just east of the mosque of Ibn Tulun) ca. 640/1242–43, there were, according to Maqrizi, no buildings on Birkat al-Fil, and nothing except gardens from the *saliba* of Ibn Tulun to Bab Zuwayla, on the west bank of the Khalij from Qanatir al-Siba' to al-Maqs, and from Qanatir al-Siba' to Bab Misr (no.104, map 3). The west bank of the Khalij we have already examined; this additional information suggests that the abandonment of Shari' al-'Azam and the former military *harat* south of Bab Zuwayla, as noted by 'Abd al-Latif, still prevailed. It does not explain, however, the sudden absence of the buildings allegedly constructed by easterners on Birkat al-Fil and on both sides of the Khalij (610–56/1213–58, v.s.).[50]

Ibn Sa'id, who lived in Egypt during the early years of the reign of al-Salih, adds some further detail. He notes that "nothing remains now of al-Qata'i' except the Tulunid mosque. It is outside al-Qahira; around it are buildings without a wall surrounding them." Birkat al-Fil, was "round like a full moon, with pavilions above it like stars. It was the habit of the sultan to ride in it by night. The lights of the owners' pavilions burned according to their ambition and their strength." Whether these pavilions were those constructed by "easterners" or by courtiers of al-Malik al-Salih seeking proximity to the sultan is open to question.[51]

Summary

While Saladin's burning of Harat al-Mansuriya and subsequent planting of the district with gardens certainly leveled a considerable area to the south of Bab Zuwayla, it is very doubtful indeed that nothing but gardens remained between that gate and the *mashhad* of Sayyida Nafisa, given 'Abd al-Latif's description of the ruins of Shari' al-'Azam and surrounding *harat* in 597–98/1201–1202. It does appear, however, that following this period of famine, the area was largely gardens, at least as far as the *saliba* of Ibn Tulun, until the time of al-Malik al-Salih. These agricultural areas included large sections of the former capitals of al-'Askar and al-Qata'i' and, to the south and southwest, probably bordered upon the northern edge of the devastation caused by the 564/1168 al-Fustat fire (particularly in the area of al-Hamra' al-Quswa).

The banks of Birkat al-Fil, which Maqrizi claimed to be empty of habitation when al-Malik al-Salih constructed his pavilion (Qal'at al-Kabsh) on Jabal Yashkur, had been occupied by pavilions of Sayf al-Islam Tughtakin and (again according to Maqrizi) settled by orientals (610–56/1213–58). It is highly unlikely that the shores of this pond were free of occupation when al-Salih commenced Qal'at al-Kabsh ca. 640/1242–43.

Finally, the construction of the citadel and, concommitantly, its associated horse market, stables, and *midan*, resulted in a new thoroughfare through a former cemetery area, Darb al-Ahmar.

Al-Fustat, al-Roda, and Giza

As noted in Chapter One, archaeological evidence suggests that the devastation from the 564/1168 fire did not extend much further east than the mosque of 'Amr and Qasr al-Sham'. The narratives of both indigenous historians and contemporary travelers, while corroborating this fire, suggest spot incursions into the then populated areas of al-Fustat, rather than the holocaust described by Maqrizi. They render us, in addition, a reasonably complete picture of the social and economic conditions of al-Fustat and its environs from the mid-sixth/eleventh to the mid-seventh/twelfth centuries.

Muhammad al-Idrisi, visiting al-Fustat ca. 549/1154–55, describes it as a city of great wealth, with all commodities readily available, and with large streets and cultivated fields. A bridge of thirty boats extended from al-Fustat to al-Roda, where there were many contiguous houses built along both river banks. A second boat bridge extended from the west bank of al-Roda to Giza, which boasted fine houses, high buildings, markets, and cultivated fields. The remainder of Idrisi's description is gleaned, almost literally, from the fourth/tenth-century narrative of Ibn Hawqal.[52]

The Spanish rabbi Benjamin of Tudela visited al-Fustat and al-Qahira during the last years of the reign of the caliph al-'Adid. Adler believes that the date of his sojourn was between 564 and 567 (1168–69 and 1171–72); in any event, Benjamin arrived in Sicily (to which he departed directly from Egypt) no earlier than A.D. 1169 (begins 30 Rabi' al-Awwal, 564). It is therefore quite possible that he visited al-Fustat after the 564/1168 fire. While largely preoccupied with local Jewish communities, Benjamin does provide some detail on al-Fustat, al-Qahira, and the surrounding areas. He describes Misraim (al-Fustat) as a large city with a community of 2,000 Jews and two synagogues. The fortress of Tso'an (al-Qahira) was enclosed by a wall, while al-Fustat was open and the Nile "washes one part of it. . . . The city [al-Fustat] is large, containing many market places, as well as inns in great number, and many wealthy Jewish inhabitants." Referring to Giza, he states that

from new [al-Fustat] to old [Giza] Misraim is a distance of two parasangs. The latter lies in ruins, but the site of the walls and the houses may still be traced to this day, as also the granaries of Joseph [the pyramids], of which there are a large number.[53]

Abu Salih the Armenian, whose personal contacts with Egypt covered a period from at least 568/1173 to 604/1208, provides us, in his *Churches and Monasteries of Egypt*, with a detailed account of the Christian institutions at al-Fustat and Birkat al-Habash. Al-Hamra', the general term for an area extending southwest from the mosque of Ibn Tulun and along the al-Fustat shore as far as the mosque of 'Amr, was divided into three sections: al-Hamra' al-Dunya, immediately to the northwest of the 'Amr mosque; al-Hamra' al-Wusta, the central area to the north of al-Hamra' al-Dunya; and al-Hamra' al-Quswa, the northern area bordering the Khalij. During the late Fatimid and Ayyubid periods there were several monasteries and churches in these districts, most of which were severely damaged, if not completely destroyed, during the years 559–64 (1163–64 to1168–69). Although one might hope to delineate the extent of the 564/1168 al-Fustat fire from this chronicle, it is unfortunately impossible. Most of the burning, pillaging, and destruction of these churches occurred as a result of mob violence spurred by anti-Christian feeling resulting from successive invasions of the Crusaders. While the churches will be discussed in detail in Chapter Seven, we will briefly examine here the vicissitudes of six al-Fustat churches and monasteries in order to demonstrate the above points.[54]

The "great" church of al-Hamra', also known as the church of St. George, was located in al-Hamra' al-Quswa. "The Ghuzz and the Kurds attacked this church, with the mob of Cairo, and razed it to the ground like the other churches, in the month of Jumada al-Awwal in the year 559/1164. Afterwards it was restored in the year 560/1164–65."[55] A church dedicated to the Angel Gabriel, also in al-Hamra', was pillaged by the "Ghuzz and the people of Cairo," and part of the roof was burned. The church was restored, however, in the caliphate of al-'Adid. Another church (no name given, but probably in al-Hamra' al-Quswa, as it commanded a view of the Khalij) was pillaged and part of its walls thrown down, "when Misr was burnt, in the month of Safar in the year 564/1168."[56] The monastery and church of St. Menas, again in al-Hamra' al-Quswa, lay near Qantarat al-Sadd.

In the month of Jumada al-Awwal, in the year 559/1164, when the Kurds and the Ghuzz came with Salah al-Din Yusuf ibn Ayyub [Saladin], and the king of the Franks was appealed to for help against them, then this monastery and this church were burned to the ground. . . . Part of the church was restored in the caliphate of al-'Adid, and in the vizierate of Shawar.[57]

The church of St. Onuphrius, in al-Hamra' al-Wusta, was burned in the al-Fustat fire of 564/1168, and later restored.[58]

The church of St. Mercurius, or Abu al-Sayfayn, occupied the present site of Dayr Abu al-Sayfayn to the northwest of the mosque of 'Amr, in the former quarter of al-Hamra' al-Dunya. According to Abu Salih, this church was burned after the 564/1168 fire by a mob of Muslims who, frustrated in an attempt to pillage the church, set fire to it until only the walls remained; it was restored in 571/1175–76. Other, smaller, churches in the immediate vicinity of Abu al-Sayfayn were also restored "after the fire," here probably referring to the mob violence following the 564/1168 al-Fustat conflagration.[59]

A cursory glance at these monasteries and churches suggests that although these establishments were damaged and/or destroyed by Ghuzz, Kurds, and local mobs during the period 559–64 (1163–64 to 1168–69), the cause of this destruction appears to be a combination of anti-Christian sentiment fostered by successive invasions of Amalric and the Crusaders, combined with the opportunities created for looting during the general disruption. Only one church, that of St. Onuphrius, was definitely burned during the 564/1168 al-Fustat fire. Thus, barring a mistake in Abu Salih's chronology, his evidence suggests that the shoreline district of al-Hamra' was left relatively unscathed by the 564/1168 fire.

Birkat al-Habash and southern areas

In addition, Abu Salih gives us some information on Birkat al-Habash and Basatin al-Wazir, currently known as Basatin. This garden had been established by Abu al-Faraj, vizier to al-Mustansir in 450/1058–59. Already a site for pavilions and promenades, several new ones were added by Saladin's brother, Taj al-Muluk Buri. A church of St. Victor was included within this garden, and other churches and monasteries were located within the immediate area.[60]

On the western side of Birkat al-Habash, between it and the Nile near the present Ribat Athar al-Nabi, was a garden known as al-Ma'shuq. According to Maqrizi, after several changes in ownership, it became the *waqf* of Shaykh Ibn al-Sabuni, which he endowed upon his sons and upon his hospice (*ribat,* near the tomb of Imam al-Shafi'i in al-Qarafa.) In another passage, Maqrizi states that the island of Jazirat al-Sabuni, opposite Ribat al-Athar and a part of Birkat al-Habash (meaning, no doubt, Bustan al-Ma'shuq), was endowed half upon Ibn al-Sabuni and his sons and half upon the above-mentioned *ribat* in al-Qarafa. The founder of this *waqf* was Saladin's father, Najm al-Din; unfortunately we have no further information on the precise location or later history of this *ribat* within al-Qarafa.[61]

Birkat al-Habash was appropriated as *waqf* and endowed upon the *ashraf* by the Fatimid vizier al-Salih Tala'i' ibn Razzayk. This *waqf* was reaffirmed by the chief *qadi* Ibn Jama'a in 640/1242–43, during the reign of al-Malik al-Salih, when it was divided equally between two groups of *ashraf,* the Aqarib and the Talibiyun. One must bear in mind that Birkat al-Habash, the largest alluvial pond in the Cairo area (over a thousand feddans), was completely flooded only during the high Nile. The remainder of the year it boasted some of the most fertile land in the vicinity, planted, as Ibn Sa'id notes, with flax, leeks, and other commodities.[62]

Ibn Jubayr's description

Ibn Jubayr's description of al-Fustat (578/1183) suggests that the city was considerably restored during the first half of Saladin's reign. Beginning with a brief description of the mosque of 'Amr, he goes on to state that while the remains of the 564/1168 fire were still very much in evidence, most of the city was restored, with buildings adjoining each other without intermission. He remarks that Giza was an important town with fine buildings and a large market; al-Roda was an island "with fine houses and commanding belvederes, which is a resort for entertainment and diversion." Al-Roda also boasted a congregational mosque.[63]

It should be noted here that, continuing previous trends, the northern end of al-Roda was the site of pavilions constructed by the amir al-Afdal ibn al-Juyushi, and, following his demise in 515/1121, the location of al-Hawdaj, the pavilion constructed by the caliph al-Amir for his Bedouin wife. The pavilions of al-Afdal, according to Ibn Duqmaq, were neglected and gradually fell into ruin, and remained so until Saladin's rule in Egypt and the end of the Fatimid dynasty. The entire island was purchased by Taqi al-Din 'Umar,

Saladin's nephew, in 566/1170–71; it was later endowed on his *madrasa* (al-Taqawiya) at al-Fustat.[64]

Famine and ruin (597–98/1201–1202)

The catastrophic results of the low Niles of 597–98/1201–1202 on al-Fustat and al-Qahira have been described above. The rehabitation and reconstruction of al-Fustat following the 564/1168 fire had suffered a definitive—but not irreparable—relapse. Although the populated area had been reduced to a narrow strip along the Nile shore, the first Islamic capital of Egypt was fated to have at least one more—if only partial—renaissance.[65]

Revival under al-Malik al-Salih

The building of the palace and fortress of al-Malik al-Salih on al-Roda, begun in 637/1239–40, was the touchstone to a new round of relative prosperity for al-Fustat, albeit short-lived. Ibn Sa'id's comparison of al-Qahira to al-Fustat (ca. 639/1241–42) has already been noted. Due to the proximity of the port facilities, al-Fustat boasted considerably cheaper prices on basic commodities. The markets had expanded; al-Malik al-Salih had built a *qaysariya* in front of the bridge to al-Roda, and the soldiers' market was moved thence from al-Qahira. Although the Nile shore was blackened and restrained in space, al-Fustat boasted dockyards in profusion, and the channel between al-Roda and al-Fustat, subject to silting, was dredged annually.[66] The markets of al-Fustat were rich not only in indigenous commodities, but in imports from the Mediterranean and the Red Sea. Here were found confectionaries, soap manufactories, foundries (*masabik*) for glass, foundries for steel and copper, and paper manufactories, all of which "did not exist in al-Qahira, and there are none other than these in Egypt."[67]

Despite these advantages, Ibn Sa'id describes al-Fustat as dirty and muddy, with foul winds, black walls, and a filthy horizon. Much of the city was ruinous, and its markets, although large, were hemmed in. Its streets were narrow, encroached upon by houses of reeds and brick, story upon story. This was, however, somewhat mitigated by the construction of houses and pavilions along the Nile shore by the amirs of al-Malik al-Salih, attracted, no doubt, by the relocation of their sovereign to the island of al-Roda. The mosque of 'Amr, still the epicenter of the community, was, although somewhat dilapidated, frequented by scholars lecturing on the Qur'an, jurisprudence, and grammar.[68]

Summary

While the al-Fustat fire of 564/1168 certainly occurred, it must have been sporadic in its area of destruction, and, given the pre-existing truncation of the city, was not of the magnitude described by Maqrizi. Recurring mob violence—especially anti-Christian—may have caused him to exaggerate the fire into a conflagration lasting fifty-five days. Ibn Jubayr's description suggests relatively swift restoration. In any case, al-Fustat's survival and resilience as an entity during the Ayyubid period, despite the devastation and depopulation of the famines of 597–98/1201–1202, was the result of three major factors. Firstly, al-Fustat was the only viable port for Cairo during the Ayyubid period. Always the primary commercial port for al-Qahira, Ayyubid Fustat (and possibly al-Roda), due to the silting at al-Maqs, became the focus for local naval activity as well. Secondly, the building of al-Malik al-Salih's citadel on al-Roda sparked a resurgence of local trade and construction. Finally, it might be assumed that a certain reverence accorded by Muslims to the mosque of 'Amr, and by Christians to the churches and monasteries of Qasr al-Sham' and al-Hamra', may well have fostered a spirit of resurgence and renaissance in these respective institutions.

Chapter Four

Defenses

The construction of the Ayyubid fortifications of Cairo can be divided into five stages: the restoration of the wall of Badr al-Jamali by Saladin in 566/1170–71; the construction of the enceinte encircling al-Qahira and al-Fustat, concomittant with that of the citadel and the *qanatir* of Giza, all begun by Saladin in 572/1176–77; the excavation of trenches on the northern and eastern perimeters of al-Qahira in 588/1192–93; successive attempts to complete the western Qahira–Fustat enceinte from 596/1199–1200 onwards; and the construction of the citadel of al-Malik al-Salih on al-Roda, ca. 638–41/1240–44. Although royal residences and public buildings are discussed in the following chapter, those of Saladin's citadel and the citadel of al-Roda will be discussed here to avoid repetition. For clarification, the citadel of Saladin will henceforth be referred to as 'the citadel,' and that of al-Malik al-Salih as 'the citadel of al-Roda.' From an architectural standpoint, the citadel and walls are discussed in detail by Casanova, and especially Creswell, and the reader is referred to those works for further study.[1] Naval dockyards, in addition, are discussed in this chapter.

Saladin's Restoration of 566/1170–71

Recurrent Crusader attacks, in addition to the ever-present threat of internal revolt, prompted the restoration of the decaying enceinte of Badr al-Jamali in 566/1170–71. Saladin, then vizier to the Fatimid caliph al-'Adid, apparently limited his repair work to the lines of Badr's walls, although, in the opinion of Casanova, the burnt brick

enceinte of Badr al-Jamali (with the exception of stone gates and minor adjacent areas) was replaced by cut stone. This construction was supervised by Saladin's major domo, Baha' al-Din Qaraqush.[2] Three.gates, Bab al-Nasr and Bab al-Futuh in the north wall and Bab Zuwayla in the southern, together with some associated wall sections, were included from the former wall of Badr. Other gates, again probably on the same sites as those of Badr, were as follows: in the western wall (overlooking the Khalij) north to south, Bab al-Qantara, Bab al-Khawkha, and Bab al-Sa'ada; in the southern wall, Bab al-Faraj (to the west of Bab Zuwayla); and in the eastern wall, north to south, Bab al-Jadid and Bab al-Barqiya.[3]

Saladin's Plan of 572/1176–77

The Qahira–Fustat enceinte

Maqrizi states, in describing the third wall of al-Qahira:

> The construction was begun by the sultan Salah al-Din Yusuf ibn Ayyub in 566/1170–71, when he was vizier to al-'Adid li-Din Allah. In 569/1173–74, when he assumed [complete] power over the kingdom, he entrusted the building of the wall to the eunuch Baha' al-Din Qaraqush al-Asadi, who built it in stone, as it is now. He intended to surround al-Qahira, Misr, and the citadel with one wall. He lengthened the wall of al-Qahira from Bab al-Qantara to Bab al-Sha'riya, and from Bab al-Sha'riya to Bab al-Bahr. He built the citadel of al-Maqs, a great tower, which he placed on the Nile near Jami' al-Maqs. The wall stopped there. He had intended to extend the wall from al-Maqs until it rejoined the wall of Misr. He increased the wall of al-Qahira [by adding] the section adjoining Bab al-Nasr, and which extended to Bab al-Barqiya, Darb Batut, and to the outside of Bab al-Wazir, [so that] it would join the wall of Qal'at al-Jabal [the citadel]. But the construction of the wall stopped at a point near the ramp [al-sawwa] which is beneath the citadel, because of the death of Salah al-Din. Until now the remains of the walls are visible to the observer in the area between the end of the [standing] wall and the area of the citadel. Therefore, the joining of the wall of the citadel with that of Misr did not occur. The perimeter of the wall which surrounds al-Qahira today is 29,302 cubits, as they are usually known, i.e. Hashimi cubits, viz: between the citadel of al-Maqs on the edge of the Nile and the tower of Kawm al-Ahmar on the shore of Misr, 10,500 cubits; between the citadel of al-Maqs and the enceinte of Qal'at al-Jabal near the *masjid* of Sa'd al-Dawla 8,392 cubits; from there to the tower at Kawm al-Ahmar 7,200 cubits; finally, behind the citadel, to the front of the mosque of Sa'd al-

Dawla [i.e. the circumference of the citadel wall], 3,212 cubits. This is the length of its curve, including its towers, from Nile to Nile.[4]

Although Saladin did indeed "assume complete power over the kingdom" in 569/1174 (the year of Nur al-Din's death), this date for the extension of the walls is almost certainly fallacious. Abu Shamah, citing 'Imad al-Din al-Isfahani, gives an almost identical account, but in his annals for 572/1176–77. Ibn Wasil corroborates this evidence. Casanova is no doubt correct in his assertion that Maqrizi has confused the relative texts, especially in view of Maqrizi's own statement in the *Suluk* for the year 572/1176–77 that Saladin had ordered the building of the citadel and the associated walls enclosing al-Qahira and al-Fustat.[5]

While Casanova's general outline of the Ayyubid fortifications of al-Qahira and al-Fustat is reasonably accurate, certain errors in his placement of gates, towers, and natural outcrops were corrected by the author himself in his later monograph on the topography of al-Fustat, and later still by Creswell. As envisaged by Saladin, the Qahira–Fustat enceinte consisted of a quasi-triangular enclosure, pivoting on the citadel and encompassing the walled city of al-Qahira in its northeast corner. For our purposes, we shall consider these fortifications in five sections, viz: the northern wall from Bab al-Futuh to al-Maqs; the section of the northern and eastern walls extending a) east of Bab al-Nasr to Burj al-Zafir and b) south from Burj al-Zafir to Bab al-Wazir, just to the north of the citadel; the citadel itself; the wall running southwest from the citadel, presumably terminating at Bab al-Qantara (on the Nile to the southeast of Qasr al-Sham'); and, finally, the western wall paralleling the Nile from Bab al-Qantara to al-Maqs, never completed.

The north wall: Bab al-Futuh to al-Maqs

While the central nucleus of the northern wall of Badr al-Jamali was maintained—i.e. Bab al-Nasr, Bab al-Futuh, and the intermediate area—the wall was extended to the Nile at the old port of al-Maqs. This western extension included two new gates: Bab al-Sha'riya, to the west of the Khalij; and Bab al-Bahr, immediately to the east of the tower (*burj*) at al-Maqs. The tower of al-Maqs, also known as Qal'at Qaraqush, was erected on or near the site of the mosque (*jami'*) of al-Maqs, constructed by al-Hakim. According to Casanova, this mosque was destroyed by Qaraqush to erect his tower, but later rebuilt; its site is currently occupied by the mosque of Awlad 'Inan, just to the south of Midan Bab al-Hadid. Given the relevant passages of Maqrizi this assertion is questionable, and will be discussed in Chapter Seven. In any case, the tower was erected overlooking the Nile near the site of the present mosque of Awlad 'Inan and was destroyed in 770/1368–69 by Shams al-Din 'Abd Allah al-Maqri, vizier to al-Malik al-Ashraf Sha'ban. We have no architectural descriptions of this tower; however, as Casanova suggests, it might well have been similar in construction to that of- the northeastern corner tower, Burj al-Zafir.[6]

The northeast section: Bab al-Futuh to Bab al-Wazir

The fortifications of Qaraqush on the northeast of al-Qahira were effectively twofold: a restoration (or rebuilding) of the enceinte of Badr al-Jamali in 566/1170–71, and an extension of the northern wall east to Burj al-Zafir, where it turned abruptly to the south, rejoining the inner wall at Bab al-Barqiya. This extension included one additional gate (Bab al-Jadid) in the eastern wall, slightly south of Burj al-Zafir. The textual information, studied in detail by Casanova, corroborates this extension, especially in view of two archaeological factors: a) the appearance of two distinct eastern walls on the French expedition map of A.D. 1798, one running south from Burj al-Zafir, and a second, internal wall, running south from the northern enceinte about 350 meters east of Bab al-Nasr; and b) Casanova's claim to have seen the juncture of the internal wall (of 566/1170–71) with that of the northern enceinte, ca. A.D. 1894. From Bab al-Barqiya southward, the eastern wall proceeded to Bab al-Mahruq, and thence to Bab al-Wazir, where it terminated approximately 300 meters north of the present citadel. The construction ended at this point, as noted above, due to the death of Saladin.[7]

Southeast section: the citadel to Bab al-Qantara

Between the citadel and Bab al-Qantara are several remnants of Saladin's curtain wall, beginning near the prison (Sijn al-Manshiya) at the southern end of the Qaramidan, and extending southwest to a point approximately 400m. southeast of Qasr al-Sham'.[8] While the exact point of connection of the southeastern enceinte with the wall of the citadel is uncertain, the enceinte runs southeast of the Qaramidan on a line with—and superimposed by—the acqueduct of al-Nasir Muhammad ibn Qalaun. At a point to the south of the mashhad of Sayyida Nafisa, this acqueduct veers to the northwest and to its intake tower (the later work of al-Ghuri) at Fam al-Khalij, while the wall continues to the southeast beneath the rubbish heaps of al-Fustat, its traces occasionally visible, to a large segment which was exposed by the excavation of 'Ali Bahgat. While some further traces are visible, only further excavation will reveal its terminus at or near Bab al-Qantara, southwest of Qasr al-Sham' on the Nile shore.[9]

Following Creswell's analysis, there remain three exposed gates in the al-Fustat wall, viz: Bab al-Qarafa, slightly southwest of the Qaramidan; Bab al-Safa', farther to the southwest near the junction with the aqueduct; and remnants of a gateway—either largely destroyed or never completed—exposed by 'Ali Bahgat in his excavations to the southeast of Qasr al-Sham'. Bab al-Qarafa, itself excavated by one of Creswell's former students, is definitively Ayyubid, but the date of Bab al-Safa' is questionable. Identified by an inscription of Qait Bay, this gate was believed by Casanova to be Bab al-Safa', during Fatimid times the major entry to al-Fustat from the northeast. His identification, however, was based on a mislocation of Kawm al-Jarih, the present site of the mosque of Abu al-Su'ud. Although Casanova corrects this mistake in his later study of al-Fustat, Creswell nevertheless suggests that the original Bab al-Safa' lies beneath this later gate of Qait Bay, a claim rather difficult to substantiate in view of the textual information gathered by Casanova.[10] The third gate, southeast of Qasr al-Sham', while architecturally compatible with others of Ayyubid date, cannot be associated with any textual or epigraphic evidence and remains, therefore, nameless.

Bab al-Qantara

The terminal gate of the southeastern wall, Bab al-Qantara took its name from the adjacent Qantarat Bani Wa'il which straddled the mouth of the canal of the same name. This canal fed, at high water, Birkat Shata, Birkat al-Sha'ibiya, and Birkat al-Habash, and entered from the Nile at a point to the southeast of Qasr al-Sham'. Bab al-Qantara was, according to Maqrizi, one of the constructions of Qaraqush.[11] This gate should not be confused with that of the same name in the west wall of al-Qahira.

Bab Misr

Located near the Nile shore (no.104, map 3), east of the intake tower at Fam al-Khalij (and close to the present intersection of the railroad to Ma'adi and the aqueduct of al-Ghuri), this gate was, according to Maqrizi, constructed by Qaraqush as one of the entries to the western wall of the Qahira–Fustat enceinte. As this wall was never finished, the gate stood isolated. Described by Ibn Duqmaq as a vaulted passageway with doors at each end, this gate, according to several passages of Maqrizi studied in detail by Casanova, straddled a north–south thoroughfare, rather than an east-west passage which its position on the western enceinte would suggest. Casanova believed that Bab Misr was the entry to al-Fustat on the western thoroughfare from al-Qahira, as Bab al-Safa' serviced the eastern approach. Furthermore, its position, set back from the Nile, appeared to Casanova as inside the projected line of the western enceinte. Finally, because of a statement of Ibn al-Mutawwaj, cited by Maqrizi, Casanova has developed a theory that Bab Misr was, in fact, a northern gateway in a separate enceinte surrounding al-Fustat.[12]

Ibn al-Mutawwaj's description of an east–west wall connecting Bab Misr to Dar al-Nahhas on the al-Fustat shore, ca. 720/1320–21, has led Casanova to believe that the Bab Misr of Qaraqush formed a north–south entry to al-Fustat in a wall perpendicular to—and designed to abut—the proposed western enceinte of the Qahira–Fustat complex. Casanova's theory is, however, untenable. In the first place, it is based on a fragment of wall, observed only once, which may easily have been misinterpreted by Ibn al-Mutawwaj. Secondly, the position of Bab Misr was not so far removed from the Nile as to be incongruous with the proposed enceinte from Bab al-Qantara to al-Maqs, as Casanova suggests. Thirdly, as Casanova admits, the north–south axis of Bab Misr may have been a sort of double entrance in the al-Fustat enceinte, with two separate passages leading to the north and south. Finally, neither Maqrizi nor any other historian or contemporary traveler has mentioned a separate enclosure for al-Fustat; indeed, several have pointedly denied its existence.[13] In sum, Bab Misr must be considered only an isolated gate constructed by Qaraqush as an entrance to the western enceinte, never consummated.

Later developments

While the western wall and the section between Bab al-Wazir and the citadel were never completed, work continued on the Qahira–Fustat enceinte until the death of Saladin in 589/1193, and, albeit sporadically, thereafter. Maqrizi states that "around the wall of al-

Qahira was a ditch. The digging of this ditch was commenced from Bab al-Futuh to al-Maqs in Muharram 588 [Jan.18–Feb.16, 1192], and, likewise, on the eastern side, from Bab al-Nasr to Bab al-Barqiya and beyond."[14] This, as Creswell points out, suggests that those sections of the enceinte from al-Maqs to Bab al-Mahruq were completed by this date.[15]

Maqrizi's *Suluk* for the year 596/1199–1200 states that al-Afdal, as regent for al-Malik al-Mansur in Egypt, ordered defensive precautions against al-'Adil's impending attack from Syria. Al-Afdal instructed Qaraqush

> to put the citadel in a state of defense and to dig the foundations for the rest of the wall surrounding Misr and al-Qahira. He ordered him to dig until he reached bedrock, and to carry the debris to the interior of the city on the edge of the ditch, in order to create bastions, and to use cattle in this work. [He ordered him] to execute these works in the part between the river and the citadel of al-Maqs in such a way that one could no longer enter the city except by its gates.[16]

These reinforcements, while possibly including unfinished sections of the Qahira–Fustat eastern enceinte, must have included extensive works on the combined city's undefended west flank paralleling the Nile. Although the western wall of al-Qahira (first constructed by Badr al-Jamali and rebuilt by Saladin in 566/1170–71) should have offered some protection to al-Qahira only some thirty years after its reconstruction, it is not, in any case, mentioned again in contemporary chronicles.

Several entries in the *History of the Patriarchs of Alexandria* note further attempts to complete the western enceinte of al-Qahira and al-Fustat. Against the impending Fifth Crusade, in 614/1217–18 al-Malik al-'Adil ordered a wall constructed at Misr along the river shore, beginning at Dar al-Mulk (near Bab al-Qantara, the southeastern point of al-Fustat) and extending along the length of the Khalij to al-Qahira. Under the direction of his son, al-Kamil Muhammad, foundations were dug and building commenced. The inhabitants of al-Fustat and al-Qahira were levied to split stones nightly, although the residents of al-Fustat appear to have been relieved of these duties earlier than the inhabitants of al-Qahira. Later, during the same crusade (615–18/1218–21), al-Malik al-Kamil and his brother al-Malik al-Mu'azzam ordered the building of a wall from Misr to al-Qahira to join the two cities. While partially a repeat of the above, we find a change here in both the laborers employed and the modus operandi. Al-Kamil and al-Mu'azzam initially planned (and, no doubt, partially built) walls having stone foundations with upper works of earth. These were the labors of Berber workmen (*maghariba*). Al-Kamil and al-Mu'azzam then reversed their decision, demolished the Berber construction, and rebuilt the wall with sun-dried bricks. "Then the order came to remove the bricks of the people in al-Qahira and Misr." In 634/1236–37 al-Malik al-Kamil ordered the foundations of the Qahira–Fustat enceinte dug along the river bank, a month's work involving forced labor for all regardless of religion or class. During the reign of al-'Adil II similar works were carried out.[17]

The western enceinte initiated by al-Malik al-'Adil "extending along the length of the Khalij to al-Qahira" could narrowly be interpreted as leaving the Nile shoreline and following the Khalij itself to join the previously constructed western wall of al-Qahira. It is more likely, however, that the wall was constructed parallel to the Khalij, but closer to the Nile, especially considering the preexisting towers/gates at Bab al-Qantara, Bab Misr, and al-Maqs. The salient point is that although the construction of the western enceinte was attempted at several points during the later Ayyubid regime—in times of political crisis, whether Crusader threats or civil wars—the wall was never completed, and the idea of its consummation lapsed into oblivion as soon as the crises passed.

The citadel (Qal'at al-Jabal)

The outcrop upon which the citadel rests, a spur of the Muqattam chain, was previously occupied by Qubbat al-Hawa' (v.s.), an Abbasid pavilion which was destroyed with the downfall of the Tulunid regime (ca.292/904–905). By the end of the Fatimid dynasty the site included a dozen mosques and tombs of various political and religious dignitaries, including the mosque of Sa'd al-Dawla, whom Casanova believes to have been *wali* of Cairo under the Fatimid caliph al-Amir. Although there is some contradiction as to their exact position, it is reasonably certain that all of these structures were located within the present citadel walls and that they ran, generally, in a northeast–southwest direction.[18] All of these structures were destroyed to make way for Saladin's citadel.

The foundation and construction of the citadel

Maqrizi's description:

> Here is the reason for its building. When the sultan Salah al-Din Yusuf ibn Ayyub had ended the Fatimid dynasty in Egypt and had assumed [complete] power, he resided at Dar al-Wizara in al-Qahira. He remained, however, troubled by partisans of the Fatimid caliphs in Egypt and al-Malik al-'Adil Nur al-Din Mahmud ibn Zanki, sultan of Syria. Initially he protected himself from Nur al-Din by sending his brother al-Malik al-Mu'azzam Shams al-Dawla Turan Shah to the Yemen in 569/1173–74, thus securing that kingdom for him and denying it to Nur al-Din. Shams al-Dawla conquered the Yemen, and God spared Salah al-Din the fear of Nur al-Din, as he [Nur al-Din] died in the same year. With his flank secure, [Saladin] wished to build himself a stronghold in Egypt. He had [already] divided the two Fatimid palaces among his amirs and quartered them there. It is said that the reason for his choice of the site of the citadel is that he hung meat in al-Qahira, and it went bad after a day and a night, while he hung the meat of another animal at the site of the citadel and it did not change until after two days and two nights. Therefore he ordered the foundation of the citadel there. He entrusted its construction to Qaraqush. He [Qaraqush] began its construction, as well as the extension to the wall of al-Qahira in 572/1176–77. He destroyed the mosques and tombs on the citadel site. He destroyed the small pyramids at Giza facing Misr—there were many in number—and he used the stone in the construction of the wall, the citadel, and the *qanatir* of Giza. He began the building of the wall surrounding al-Qahira, the citadel, and Misr, but the sultan died before the wall and the citadel were completed. These works were neglected until the reign of al-Malik al-'Adil who placed his son al-Malik al-Kamil in the citadel, appointed him his deputy in Egypt, and named him his successor. He [al-Kamil] completed the citadel, and he built within it the palace of the sultan [al-Dar al-Sultaniya]; that was in 604/1207–1208. Al-Kamil lived in it until his death, and it remained the seat of government for Egypt until our times. The sultan Salah al-Din Yusuf ibn Ayyub stayed at the citadel occasionally, as did his son al-Malik al-'Aziz during his father's lifetime; then he moved from there to Dar al-Wizara.[19]

Choice of the site

The spur of the Muqattam on which the citadel rests was the natural pivot point for the Qahira–Fustat enceinte. Almost equidistant from the northern wall of al-Qahira and Bab al-Qantara at al-Fustat, this promontory provided a vantage point from which to ward off attacks from the northeast, as well as a zone of security against insurrections from within the city itself. Although considerably higher, the main bulk of the Muqattam to the east and southeast presented no significant threat, as no catapults of Saladin's day were capable of spanning the gap between the two hills.[20]

Construction during Saladin's reign

The citadel was, as Casanova points out, divided into two distinct sections, eastern and western. The eastern section was a massive military/defensive complex while the western section, considerably less fortified, provided a residential and administrative complex for the sultanate. In time of crisis, the eastern section served as an immediate refuge for the sultan and his entourage. The work of Saladin was largely, if not strictly, limited to the eastern enceinte. A possible exception was the well of Joseph, within the western enclosure and excavated or enlarged by Qaraqush. The foundation inscription of the citadel, above Bab al-Mudarraj, is dated 579/1183–84. This, as Casanova suggests, is probably the terminal date for work accomplished during Saladin's reign, especially since he permanently left Egypt in the previous year. Based on Casanova's historical research and Creswell's architectural survey, Saladin's work on the eastern enclosure consists of the following: the enceinte with half-round towers, two postern gates, and the two major gates which remained in Maqrizi's time, Bab al-Mudarraj and Bab al-Qarafa. In addition, two major trenches were excavated, still largely extant, against the northern and eastern walls of the enceinte. Bab al-Mudarraj, on the northwestern side, was the main entrance from the city, while Bab al-Qarafa, the inner part of which is thought to have been constructed by Saladin, faced the cemetery areas to the south and southeast and was considerably less frequented.[21]

Bi'r Yusuf (Joseph's well) within the western enclosure and immediately to the south of the mosque of al-Nasir Muhammad ibn Qalaun, was, according to Ibn 'Abd al-Zahir

> among the wonders of construction. At the top of the well cattle move in a circle to raise the water from a reservoir located at its midpoint [in depth], where other cattle raise the water from the lowest depths of the well. It has a path to the water by which the cattle descend to its spring. All of this is cut into the rock; there is no building in it. It is said that [it is dug] to the same level as Birkat al-Fil, and that its water is sweet. I have heard from some older men, that when the well was dug, its water was very sweet. Qaraqush and his assistants, wishing to augment the water supply, widened the excavation into the bedrock, and encountered a saline spring which contaminated the earlier source. The *qadi* Nasir al-

Din Shafi'i ibn 'Ali, in *Kitab 'aja'ib al-bunyan,* mentioned that he descended into this well by a staircase of about three hundred steps.[22]

Joseph's well, then, was constructed in two shafts, not directly above each other, which were separated at midpoint.[23] Casanova makes several further observations. First, the well is located within the western enclosure outside of Saladin's enceinte. Although this might suggest that the well was excavated as part of the later residential complex, this is negated by three factors. Firstly, Qubbat al-Hawa' and the Fatimid mosques and tombs which previously occupied the citadel site would have needed water, probably from local wells. Secondly, according to Ibn 'Abd al-Zahir, the well was enlarged by Qaraqush. Finally, in the same passage, Ibn 'Abd al-Zahir relates from hearsay that the well was formerly descended by a series of steps, suggesting that the present ramp existed in his time, and may well have been part of the renovations of Qaraqush.[24]

Casanova further points out that the name Yusuf, as applied to this well, should probably be attributed to the patriarch Joseph rather than to Saladin. His argument is based on the following points: that it would be unusual to name the well Yusuf rather than al-Salahi or al-Nasiri; that Ibn Khallikan states that Saladin made numerous foundations, none of which was known under his name; that the story of the Patriarch Joseph was associated with many places in the area of the citadel; and, finally that the name Yusuf was attached to several buildings at the citadel which were constructed after the Ayyubids, such as Diwan Yusuf built by al-Nasir Muhammad ibn Qalaun. His argument, on the whole, is tenable.[25]

Less acceptable, however, is Casanova's suggestion that Joseph's well was dug after Saladin's campaign of 583/1187–88 during the Third Crusade. A statement of Ibn 'Abd al-Zahir (620–92/1223–92) cited by Ibn Taghribirdi, maintains that Saladin used thousands of Frankish prisoners on the building of the wall of al-Qahira and the digging of the well at the citadel.[26] A second statement of the same author, cited by Maqrizi, suggests that Qaraqush used fifty thousand prisoners-of-war on the building of the citadel. Casanova believes that such a large number of prisoners would have been unavailable before the Third Crusade; this however, is belied by Ibn Jubayr's statement in 578/1183:

> We also looked upon the building of the citadel, an impregnable fortress adjoining Cairo which the sultan thinks to take as his residence, extending its walls until it enfolds the two cities of Misr and Cairo. The

forced laborers on this construction, and those executing all the skilled services and vast preparations such as sawing the marble, cutting the huge stones, and digging the fosse that girdles the walls of the fortress noted above—a fosse hollowed out with pickaxes from the rock to be a wonder among wonders of which trace may remain—were the foreign Rumi prisoners whose numbers were beyond computation. There was no cause for any but them to labor on this construction. The sultan has constructions in progress in other places and on these too the foreigners are engaged so that those of the Muslims who might have been used in this public work are relieved of it all, no work of that nature falling on any of them.[27]

Thus Frankish prisoners were employed en masse on Saladin's construction projects at least five years prior to the Third Crusade and certainly could have been used on the excavation and/or enlargement of Joseph's well.

The *History of the Patriarchs* states that among the construction works of Qaraqush were a well and cistern at the citadel of Cairo.

[Qaraqush] dug a well in it, using iron tools, from the top of the *jabal* to its base, reaching water at a depth estimated as two hundred cubits. In addition, he constructed [*'amala*] there a cistern [*sihrij*] to be filled from tanks [which] he had constructed outside the citadel.[28]

Despite such contradictory evidence, the well probably existed in Fatimid times and, since it was not included within Saladin's eastern enceinte, it was enlarged, at some point during his reign, with the intention of serving the western or residential complex.

Building materials and construction processes

Maqrizi, in his description of the pyramids, relates:

There were formerly at Giza, opposite Misr, a great number of pyramids, all of them small. They were destroyed in the time of the sultan Salah al-Din Yusuf ibn Ayyub, under the auspices of Qaraqush. With these materials he built the citadel [Qal'at al-Jabal], the wall surrounding al-Qahira and Misr, and the *qanatir* of Giza.[29]

'Abd al-Latif al-Baghdadi, writing ca. 597–99/1200–1203, states:

One saw formerly at Giza a large number of pyramids, small, to be truthful, which were destroyed in the time of Salah al-Din Yusuf ibn Ayyub. Their destruction was the work of Qaraqush, a Greek [*rumi*] eunuch, who was one of the amirs of the army of this prince, and a man of genius. He supervised the building projects of the capital, and it was he who erected the wall of stone which surrounds al-Fustat, al-Qahira, the land between the two cities, and the citadel built on Jabal Muqattam. It was also he who constructed this citadel and the two wells that one sees there today. [Joseph's well and the accompanying cistern?]. . . . Qaraqush [also] used the stones from the small pyramids, which he destroyed, for the construction of the arches one presently sees at Giza. . . . One can still see today the remains of the pyramids destroyed by Qaraqush; I mean to say the materials, the cores, and the interiors of these edifices. As these were only the building debris and small stones which were of no use to the construction of the aforementioned arches, they were left in place.[30]

It is unacceptable to this writer that the building stone for the three projects of the citadel, the Qahira–Fustat enceinte, and the *qanatir* of Giza (v.i.) was supplied solely by the destruction of the minor pyramids of Giza. Given the size of the smaller pyramids still remaining at Giza, the number of structures requisite to supply the materials for a construction project of this size would be legion and the task of transporting the stones ten to fifteen miles from Giza to the Muqattam a herculean, although not impossible, task. We unfortunately lack pre-Ayyubid Arabic texts as to the number of small pyramids extant at Giza, and current archaeological evidence renders us no traces of the specific pyramids destroyed as noted by 'Abd al-Latif. While the *qanatir* of Giza were probably built from destroyed pyramids in the immediate area, it is also likely that most of the stone for the citadel was quarried in its vicinity. Ibn Jubayr, while noting the transportation of stone from dismantled structures near Abu Sir, stresses the Frankish prisoners excavating the huge trench girdling the northern and eastern sides of the citadel, cutting and sawing the huge stones thereat.[31] As Casanova points out, the occasional block inscribed with hieroglyphics is observed in the north wall and its extension east to Burj al-Zafir,[32] but reused blocks are common throughout antiquity and these are not necessarily remnants of the smaller pyramids. (Indeed, most of the remaining pyramids are without inscriptions.) Then, as Creswell points out, the citadel was built on a small spur of the Muqattam which was "separated from the main mass by Saladin who purposely quarried stone here."[33] Although he supplies no historical reference for this statement, the size of the trenches dug (cf. Ibn Jubayr), which may have included at least part of the quarried gap between the citadel and the Muqattam, and the far more practical approach of using local stone rather than hauling it from Giza, render Creswell's view highly plausible. Thus, given the testaments of 'Abd al-Latif and Maqrizi, while some of the stone for the building of the citadel and the Qahira–Fustat enceinte may indeed have come from the small pyramids of Giza, it is far more reasonable to assume that the lion's share of building materials was quarried in the immediate area of the Muqattam.

Occupation of the citadel

Casanova, based on a series of citations from Maqrizi's *Khitat* and al-Bakri al-Siddiq, draws the following conclusions: that although Saladin had intended to complete the residential portion of the citadel, this section was incomplete (or perhaps not even begun) at the time of his death, largely due to his absence from Egypt; that Saladin and his successors (al-'Aziz, al-Mansur Muhammad, and al-'Adil) lived at Dar al-Wizara in al-Qahira until the reign of al-Malik al-'Adil, although they occasionally sojourned at the construction site of the citadel; that the first to build residences in the palace complex was al-Malik al-Kamil as *na'ib* to al-'Adil in Egypt; and that "al-Malik al-Kamil was the first Ayyubid ruler who, after completing the plan of his uncle, Saladin, definitively established the royal residence at the citadel in 604/1207–1208."[34] Maqrizi further notes, in the *Suluk*, that the remaining members of the Fatimid family were transferred to the citadel at this time (from Dar al-Muzaffar in al-Qahira), where they were lodged "in a house which had the appearance of a prison."[35] The Ayyubid and Mamluk sultans, with the exception of a brief period under al-Malik al-Salih (v.i.), resided at the citadel thereafter.

Renovation and addition by al-Malik al-Kamil

'Imad al-Din al-Isfahani, cited by Abu Shamah, states that the circumference of the citadel was 3,210 Hashimi cubits or, as calculated by Creswell, 2,103.73 meters. In his architectural survey, Creswell concludes that the original enceinte—i.e. the eastern fortified enclosure of Saladin—measured approximately 1,400 m., leaving ca. 650 m. to be accounted for (his calculation). Creswell believes, therefore, that at least some of the western palace complex was constructed during Saladin's reign, particularly since 'Imad al-Din, as Saladin's personal secretary, had both access to the architect's plans and personal familiarity with the site.[36] Since the western enclosure is almost completely covered with later construction, there is, as Creswell admits, no archaeological evidence to back this assertion.[37]

Casanova, on the other hand, suggests that nothing related to the western enclosure was the work of Saladin, with the possible exception of Joseph's well. He believes that the eastern enceinte constructed by Saladin measured 1,800 m. in circumference, as opposed to Creswell's 1,400 m., thus leaving only ca. 300 m. to be accounted for. Erroneously, however, as effectively proven by Creswell, Casanova has included in his measurements the major square and round towers of the eastern enclosure, all of which were built under the administration of al-Malik al-Kamil. In any case, while it is a certainty that the measurements of 'Imad al-Din suggest a total enclosure of a greater circumference than that of the eastern enceinte, any suggestion of Saladin's work on the palace complex, with the exception of Joseph's well, can be proven only by intensive—and unfeasible—excavations. The textual evidence—as compiled by Casanova—indicates that any construction in the western enclosure prior to al-Kamil must have been very minimal indeed. We must conclude, for lack of further evidence, that most if not all of the western enclosure was the work of al-Malik al-Kamil and his successors.[38]

As Creswell points out, Saladin's enclosure was "as complete and as strong as the time at his disposal to make it."[39] The major square and round towers of al-Kamil, discussed in detail by Creswell, were constructed in an architectural style similar to that of the Ayyubid citadels of Damascus and Basra, and spaced at such intervals as to break the uniform spacing of the half-round towers of Saladin. Al-Kamil's work on the eastern enclosure amounted to a strengthening, but not an enlargement, of the enceinte completed some forty years earlier by Qaraqush.

Burj al-Matar, the twin towers flanking the southern wall of the eastern enceinte, was utilized as pigeon-cotes which, along with Burj al-Fayyum outside the Barqiya quarter of al-Qahira, housed the carrier pigeons which delivered messages throughout the sultanate. According to Maqrizi:

> In the citadel were pigeon-cotes intended for carrier pigeons. According to Ibn 'Abd al-Zahir . . . at the end of Jumada al-Akhira of 687/1288 there were 1,900 of these birds. They were under the supervision of a number of overseers, each overseer supervising a fixed number. All of these birds were kept in the towers of the citadel with the exception of a certain number which were kept in the tower at Burj al-Barqiya outside of al-Qahira which was known as Burj al-Fayyum. This tower was established by the amir Fakhr al-Din 'Uthman ibn Qizil, major domo [*ustadar*] to al-

Malik al-Kamil. . . . It was called Burj al-Fayyum since that entire province was the *iqta'* of Ibn Qizil.[40]

Casanova believes, not unreasonably, that the citadel pigeon-cotes were established by al-Malik al-Kamil as well, although Burj al-Matar was constructed under Saladin, as later proven by Creswell.[41]

In Casanova's opinion, al-Kamil's work on or near the western enclosure consisted of the following: an *iwan*; two gates, Bab al-Sirr and Bab al-Qulla; the royal stables; a library (Khizanat al-Kutub); a vizier's residence (Qa'at al-Sahib), and a mosque.

The iwan

On the evidence of an unidentified Coptic author, Casanova—citing Amelineau and Quatremere—establishes the existence of an *iwan* (throne-room, court of justice) on the citadel during the administration of al-Malik al-Kamil.[42]

Bab al-Sirr and Bab al-Qulla

A secret, or private gate, entered the western enclosure from the north, leading directly to the great *iwan*. This gate (Bab al-Sirr), according to Qalqashandi, was kept closed, and opened only for those authorized to pass, presumably court officials. Casanova believes this gate to be an integral part of the constructions of al-Malik al-Kamil for access to the *iwan*, palaces, and administrative buildings within.[43] Bab al-Qulla, centrally placed in the wall common to both the eastern and western enclosures, was the main path of communication between the two. This gate existed in the time of Baybars, and Casanova believes it a consequence of al-Kamil's construction and renovation.[44]

The royal stables

As mentioned above, al-Malik al-Kamil's transferal to the citadel fostered the relocation of the market of horses, donkeys, and camels to al-Rumayla; the probable establishment of the royal stables at the citadel; and the establishment of a *midan* on the site of the present Qaramidan. These stables, according to Quatremere, existed during the reign of Baybars.[45] Casanova believes that the stables were transferred to the citadel under al-Kamil for two reasons; firstly, that the distance from the former political centers of al-Qahira and al-Fustat would require a ready access to mounts near at hand, and secondly, that the continuing wars against the Crusaders accentuated the need for these mounts. These stables were located at the foot of the citadel between al-Rumayla and the Qaramidan. Casanova continues:

> In the time of Qalqashandi, the stables connected with the citadel by a special gate. Already in the time of Baybars this connection seems to have existed. It is even reasonable to suppose that it existed in the time of al-Kamil.[46]

Khizanat al-Kutub

Khizanat al-Kutub, the royal library, was, under the Fatimid dynasty, one of the most important depositories of books and manuscripts in the mediaeval world. While not a defense-related institution, we will nonetheless discuss it here because of its later and final location within the western enclosure of the citadel.

In his *Khitat*, Maqrizi gives extensive detail on the contents and vicissitudes of this library from the time of its founding by the Fatimid caliph al-'Aziz. Located, apparently, in several areas within the Fatimid palace(s), the library was severely damaged during the Turkish uprisings of the reign of al-Mustansir. At some point, according to Ibn Tuwayr, this library was relocated to one of the conference rooms (*majalis*) of Maristan al-'Atiq, the hospital established by Saladin in an assembly hall (*qa'a*) constructed by al-'Aziz bil-Allah south of the eastern palace. It was, presumably, there at the end of the Fatimid dynasty.[47] Maqrizi continues:

> Ibn Surah supervised the sale of the library in the days of al-Malik al-Nasir Salah al-Din. . . . Ibn Abi Tayy said, concerning Salah al-Din's takeover of the palace, that Khizanat al-Kutub was among what was sold. It was one of the marvels of the world. It is said that there was not, in all the lands of Islam, a library larger than the one in the palace at al-Qahira. Among its wonders were twelve hundred copies of *Tarikh al-Tabari* . . . and [many things] other than that. It is said that it contained 601,000 volumes, and many attributed manuscripts [*khutut mansuba*]. . . . To corroborate this, when al-Qadi al-Fadil 'Abd al-Rahim ibn 'Ali founded al-Madrasa al-Fadiliya in al-Qahira, he placed in it 100,000 bound volumes [*kitab mujallad*]. The auctioneer of books, Ibn Sura, sold all the books [of the Fatimid library] over a period of years. Ibn Abi Wasil mentioned that Khizanat al-Kutub consisted of more than 120,000 volumes.[48]

In *Kitab al-suluk* for the year 626/1288–89, Maqrizi states that

> on Sunday, the fifth of Jumada al-Awwal, the palace [*dar*] of the *qadi* al-Ashraf Ahmad, son of al-Qadi al-Fadil, was sequestrated, and on the twenty-sixth, the entire library [Khizanat al-Kutub] was transported to the

citadel. There were sixty-eight thousand volumes. On the third of Jumada al-Akhira, the cabinets [*khashab*] of the removed libraries were transported to the citadel on forty-nine camels. On Saturday 22 Rajab of this year the books and libraries from the citadel were transported back to his [al-Fadil's] palace. The number [of books] was, it is said, 11,808. Among the books taken was the *Book of Atabegs and Eras* by Abu 'Ala' al-Ma'arri in sixty volumes.[49]

Casanova further mentions a celestial sphere in brass, located in the Borgia museum at Velletri. The inscription on this globe indicates that it was made for the library (*khizana*) of al-Malik al-Kamil by Qaysar ibn Abu al-Qasim ibn Musafir in 622/1225–26. Based on several citations, including one from Abu al-Fayda referring to Qaysar as *muhandis* (geometrician, engineer), Casanova believes that Qaysar may have been employed on al-Kamil's citadel construction as well.[50]

In summary, Khizanat al-Kutub, after being depleted at the hands of the Turks under al-Mustansir, was sold, apparently in totality, by Saladin. The largest known collection of these volumes to survive the sale was that purchased by al-Qadi al-Fadil and deposited in his *madrasa*. Judging from the inscription on the celestial globe at Velletri, al-Kamil maintained a library at least as early as 622/1225–26. The sequestration of 68,000 volumes from the palace of al-Ashraf Ahmad ibn . al-Qadi al-Fadil to the citadel library is tenable; as Casanova points out, al-Kamil was a lover of the sciences, and if a certain number of volumes were returned to al-Ashraf Ahmad, they must have been especially selected.[51] However, Maqrizi, in his description of al-Madrasa al-Fadiliya (v.i.), states that the primary loss of books from this *madrasa* resulted from the famine of 694/1294–95, when students sold the books, often for a loaf of bread, until most of them dissappeared. "They then passed from hand to hand—in borrowing among the *fuqaha'*—and became separated."[52] The possibility exists, then, that al-Qadi al-Fadil—and, perhaps, his son al-Ashraf Ahmad—formed two separate libraries, one at al-Madrasa al-Fadiliya and one at al-Qadi al-Fadil's palace which, according to Maqrizi, was in the neighborhood of the *madrasa*.[53] Although not specifically stated, it can be assumed that the palace collection—which was transferred to the citadel—emanated from the Fatimid libraries as well. A major fire at the citadel destroyed Khizanat al-Kutub in 691/1291–92.[54]

A vizier's residence (Qa'at al-Sahib) and a mosque

Casanova states:

> I also attribute to al-Kamil the construction of the edifice called the hall of the Sahib [Qa'at al-Sahib]. The title *sahib* was given to viziers from the time of Safi al-Din ibn Shukr, who was vizier to al-Kamil. In the time of Baybars, there was a mosque here; the caliph al-Hakim gave the Friday sermon [*khutba*] in it. It probably dated from the time of al-Kamil, and must have stood on the site of the mosque rebuilt by Muhammad ibn Qalaun.[55]

Qa'at al-Salihiya

For the remainder of the Ayyubid dynasty, the only known additional structure on the citadel is that of Qa'at al-Salihiya, an audience hall constructed by al-Malik al-Salih. The move of al-Malik al-Salih to the island of al-Roda fostered, no doubt, a period of relative neglect for the citadel—until the assumption of the first Mamluk sultan, al-Mu'izz Najm al-Din Aybak.[56] Thenceforth, with the exception of the French occupation, the citadel remained the focal point of Egyptian administration through the reign of Muhammad 'Ali in the nineteenth century.

The *qanatir* of Giza

Ibn Jubayr, 578/1183, states:

> Another of the Sultan's [Saladin] benefactions, and a monument of enduring usefulness to Muslims, are the bridges [*qanatir*] he has begun to construct seven miles west of Misr at the end of a causeway that begins at high-Nile beside Misr [i.e. opposite, on the Giza shore]. This causeway is like a mountain stretched along the ground, over which it runs for a distance of six miles until. it reaches the aforesaid bridges. These have about forty arches of the biggest type used in bridges, and reach the desert which extends from them to Alexandria. It is one of the most excellent measures taken by a prudent king in readiness against any sudden onslaught by an enemy coming through the breach of Alexandria at the time of the Nile's overflow, when the countryside is in flood and the passage of soldiers thereby prevented. He prepared this as a passageway for any time it may be needed. . . . To the Egyptians, the construction of these bridges is a warning of a coming event, for they see in it an augury that the Almohades will conquer it and the eastern regions. . . . Near to these bridges are the ancient pyramids.[57]

'Abd al-Latif al-Baghdadi, writing in 597/1200–1201, notes:

> Qaraqush used the stones from the small pyramids which he had had destroyed in the construction of the arches which are now to be seen at

Giza; these arches themselves are edifices worthy of the greatest admiration and deserve to be counted among the works of the giants. There were more than forty similar arches; but in the present year of 597/1200–1201, the responsibility for the arches having been entrusted to the hands of an ignorant and foolhardy man, he decided to have them stopped up. He imagined that this would make the waters, held back from their normal course as though by a dam, spill over onto the land of Giza, which would thereby share in the benefits of the inundation. Just the opposite happened: the force of the waters against the arches weakened three of them, which crumbled and fell, without the lands which this man had hoped to flood having gained that advantage.[58]

Ibn al-Wardi, cited by DeSacy, states that "at Giza are the bridges; nothing similar to this work has ever been built. There are forty arches in a single line." It is DeSacy's further belief that the causeway built by Qaraqush, and which extended to the arches, "furnished, at all times, a commodious route for the transport of materials destined for the construction of the wall of Cairo and the citadel of the mountain."[59]

Maqrizi, in his *Khitat*, renders us the following description:

> The author of *The Book of Marvels of Construction* [*Kitab 'aja'ib al-bunyan*] said that the bridges existing today at Giza are among the marvels of building and [like] the works of giants. There are more than forty arches. The amir Qaraqush, the eunuch, built them. He supervised the building operations in the days of the sultan Salah al-Din Yusuf ibn Ayyub, using the rubble from the pyramids which he had destroyed at Giza. With the stone from these pyramids, he built these bridges. He also built the wall of al-Qahira and Misr and the area between them, and the citadel of the mountain. . . . In the year 599/1202–1203 a man took charge of these bridges who did not understand them properly, and he dammed them as a block to defer the water. The pressure of the water increased to such an extent that three of the arches collapsed and split apart. The anticipated water flow did not occur. In 708/1308–1309 al-Malik al-Muzaffar Baybars al-Jashankir undertook their repair. He rebuilt what was ruined and restored what was unsound in it. This [undertaking] brought major improvement. When Qaraqush built these bridges, he [also] built a causeway [*rasif*] of stone. He built it from the edge of the Nile opposite Misr. It resembled a mountain stretching along the ground, for a distance of six miles until it reached the bridges.[60]

The suggested primary roles for the *qanatir* of Giza are the transport of troops and building materials, both of which may have been valid. A secondary and later role, irrigation, failed. The suggestion of Ibn Jubayr that the causeway and arches were constructed for troop transport is, to this writer, the most valid. That the causeway and arches were largely constructed of rubble from the smaller pyramids is acceptable, largely due to proximity; that masses of stone were removed from Giza to build the Qahira–Fustat enceinte and the citadel is very questionable indeed. It is possible that some stone was transported along this bridge/causeway to the western shore of the Nile, and thence to al-Fustat by boat bridges which traversed the river via the southern tip of al-Roda. However, logistics would dictate that most of the building stone for the fortifications of al-Qahira and al-Fustat emanated from local quarries in the vicinity of the Muqattam. That the arches were originally designed for irrigation purposes is effectively negated by 'Abd al-Latif and Maqrizi, in their almost identical descriptions of the disastrous attempt to dam the area ca. 597/1200–1201.

Naval Facilities

While the al-Fustat area was replete with commercial dockyards and, despite massive alluviation, some trading facilities still existed at al-Maqs, information on the exact locations of naval shipyards under the Ayyubids remains somewhat vague. As noted in Chapter One, naval arsenals existed at both al-Roda and al-Fustat during the reign of the Fatimid caliph al-Amir, with that of al-Fustat (near Fam al-Khalij) lasting until ca. 700/1300–1301. The *History of the Patriarchs* mentions Ayyubid naval dockyards in three instances. In 614/1217–18, during the reign of al-Malik al-'Adil, a boat bridge was constructed from al-Roda to Giza, beginning "in front of the new dockyard" (*al-sana'a al-mustajidda*), suggesting a dockyard either at the southern tip of al-Roda or on the opposite bank at al-Fustat. In 637/1239–40, as part of a campaign to the Yemen, al-Malik al-Salih had forty ships constructed in dockyards (*masani'*) at al-Fustat, thence transported to the Red Sea (in sections) by camelback. Finally, in 640/1242–43, al-Malik al-Salih ordered the transfer of the dockyards for both Nile ships and warships from al-Fustat to Giza, as part of an attempt to isolate himself at his new citadel on al-Roda. There is no evidence that such a transfer actually took place.[61] It is reasonably safe to assume that naval dockyards existed at several points along the shore of al-Fustat and at the southern end of al-Roda either simultaneously or at different times under the Ayyubids, with commercial dockyards sequestered during military emergencies as well.

The Citadel of al-Roda

The citadel of al-Roda, which encompassed the southern half of the island, was constructed by al-Malik al-Salih ca. 637–41/1239–44. This vast enclosure served two functions: firstly, as a palace-administrative complex temporarily supplanting Saladin's citadel (Qal'at al-Jabal) and secondly, as the barracks of al-Salih's Bahri (riverine) *mamalik*, the nucleus of the ensuing dynasty. While certain activity must have continued at Qal'at al-Jabal (Qa'at al-Salihiya was founded during this reign, v.s.), the focal point of administrative and military activity was definitely transferred to the river for almost a decade.

As noted in previous chapters, the island of al-Roda, although the site of military installations from the Umayyad through the Fatimid dynasties, was primarily a center for gardens, recreation, and pavilions, including al-Hawdaj, a pavilion constructed by the Fatimid caliph al-Amir on the northern end of the island.

According to Ibn al-Mutawwaj, the island was purchased by al-Malik al-Muzaffar Taqi al-Din 'Umar ibn Shahanshah ibn Ayyub (nephew of Saladin) in 566/1170–71. When appointed to the governorate of Hama in 574/1178–79, Taqi al-Din endowed the entire island upon his *madrasa* (al-Taqawiya) at al-Fustat (v.i.). Al-Malik al-Salih on his assumption of the sultanate rented the island from the *qadi* Fakhr al-Din al-Sukri, shaykh of the above-mentioned *madrasa*,

> for a period of sixty years in two payments, each payment for a part of the island. The first section [*qit'a*] was from Jami' Ghayn [a congregational mosque built during the reign of al-Hakim] north to the pavilions, and in width from shore to shore. He [also] rented the second part—the remaining land of the island—which included date palms, sycamores, and plants. When al-Malik al-Salih built the pavilions of Qal'at al-Jazira the date palms were removed and their site was included in the area of the buildings.[62]

Maqrizi continues:

> Know that the royal pavilions [i.e. al-Hawdaj] and other residences, as previously mentioned, remained at al-Roda until the reign of al-Malik al-Salih. . . . He established the citadel of al-Roda. It was known as Qal'at al-

Miqyas, Qal'at al-Roda, Qal'at al-Jazira, and Qal'at al-Salihiya. He began digging the foundations on Wednesday the fifth of Sha'ban and began the construction . . . on Friday the sixteenth. On the tenth of Dhu al-Qa'da began the destruction of the houses, palaces, and mosques on the island of al-Roda. The people left their houses. He destroyed the Jacobite church near the nilometer, and included its place within the citadel. He spent much on its building. Within the citadel he constructed houses and palaces. He built [on the citadel wall] sixty towers. He built a mosque in it. Within the citadel he planted every [kind] of tree. He removed to it granite columns from temples, as well as marble columns, and sent to it arms, tools of war, and necessities in grains, supplies and foods, fearing an attack of the Franks. They were at the time headed for Egypt. He spent such effort and expense towards its completion that it was said that he raised each stone as a dinar and each brick as a dirham. The citadel became a wonder in the amount of its ornament, and the observer was bewildered by the excellence of its decorated ceilings and that of its marble. It is said that he removed a thousand palm trees from the site of the citadel. . . . He destroyed al-Hawdaj and Bustan al-Mukhtar. He also destroyed thirty-three mosques built by the caliphs and nobility of Egypt.[63]

That the wholesale destruction of mosques did not meet with universal approval is attested by the narrative of al-Jawad Jamal al-Din, an amir of al-Malik al-Salih. When al-Jawad asked to be excluded from the supervision of the destruction of a certain mosque, al-Salih deputized another in his place who removed the mosque and erected a *qa'a* in its stead. Al-Malik al-Salih never entered this *qa'a* alive but, following his death at the battle of Mansura, he was interred therein pending the completion of the tomb at his *madrasa* in Bayn al-Qasrayn. While the cause and effect relationship may be somewhat questionable, the antipathy towards the destruction of Islamic religious structures is certainly evident, and the point made.[64]

Further on Maqrizi states:

When al-Malik al-Salih ordered the building of the citadel of al-Roda, the Nile was [only] on the western side between al-Roda and Giza. It did not surround al-Roda except during the flood season. [Al-Malik al-Salih] continuously sank ships on the western bank [of the Nile]. He dredged the sands between al-Roda and Misr until water returned to the shore of Misr and remained there. He built a great bridge from Misr to al-Roda—its width was three *qasabat* [about 11.5 m.]. When amirs rode to attend the sultan at the citadel of al-Roda, they dismounted and walked the length of this bridge to it. Only the sultan could cross this bridge on horseback. Upon [the citadel's] completion, [al-Malik al-Salih] moved to it with his family and his harem, and he used it as the royal palace [Dar al-Mulk]. With him were quartered his Bahri *mamalik*; they numbered about one thousand.[65]

The learned 'Ali ibn Sa'id said in *Kitab al-Maghrib* that al-Roda faces al-Fustat, and is situated between it and the pavilions of Giza. The nilometer is there. It had been a promenade for the people of Misr. Al-Salih ibn al-Kamil chose it as the seat of the sultanate. He built there a citadel surrounded by a wall [which is] luminous in color, sturdy in construction, and high in elevation; I have seen nothing more impressive than it. On this island was al-Hawdaj, which the caliph al-Amir built for his Bedouin wife. . ., and al-Mukhtar, [which was] the garden of al-Ikhshid, and his palace [*qasr*].

In extended hyperbole, Ibn Sa'id continues:

I walked several nights along the al-Fustat shore, and the laughter of the full moon shone upon me from the Nile bank before the wall of this island, glittering in color. I did not leave Egypt until the wall of this citadel had been completed. Inside were the palaces [*dur*] of the sultan; nothing was of greater importance to him than their construction. [Al-Malik al-Salih] was one of the greatest builders among the sultans. I saw on this island a throne room—I had never seen its like before, and I cannot assess its cost. In it are gilt surfaces and marble—ebony, camphor, and veined—which boggle the mind, paralyze the eyesight, and even confer benefit on the blind. The enceinte encompassed a large tract of land. Part of this area was enclosed by a fence, which preserved the sultan's wild game, and beyond this were meadows leading to the Nile. . . . At high Nile the island was separated from al-Fustat like a kidney. In the days of low Nile its bank became attached to that of al-Fustat south from the area of Khalij al-Qahira, and boats remained in the place of the bridge [i.e. the components of the boat bridge at the southern end of the island between it and al-Fustat, remained high and dry].[66]

Maqrizi goes on:

This citadel [Qal'at al-Roda] remained in use until the end of the Ayyubid dynasty. When the sultan al-Malik al-Mu'izz 'Izz al-Din Aybak al-Turkmani, first of the Turkish rulers, assumed the rule of Egypt, he ordered its destruction. From its remains he built his *madrasa*, al-Mui'zziya, at Rahbat al-Huna' in Misr. . . . A group of people [*jama'a*] took from the citadel of al-Roda a number of ceilings, many windows, and other things, and magnificent woods and marbles were sold from it. When the sultan al-Malik al-Zahir Rukn al-Din Baybars al-Bunduqdari assumed the rule of Egypt, he concerned himself with the building of the citadel of al-Roda; he entrusted the amir Jamal al-Din Musa ibn Yaghmur with its restoration. [Jamal al-Din] restored some of its destroyed areas, assigned them to the cavalry, and restored it to its former esteem. He was entrusted with its towers; they were assigned to the amirs. . . . He planned that there would be [at the citadel of al-Roda] houses and stables for all the amirs and handed over the keys to them.

When al-Malik al-Mansur Qalaun became sultan and began construction of his hospital [*maristan*], dome, and *madrasa* [al-Mansuriya], he removed from Qal'at al-Roda granite and marble columns, which had already been reused from pharaonic remains. He also took much marble and many fine lintels which were, again, reused from pharaonic times. Then the sultan al-Malik al-Nasir Muhammad ibn Qalaun removed granite columns for the construction of the *iwan* known as Dar al-'Adil on the citadel [Qal'at al-Jabal] and Jami' al-Jadid al-Nasiri outside of Misr. He removed other materials until there was practically nothing left. There remained from the citadel of al-Roda a fine vault, popularly known as al-Qus; it stood on the western side. We remember its standing until about the year 820/1417–18. There also remained a number of towers; many of them were overturned, and the people built their houses above their remains, paralleling the Nile.[67]

Ibn Duqmaq adds that the construction materials of the citadel of al-Roda were gypsum, baked brick, mud, and lime. This suggests that the actual materials were limestone and baked brick, cemented by mud and/or lime mortar. His statement, however, that the citadel of al-Roda was constructed in 646/1248–49 and destroyed three years later by the order of al-Malik al-Mu'izz Aybak, is unacceptable, given the testimony of Ibn Wasil and Maqrizi.[68] In the *Suluk* for the year 638/1240–41, Maqrizi states that a son was born to al-Malik al-Salih by one of his concubines. As a fitting remembrance, al-Salih ordered the construction of the citadel of al-Roda.[69] Ibn Wasil notes, in his annals for the same year, that al-Malik al-Salih built the citadel as a center [*markaz*] for his *mamalik* and amirs, and that it was three years in construction.[70] Given the general reliability of Ibn Duqmaq's narrative, the 646/1248–49 date is most likely an error in copy.

The citadel of al-Roda was constructed as a fortress–palace–administrative complex which temporarily—indeed little longer than the reign of al-Malik al-Salih—served as the administrative seat of Egypt. Having lived at Qal'at al-Jabal for three years prior to the new citadel's completion, al-Malik al-Salih removed his court, family, harem, and his personal contingent of *mamalik* to the new citadel on the Nile. The site of numerous fortresses, arsenals, and shipyards in pre-Fatimid and Fatimid times, the island of al-Roda had served—at least periodically—as a base for military offense and defense for over five centuries prior to the Ayyubid regime. It must be remembered, however, that when al-Roda served as a fortress—specifically during the Byzantine and Ummayad eras—this fortress was established primarily for the defense of Babylon and al-Fustat. During the 270 years prior to the establishment of the citadel of al-Roda, the nucleus of defense had shifted; first, under the Fatimids, to the walled city of al-Qahira; and then, under Saladin, to the citadel (Qal'at al-Jabal), the focal point of the Qahira–Fustat enceinte. Qal'at al-Jabal remained the seat of government until the reign of al-Malik al-Salih and, almost immediately thereafter, through the reign of Muhammad 'Ali (broken briefly by the French occupation). As a bastion of defense it was, simply by nature of its situation, far superior to any fortress which could have been erected on the island of al-Roda. Despite sixty towers the al-Roda citadel, with its low-lying position, separated from the mainland only by a narrow channel (when it was flooded), could hardly be compared to the great bastions some two miles to the northeast on the Muqattam spur.

Why, then, the shift? That the citadel of al-Roda was built merely as a remembrance to al-Malik al-Salih's newborn son, as Maqrizi suggests, is hardly tenable. The narratives of Ibn Sa'id, Ibn Duqmaq, and Maqrizi, describe—other than a cursory mention of the fortifications—a palace of vast sumptuousness, extravagant in construction and embellishment, in conjunction with parks and game preserves running to the water's edge. Nothing of similar elegance is recorded at Qal'at al-Jabal during the Ayyubid dynasty; during al-Malik al-Salih's three years of residency, his only structure of note at Qal'at al-Jabal was Qa'at al-Salihiya, presumably a throne room. Worthy of note, however, are al-Malik al-Salih's other building projects to the west: the revitalization of the Qaramidan beneath the citadel (v.i.); the pavilions, polo grounds, etc. at Bab al-Luq; the pavilions of Qal'at al-Kabsh overlooking Birkat al-Fil (v.i.); and, finally, the citadel of al-Roda. All four of these establishments suggest his attraction to parks, open spaces, and, especially, to water, be it that of the *saqiya* of the Qaramidan, Birkat al-Fil (and, adjacently, Birkat Qarun), or the Nile itself, which at that time washed the confines of both Midan al-Luq and the citadel of al-Roda. The citadel of al-Roda may well have been the culmination of two desires on the part of al-Malik al-Salih: firstly, to establish a fortress–palace–administration complex in a suburban setting, and secondly, a wish to continue the process followed by the successive rulers of al-Fustat and al-Qahira—to establish a new center of administration separate from the previous sites, viz: al-Fustat, al-'Askar, al-Qata'i', al-Qahira, and Qal'at al-Jabal. While admittedly the citadel of al-Roda was probably of extremely limited value as a fortress, there is no evidence to suggest that the infinitely more secure Qal'at al-Jabal ceased to function as an entity and could not be relied upon to serve as an ultimate refuge against attack. Al-Malik al-Salih's Nilotic castle was ultimately a one-man show, relegated to destruction by the dynasty he spawned. Although the relocation fostered a temporary respite to the economic and social life of al-Fustat due to the proximity of the sultan, it was only a brief halt on al-Fustat's decline to a relatively insignificant suburb.

Summary

The defensive measures of the Ayyubids at Cairo served three basic functions: the general protection of the Qahira–Fustat municipal area; the specific protection of the sultan, his troops, and entourage, concommitant with administrative facilities, within a given area, usually a citadel; and facilities for troop movement. In terms of basic protection, the restoration of the walls of Badr al-Jamali served as a temporary measure pending the construction of the citadel and the Qahira–Fustat enceinte, while the Qahira–Fustat enceinte, supplemented by trenches, was intended to render protection to Saladin's new metropolitan entity, effectively including the four previous Islamic capitals of Egypt. Specific facilities included the citadel (Qal'at al-Jabal), the citadel of al-Roda, and, perhaps, the tower at al-Maqs, sometimes referred to as *qal'a*. The *qanatir* of Giza apparently served primarily as a means of rapid deployment of troops, especially in times of high Nile, against any threatened invasion.

The projects of the citadel and the Qahira–Fustat enceinte, both undertaken by Saladin, were not finished during his lifetime; the enceinte, indeed, was never completed. While work continued on these projects and, later, the citadel of al-Roda, throughout the Ayyubid regime, the construction was sporadic, and followed certain patterns worthy of note here. The citadel (Qal'at al-Jabal) and the Qahira–Fustat enceinte were begun by Saladin from a position of strength, and largely discontinued following his final departure to Syria. The fortress/palace complex of the citadel, as envisaged by Saladin, was completed under al-Kamil, deputized as ruler of Egypt under his father, al-Malik al-'Adil, and the citadel of al-Roda was constructed by al-Malik al-Salih. In the case of the Qahira–Fustat enceinte, however, later work took place only during times of civil war or of external threat. Beyond the initial construction of the Qahira–Fustat enceinte, then, major work on the citadels would appear to have been undertaken in times of relative security, while that on the enceinte occurred during times of crisis, principally as stopgap measures on the undefended western flank of the Qahira–Fustat combined area. That the enceinte on this western flank was never completed can probably be explained by two factors; first, that as the Nile itself rendered a certain amount of protection, Qaraqush left the construction of the western wall until last and, secondly, that the death of Saladin and/or Qaraqush ended the impetus for its completion.

The construction of the citadels of Saladin and al-Malik al-Salih fostered a certain amount of social and economic growth in their respective areas in terms of a) population growth, the natural clustering of nobility, bureaucrats, and military personnel within the immediate proximity of the sultans and b) the support personnel and facilities to render goods and services to those groups. While this was a very temporary situation in the case of the citadel of al-Roda, which, as mentioned above, brought about a short respite in the ongoing decline of al-Fustat, Qal'at al-Jabal, as the major center of Egyptian administration for some 650 years, engendered the development of a new and relatively prosperous district of Cairo, Darb al-Ahmar.

Finally, it should be remembered that despite the religious zeal which both Saladin and al-Malik al-Salih at least ostensibly professed, their respective citadels were built at the cost of the wholesale destruction of the mosques and tombs which previously occupied the sites. The sanctity of religious property had, out of practical necessity, taken second place to the dictates of secular power.

Chapter Five

Major Governmental and Private Buildings

The Ayyubid domination of al-Qahira resulted in the assignment of the former royal living quarters to Ayyubid magnates and the continued use (or reuse) of various Fatimid administrative centers. With the Fatimid palaces allocated to Saladin's amirs and family, smaller residences—*dur, qusur, manazir,* etc.—were also appropriated by leading members of the new regime. Major governmental buildings included centers for administration, housing for visiting ambassadors, the mint, the bureau of weights and measures, and several prisons. Similar residences and administrative centers also existed at al-Fustat, again often residual from the Fatimids. In addition to the continued use of Fatimid structures, smaller private buildings were often built on or within the sites of the earlier constructions, particularly in the areas of the great western and eastern Fatimid palaces.

As previously stated, the eastern and western Fatimid palaces were divided among Saladin's amirs and family. The greater (eastern) palace was allotted to the amirs,[1] although not in its entirety, since Maqrizi states that the Fatimid palaces "were reduced in extent; some of them were allocated as living quarters and some of them destroyed."[2] The western palace, assigned to al-Malik al-'Adil, was the birthplace of his son al-Malik al-Kamil.[3] Saladin and his successors, until al-Malik al-Kamil moved permanently to the citadel, maintained their residence and administrative center at Dar al-Wizara.

Dar al-Wizara

Established by al-Afdal ibn Badr al-Jamali, Dar al-Wizara (no.80, map 1) stood to the northeast of the eastern Fatimid palace on the approximate site of the *khanqah* of Baybars al-Jashankir.[4] As the residence of Fatimid viziers and Ayyubid sultans, it remained an important center of administration until the completion of the citadel in 604/1207–1208. "Then," according to Ibn 'Abd al-Zahir, "Dar al-Wizara became a hostel for diplomats and emissaries from the caliphate until this time."[5] Maqrizi adds that until the move to the citadel, Dar al-Wizara was known (presumably only under the Ayyubids) as Dar al-Sultaniya, following which it became a *manzil* (stopping place, hotel) for envoys (*rusul*).[6]

Dar al-Diyafa

Located in Harat Barjwan to the north of the western Fatimid palace, Dar al-Diyafa was originally the residence—or, perhaps, a residence—of Badr al-Jamali. Upon the succession to the vizierate of al-Afdal, this palace was assigned to his brother al-Muzaffar (ibn Badr al-Jamali), and thence known as Dar al-Muzaffar. Following al-Muzaffar's death, the structure assumed the role of Dar al-Diyafa, or guest house, for visiting emissaries. Upon Saladin's accession to the sultanate Dar al-Diyafa became the residence of the deposed Fatimid royal family, until its transferral to the citadel in 604/1207–1208.[7]

Mints

Maqrizi's comments and quotations on the mint (Dar al-Darb) are somewhat confusing. In 516/1122–23, during the caliphate of al-Amir, a mint was founded near Suq al-Kharratin and the greater Khan Masrur (southeast of the present mosque of al-Ashraf Barsbay). He then gives it a more southern location at Darb al-Shamsi, between the main thoroughfare (*qasaba*) and al-Azhar. Whether this is a confusion, a rebuilding, or the opening of a second mint is open to question. Howbeit, Maqrizi states that the mint lasted until the rule of Saladin, "when it was moved to its present location," a storehouse near the great *iwan* of the eastern Fatimid palace.[8]

The *History of the Patriarchs*, for the year 622/1225–26, states that al-Malik al-Kamil ordered that mints be opened at the citadel and at Misr, in addition to the mint at al-Qahira. The mint at the citadel was in fact opened during that year.[9]

Dar al-'Iyar

Dar al-'Iyar, the bureau of weights and standards, lasted, according to Maqrizi, throughout the Fatimid period. "When Saladin took power he established this *dar* as a *waqf* on the wall of al-Qahira, in association with [other] *awqaf* on the wall in houses [*riba'*] and districts [*nawahi*] in the *diwan* of the walls. This *dar* continued." While Maqrizi does not give us the location, it can reasonably be assumed that Dar al-'Iyar was located within al-Qahira, perhaps in the immediate vicinity of Dar al-Darb.[10]

Prisons

Ayyubid prisons were largely continuations from Fatimid times, and were located in both al-Qahira and al-Fustat. They would appear to have been divided into two categories: one for amirs and other political prisoners, the other for common criminals.

Habs al-Ma'una at al-Fustat

Located in front of the mosque of 'Amr ibn al-'As, Habs al-Ma'una was, in pre-Fatimid times, an administrative/police center (*shurta*). A prison from 381/991–92, it remained such until the reign of Saladin, when it was reestablished as al-Madrasa al-Sharafiya.[11]

Habs al-Siyar

Habs al-Siyar succeeded Habs al-Ma'una at al-Fustat, after the latter had been reestablished as a *madrasa* by Saladin. It was, according to Maqrizi, a prison for notables (*wulat*). Its name derived from a shopkeeper in the immediate area of the prison, Mansur al-Tawil, known as al-Siyar due to his trade in salt fish. Maqrizi does not give its exact location.[12]

Khizanat al-Bunud

A storehouse for banners and weapons, Khizanat al-Bunud (no.81, map 1) was founded by the Fatimid caliph al-Zahir, and adjoined the great eastern palace between Qasr al-Shawq and Bab al-'Id. Following its burning in 461/1068–69, it became a prison for amirs and notables until the end of the Fatimid dynasty. Khizanat al-Bunud remained a prison under the Ayyubids, and served as a residence (*manzil*) for the Frankish prisoners and their families captured at Karak during the reign of al-Nasir Muhammad ibn Qalaun. The prison was destroyed in 744/1343–44.[13]

Habs al-Ma'una at al-Qahira

Located just south of the present mosque of al-Ashraf Barsbay, Habs al-Ma'una (no.82, map 1) was a Fatimid prison for thieves and brigands. "A narrow, oppressive prison, one smelled an abominable odor in its vicinity." This prison, destroyed by al-Nasir Muhammad ibn Qalaun, was presumably functioning under the Ayyubids.[14]

Khizanat Shama'il

Khizanat Shama'il (no.83, map 1) stood on the site of the mosque of al-Mu'ayyad Shaykh, immediately within Bab Zuwayla. It took its name from 'Ilm al-Din Shama'il, *wali* of al-Qahira under al-Malik al-Kamil.

> Imprisoned there were murderers, thieves, highway robbers, and other serious criminals and *mamalik* whom the sultan wished incarcerated. It was one of the most atrocious of prisons, grotesque in appearance. The warden of this prison received a daily allowance [for its upkeep] from the *wali* of al-Qahira. . . . The prison was destroyed by al-Mu'ayyad Shaykh in 818/1415–16.[15]

Major private residences and palaces

Qasr al-Hijaziya

Located (no.84, map 1) in Khatt Rahbat Bab al-'Id, at the northeast of the eastern Fatimid palace near al-Madrasa al-Hijaziya, this palace was originally known as Qasr Zummurud. This was due to its proximity to Bab al-Zummurud, a gate to the Fatimid palace nearby. At the end of the Fatimid dynasty it became Ayyubid property, and changed hands until the chamberlain (*hajib*) Ibn Khatir purchased it from the descendants of the Ayyubids. The palace remained Ibn Khatir's property until he was appointed the sultan's representative at Gaza in 741/1340–41.[16]

Qasr Awlad al-Shaykh

Formerly a *qa'a* of the greater Fatimid palace, Qasr Awlad al-Shaykh (no.85, map 1) stood between the mosque of al-Aqmar and the *khanqah* of Sa'id al-Su'ada' and near Bab al-Rih, the northern gate to the eastern palace. This *qasr* was the residence of Mu'in al-Din Husayn ibn Shaykh al-Shuyukh, vizier to al-Malik al-Salih.[17]

Dar *of al-Qadi al-Fadil*

This *dar* (no.86, map 1) of al-Qadi al-Fadil, along with his *madrasa*, was located in Darb al-Mulukhiya in al-Qahira, to the northeast of the eastern Fatimid palace.[18]

Pavilions

Pavilions (*manazir*, singular *manzara*) were scattered throughout the outskirts of al-Qahira and al-Fustat, particularly in the areas bordering the Nile, the Khalij, and the alluvial ponds. Especially common under the Fatimids, these pavilions continued under the Ayyubids in approximately the same locations, in addition to those established in newer alluvial lands on the east bank of the Nile. With few exceptions we have no descriptions of these structures, but it may be generally assumed that they boasted large porches or porticoes to take advantage of both the view and the breezes, especially at high Nile during September and October. Most pavilions probably included walled living quarters; some of the larger ones such as Qal'at al-Kabsh, Lu'lu', and perhaps, that of Taj al-Muluk Buri at Birkat al-Habash, were de facto palaces. In discussing those in use under the Ayyubids, we shall examine these pavilions chronologically, with only cursory mention of those discussed in previous chapters.

Reign of Saladin

The pavilions of two of Saladin's brothers, Sayf al-Islam Tughtakin and Taj al-Muluk Buri, were located at Birkat al-Fil and Birkat al-Habash respectively. According to Abu Salih, Taj al-Muluk Buri founded several pavilions near the church of St. Victor at Birkat al-Habash. These pavilions were lavish in construction, and Taj al-Muluk went to considerable expense in embellishing them with marble and gilding.[19] That of Sayf al-Islam, on the eastern bank of Birkat al-Fil, boasted spacious galleries and kiosks (see Chapter Three).[20] Further pavilions noted during Saladin's reign were: that of Lu'lu', located between the western wall of al-Qahira and the Khalij and occupied by Najm al-Din Ayyub; those described by Ibn Jubayr on the island of al-Roda; and several mentioned by Abu Salih at al-Hamra' in the general area of Birkat Qarun.[21]

Al-'Adil and al-Kamil

A major pavilion was constructed near Bab al-Luq by Fakhr al-Din ibn Tha'lib (an amir of al-Malik al-'Adil, and *sahib* of al-Madrasa al-

Sharifiya in al-Qahira; see Chapter Three). Ibn Wasil notes that prior to the establishment of the citadel of al-Roda by al-Malik al-Salih, the island of al-Roda was used as a promenade by al-Malik al-Kamil, and that he had a palace (*dar*) there solely for that purpose.[22]

Al-Malik al-Salih

Among the many constructions recorded in the greater al-Qahira area during the reign of al-Malik al-Salih were several pavilions, located to the south and southwest of the city. Discussed earlier were those of al-Luq and Birkat al-Shiqaf on the western bank of the Khalij, those on the Khalij itself, and those surrounding Birkat al-Fil (see Chapter Three).

Bustan al-'Alima

Located between Bab Misr and Fam al-Khalij, this garden was given by al-Malik al-Salih to a noble woman named 'Alima. A pavilion was built adjacent to it, facing the Nile. The property reverted to her heirs upon her death, and ultimately became the property of the heirs of al-Zahir Baybars al-Bunduqdari.[23]

Qal'at al-Kabsh (Manazir al-Kabsh)

A major construction on Jabal Yashkur (west of the mosque of Ibn Tulun), Qal'at al-Kabsh ('citadel of the ram') was erected by al-Malik al-Salih ca. 640/1242–43. This pavilion, above Jisr al-A'zam (the 'great dam', v.i.) dominated both Birkat al-Fil and Birkat Qarun, and, according to Maqrizi, boasted an unobstructed view of Bab Zuwayla, Bab Misr, Misr, and the Giza shore. It was "among the most splendid pavilions of Egypt." During the reign of al-Zahir Baybars, Qal'at al-Kabsh became the temporary residence of at least two of the Abbasid caliphs of Baghdad, transferred thence following the Mongol invasion. The pavilion was also occupied, in 673/1274–75, by several of the Ayyubid princes of Hama on a visit to Egypt. It was destroyed by al-Nasir Muhammad ibn Qalaun in 723/1323–24.[24]

Chapter Six

Water Resources and Health

Nile Changes: Channels, Islands, and Shores

From the late Fatimid through the Mamluk period, the basic shift in the Nile and its associated water resources was one of east to west. While the shore of Giza and the island of al-Roda remained relatively stable, on the eastern bank of the Nile alluvial deposits blocked the channel between al-Roda and al-Fustat, and the port of al-Maqs was rendered inoperable by the formation of the islands of Bulaq and Jazirat al-Fil. The creation of Jazirat al-Fil by sands coalescing around a sunken ship in the later Fatimid period—in addition to alluvial deposits on the Nile shore itself—necessitated the removal of the "sand islands" in that area by Saladin and his amirs in 577/1181–82 (see Chapter Three). Al-Maqs, dockyard and arsenal for the Fatimid fleet and immediate port to al-Qahira, is not specifically mentioned as either a military or a commercial port from this date forth. Some utility, however, is suggested by two factors: firstly, the dredging action in itself, and secondly the almost regular annual silting of the Nile between al-Roda and al-Fustat. A more practical substitute might have been the port facilities at Giza, generally free of silting with established markets and boat bridges to al-Roda and al-Fustat.

The silting of the Fustat–Roda channel, concommitant with the general alluviation along the eastern bank of the Nile, augmented the Fustat shore. Beginning near Dar al-Mulk, almost opposite the nilometer, the alluvial deposits gradually extended westward, reaching their most western point almost opposite the northern end of al-Roda. The alluvial lands west of the Khalij (including al-Luq, v.s.) then continued on a relatively uniform line north to al-Maqs. At the time of the Islamic conquest, al-Roda was situated approximately

85

in the middle of the Nile. Alluviation at al-Fustat was noted as early as the governorship of 'Abd al-'Aziz ibn Marwan (65–86/684–705), when construction was undertaken on the new lands.[1] The first excavation of the al-Fustat shore, according to Maqrizi, took place under Kafur al-Ikhshidi in 336/947–48. The branch of the Nile between al-Roda and al-Fustat (henceforth referred to as the Fustat channel) was dry, forcing both men and animals to seek water at the western bank of al-Roda. Kafur dug a canal which joined Khalij Bani Wa'il (the canal leading from the Nile to Birkat al-Habash), and the Nile once again reached the Fustat shore.[2] During the vizierate of al-Afdal ibn al-Juyushi (487–515/1094–1121), a major drainage and canalization project was undertaken to remove a sand island in front of Dar al-Mulk. This may refer to Jazirat al-Sabuni, now known as Jazirat al-Dhahab.[3]

The gradual alluviation of the Fustat shore is further demonstrated by Nasir-i Khusraw's description of the boat bridge between al-Fustat and al-Roda (thirty-six boats), compared with that of Idrisi over two centuries later (thirty boats). This bridge, located at the southern end of al-Roda near the nilometer, traversed the entrance to the al-Fustat channel, water relatively free of silting. Points to the north, especially the naval dockyard at Bustan al-Jurf (near the entrance to the Khalij, see Chapter One), would have been especially hampered by this alluviation. Since the dockyard allegedly survived until shortly before 700/1300–1301, regular dredging must have been necessary to maintain its use, as well as access to the port facilities of al-Fustat, and to insure the flow of water into the Khalij at high Nile.[4]

The silting of the Fustat channel was a frequent occurrence under the Ayyubids. Clerget notes two instances when locals were forced to obtain water from the Giza branch in A.D. 1199 and 1203.[5] While his source is questionable, this is the approximate time of the famine years described by 'Abd al-Latif al-Baghdadi (597–98/1201–1202), when the nilometer itself was high and dry.[6] Maqrizi corroborates this: "Then, shortly before 600/1203–1204, the water withdrew from the old bank of Misr, and, during the low Nile, the route of the nilometer [i.e. the Fustat branch] was dry." He continues:

> In the year 628/1230–31 the sultan al-Malik al-Kamil . . . fearing the withdrawal of the river from the houses of Misr, undertook the dredging of the river from Dar al-Wikala at Misr to Sana'at al-Tamr al-Fadiliya. He worked on the project himself. All were levied for this work, amir and rabble alike. The expenses of the dredging were distributed

proportionately on the houses of al-Qahira, Misr, al-Roda, and the nilometer. The work lasted from the beginning of Sha'ban until the end of Shawwal, a period of three months. Thereafter the water surrounded the nilometer and the island of al-Roda so that, even during extreme dryness, a small stream was retained at the lower [northern?] end of al-Roda. When the Nile rejoined the Bulaq branch, in the month of Abib, it was a famous day in Misr.

During the reign of al-Malik al-Salih—who constructed the citadel of al-Roda—he desired that al-Roda be surrounded with water in abundance throughout the year. He concentrated on this project. He sank a number of ships filled with stones on the Giza bank opposite Bab al-Qantara which is outside the city of Misr and south of the island of al-Roda. Thus, the water was restored and the river, from that time, flowed little by little and its flow increased gradually on the bank of Misr from Dar al-Mulk to the neighborhood of al-Maqs, and cut into [qata'a] Minsha'at al-Fadiliya. Ibn al-Mutawwaj said, on the emplacement of Jami' al-Jadid [a mosque constructed by al-Nasir Muhammad ibn Qalaun, formerly located just south of Fam al-Khalij]: "Under the Salihi dynasty—i.e. al-Malik al-Salih Najm al-Din Ayyub—sands were there in which animals would wallow during the time of low Nile and the dryness of the branch of the river which [passed] in front of it. When al-Malik al-Salih built the citadel of al-Roda, he and his soldiers undertook to dredge this river [the Fustat channel] annually. Some of the sand was thrown upon this site, and the leading notables [khawas] of the sultan began construction along the banks of this branch."[7]

Ibn al-Mutawwaj then mentions those who built from in front of the site of Jami' al-Jadid to al-Madrasa al-Mu'izziya. He adds: "The site of Jami' al-Jadid, before the construction of the mosque, was allocated as granaries—for straw—of the sultan."[8]

In sum, east bank alluviation during the Fatimid and Ayyubid periods supplemented the primarily agricultural areas between Fam al-Khalij and al-Maqs. However, it also resulted in the gradual eclipse of the port of al-Maqs, and the necessity for continuous dredging in the Fustat channel, both to preserve the viability of al-Fustat as a port and to allow the Nile flow into the Khalij. During the reign of al-Malik al-Salih, a secondary motive for dredging may have been his desire to isolate the al-Roda citadel. As the construction at al-Fustat did not extend farther south than Dar al-Mulk, port facilities at al-Fustat under the Ayyubids must have been almost exclusively between that point and the entrance to the Khalij, since the new lands created to the north at Minsha'at al-Fadil were primarily gardens, and the administrative and commercial areas of al-Fustat were maintained, traditionally, in the southern section bordering the Nile.[9]

While the general pattern of Nile flow during this period resulted in erosion on the western shore and alluviation on the eastern, there are two notable examples of undercutting the eastern bank. In Ramadan of 587/1191–92 the *zariba* (cattle yard? stockade?) of the mosque of al-Maqs broke away, undermined by the Nile, and had to be rebuilt.[10] The mosque of al-Qadi al-Fadil at Minsha'at al-Mahrani (north of Fam al-Khalij), in addition to its associated houses and gardens, was destroyed by the aggressions of the Nile after 660/1261–62.[11] With these exceptions, however, east bank alluviation and the concomitant necessity for continuous dredging was maintained.

Canals and Alluvial Ponds

Under the Ayyubid dynasty, the canals and ponds in the area of al-Qahira and al-Fustat were fed, directly or indirectly, by the Nile. These alluvial ponds, between the Muqattam and the river, were either fed directly by major canals or appeared in depressions during a high water table. While many of these ponds surfaced in the new lands on the west bank of the Khalij, others, such as Birkat al-Habash and Birkat al-Fil, had existed from the time of the Islamic conquest. It is difficult to ascertain which of those ponds on the west bank of the Khalij existed during the Ayyubid era, and only those specifically noted by the chroniclers will be mentioned here.[12] As the settlement patterns for Birkat al-Fil, Birkat al-Habash, and the Khalij have been discussed at length in Chapter Three, we shall limit our scope here to general discussion of the canals with their associated alluvial ponds, together with particulars not previously mentioned.

Three major canals (*khuljan*, singular *khalij*) served the Qahira–Fustat area: Khalij Bani Wa'il, Khalij al-Qahira (heretofore and henceforth referred to simply as 'the Khalij'), and Khalij al-Dhikr.

Khalij Bani Wa'il

Running southeast from Bab al-Qantara at al-Fustat, Khalij Bani Wa'il fed three alluvial ponds, Birkat Shata, Birkat al-Shu'ibiya, and Birkat al-Habash. Proceeding southeast from Bab al-Qantara it entered the smallest of the three, Birkat Shata, whence the water flowed through a dike (*jisr*) to Birkat al-Shu'ibiya, thence through a short canal and a second dike into Birkat al-Habash. While Birkat Shata was relatively minuscule, Birkat al-Shu'ibiya covered an area of fifty–four feddans, and Birkat al-Habash over a thousand.[13] Although there is no mention of a seasonal opening of this canal (similar to that of Khalij al-Qahira), it may be assumed that it functioned primarily at high Nile, since Birkat al-Shu'ibiya and Birkat al-Habash were planted during the dry season.

Khalij al-Qahira (the Khalij)

Khalij al-Qahira, the former Amnis Trajanus, had, during Roman times, extended to the Red Sea at Qulzum (Suez). A combination of silting and the hostility of both Bedouins and local people rendered the continuous use of this canal uncertain at best, although it was restored to full use under the caliph 'Umar. In 144/761–62, however, during the reign of the caliph al-Mansur, the canal was blocked to prevent its seizure by an 'Alid pretender at al-Madina, which would have diverted the grain supply of Baghdad. Thereafter, the terminal point of the Khalij gradually receded westward, until it ended only slightly north of Cairo at Matariya. Under the Ayyubids, however, the Khalij apparently terminated at al-Sadir (the entrance to Wadi Tumayla, southeast of Zagazig), whence eastern transport continued by camel.[14] The extent of its commercial use in this period is, however, very much in doubt. For al-Qahira itself, it served primarily as a reservoir, especially during the three to four months of high Nile, considerably shortening the itinerary of the water carriers.[15]

Birkat al-Fil and Birkat Qarun, to the east of the Khalij in the general area of what is now al-Sayyida Zaynab and the district of Birkat al-Fil, were separated by the grand dike, al-Jisr al-A'zam. These alluvial ponds existed, apparently, from the time of the Islamic conquest; they appear to have been fed by ground water, rather than directly from the Khalij. On the west bank Birkat al-Shiqaf, near Bab al-Luq, boasted numerous pavilions by 600/1203–1204. While other ponds associated with the Khalij probably existed at this time, none is specifically mentioned by the chroniclers.[16] It can be assumed that these ponds were low to dry during the winter and spring seasons, and were at least partially cultivated.

Khalij al-Dhikr

According to Maqrizi, Khalij al-Dhikr was a short canal extending directly from the Nile to Birkat Batn al-Baqara (later Birkat al-

Azbakiya). This pond was originally a garden, Bustan al-Maqsi. Although Maqrizi's chronology is somewhat confused, the original canal was allegedly dug by Kafur al-Ikhshidi. Under the Fatimid caliph al-Zahir, the garden was transformed into a pond, Batn al-Baqara, which faced the pavilion of Lu'lu', and was supplied by water from the same canal. The annual opening of Khalij al-Dhikr took place before that of Khalij al-Qahira, due, perhaps, to a more direct approach of the Nile flow. According to Ibn 'Abd al-Zahir, the canal was fed by the Nile through culverts (*barabikh*), and was widened by al-Malik al-Kamil.[17] The *History of the Patriarchs* states that in the year 623/1226 Khalij al-Dhikr actually penetrated Khalij al-Qahira, suggesting that it flowed *through* the area of Batn al-Baqara, and was blocked by a dam near Bab al-Qantara.[18] Batn al-Baqara underwent further changes. Having become dry during the famines under al-Mustansir, houses were built in the area of the pond, and it became an unsavory quarter known as Harat al-Lusus ('quarter of thieves'). During the reign of al-Amir (495–524/1101–1130) the vizier al-Bata'ihi destroyed the buildings, excavated the area, and restored the pond, again channeling water to it from Khalij al-Dhikr. The name Batn al-Baqara apparently emanates from this time. This continued, according to Maqrizi, until after 700/1300–1301.[19] While no further information is available on this pond during the Ayyubid era, it can be assumed that Birkat Batn al-Baqara, on the site of the present Azbakiya gardens, functioned as a site for pavilions and promenades, and, during low Nile, as an agricultural area.

Bridges

Bridge construction and specific bridge use recorded in the Cairo area under the Ayyubids are limited to the boat bridges between al-Fustat and Giza, and three bridges (*qanatir*) spanning Khalij al-Qahira. (The *qanatir* of Giza are discussed in Chapter Three.)

The boat bridges between al-Fustat and Giza

Dating at least from the caliphate of al-Ma'mun (198–218/813–33), a boat bridge (*jisr*) connected al-Fustat with al-Roda (just north of the nilometer), while a second continued from the west bank of al-Roda to Giza. These bridges consisted of a chain of boats placed side to side supporting a roadwalk of wood (planks?) covered with mud.[20] In 614/1217–18, during the reign of al-Malik al-'Adil, a boat bridge of fifty-three boats was constructed (or reconstructed) from al-Roda to Giza, with men employed to repair it and to open it for river traffic.[21] That section between al-Fustat and al-Roda was reconstructed by al-Malik al-Salih when he built the citadel of al-Roda, and was three *qasabat* (ca. 11.5 m.) in width. The Roda–Giza section was rebuilt as well.[22] Ibn Sa'id states:

> Most of the traffic—both people and their animals—is in boats, because these two bridges were near the citadel of the sultan. No one passed riding on the bridge between al-Fustat and the island out of respect to the sultan.[23]

The presence of al-Malik al-Salih, then, limited the use of these bridges for cross-river traffic. It should, in addition, be noted that certain sections of these bridges must have been easily separable in order to allow longitudinal river traffic.

Qantarat al-Muski

Spanning the Khalij to the western wall of al-Qahira, Qantarat al-Muski (no.89, map 2) stood at the present intersection of Shari' al-Muski and Shari' Port Sa'id. This bridge was constructed by the amir 'Izz al-Din Musk (a relative of Saladin) who died at Damascus in 584/1188–89.[24]

Qantarat Bab al-Kharq

Located at the modern *midan* of the same name, Qantarat Bab al-Kharq (no.88, map 2) crossed the Khalij at a point used as a quay for the water-carriers of al-Qahira under the Fatimids. "When al-Malik al-Salih founded Midan al-Sultani in the land(s) of al-Luq, he built there pavilions in 639/1241–42. He built this bridge to cross the mentioned *midan*."[25] This bridge became a lynchpin in a west-east thoroughfare connecting Midan al-Luq and its associated alluvial lands with Bab Zuwayla and the southern sections of al-Qahira.

Qantarat al-Sadd

Qantarat al-Sadd ('bridge of the dam') was constructed at or near the dam blocking the mouth to the Khalij. During the reign of al-Malik al-Salih, this was located in the new alluvial lands adjoining Bustan al-Khashshab (in modern terms, on Shari' al-Sadd about halfway between Fam al-Khalij and Midan al-Sayyida Zaynab). The building of this bridge, which had two arches, was begun by al-Malik al-Salih in 638/1240–41, and occupied the position of Qantarat al-Ghyr (sic) on the Napoleonic map of A.D. 1798.[26]

Channeled and Corralled Water

Several instances of cisterns and channeled water are noted under the Ayyubids.

'Ayn 'Arafa

An inscription of 594/1197–98 contains the order (allegedly from the caliph al-Nasir) for the building of 'Ayn 'Arafa and the cisterns surrounding it, directed to Muzaffar al-Din Kukburi. The exact location in the Cairo area is, however, uncertain.[27]

The Qaramidan

In the *midan* beneath the citadel (see Chapter Three) several substantial waterworks were undertaken during the later Ayyubid period. According to Ibn 'Abd al-Zahir:

> Al-Malik al-Kamil ibn al-'Adil ibn Ayyub built this *midan* underneath the citadel when he lived there [in the citadel] and he caused rivulets to flow [*ajra al-sawaqi al-naqqala*] to it [the *midan*]. He built on its side three ponds which were filled for drinking. Then it became neglected for a period of time during al-Kamil's days. His son al-Malik al-'Adil renewed it. Then al-Malik al-Salih Najm al-Din Ayyub became greatly concerned with its care. He added another *saqiya* to it, planted trees on its sides . . . and it became a fine place. When al-Salih died, its condition gradually became ruinous until it was destroyed in 650/1252–53 or 651/1253–54 during the Mu'izzi period [al-Malik al-Mu'izz Aybak]. The *sawaqi* [rivulets? waterworks?; v.i.] and the bridges [*qanatir*] were destroyed and their traces erased. It remained in this state until the sultan al-Malik al-Nasir Muhammad ibn Qalaun . . . rebuilt it, and he improved its construction and paved it with superior workmanship. This is its present situation.[28]

The term *saqiya* (plural *sawaqi*) can be translated either as a ditch, rivulet, irrigation canal or in its second sense as a water scoop or waterwheel. *Sawaqi naqqala* (the work of al-Malik al-Kamil) probably refer to some sort of channel—possibly elevated—from the Nile to the *midan*, supplying water to the three ponds. The *saqiya* added by al-Malik al-Salih may have been either an addition to the Nile channel or some sort of water raiser in the *midan* itself. The fact that al-Mu'izz Aybak destroyed both *sawaqi* and *qanatir* in 650/1252–

53 suggests the possibility of some sort of aqueduct from the Nile, perhaps similar to that later constructed by al-Nasir Muhammad ibn Qalaun. The route followed, however, from the Nile to al-Rumayla, is uncertain.

Water supply to the tomb of Imam al-Shafi'i

The dome and reconstruction of the tomb of Imam al-Shafi'i (v.i.), undertaken by al-Malik al-Kamil in 607/1210–11, was provided with a *sabil* and *saqiya* at its doorway. "He caused water to flow from Birkat al-Habash to the cistern [*hawd*] for the *sabil* and *saqiya* at the door of the mentioned dome."[29] It is possible that the former aqueduct of Ahmad ibn Tulun, running from Birkat al-Habash to 'Ayn al-Sira, may have been partially used in this canalization.

Hawd Ibn Hanas

This *hawd* (no.90, map 2) was located slightly to the east of Birkat al-Fil, adjoining Harat Halab. This was the *waqf* of Sa'd al-Din Mas'ud, son of the amir Badr al-Din Hanas ibn 'Abd Allah. Sa'd al-Din was one of the special chamberlains (*hujjab khas*) during the reign of al-Malik al-Salih. The water for the *hawd* was supplied by a neighboring spring well, equipped with a *saqiya*. It is probable that this cistern was essentially a trough, as it was frequented by animals. In addition, he built a tall mosque "above it [*bi-'alahu*]." It can be assumed that this indicates the immediate vicinity of, rather than immediately above, the *hawd*. This *waqf* was established in 647/1249–50, the year of Sa'd al-Din's death. He was buried in the vicinity of the *hawd*.[30]

Public Baths

André Raymond, discussing the baths of Cairo as described by Maqrizi, notes fifty-one baths listed by that writer. He adds another seven, from other sources, which must have existed in Maqrizi's time (the *Khitat* dates from ca. 824/1421). Of these fifty-eight baths, forty-eight were located within al-Qahira, one slightly to the west of al-Qahira on the Khalij, and nine in the area between al-Qahira and the mosque of Ibn Tulun.[31] Of relevance to this study are twenty-five baths described by Maqrizi, all within the enclosure of al-Qahira, and another seven at al-Fustat discussed, primarily, by Ibn Duqmaq. Of those twenty-five baths at al-Qahira (many of which were in ruins at the time of Maqrizi), two date from the Fatimid period, ten more from the Fatimids but with documented continuation under the Ayyubids, and another thirteen were founded under the Ayyubid dynasty. The seven baths at al-Fustat will be discussed separately.

Most public baths were established within al-Qahira. That these baths suffered the vicissitudes of economic and political life is evidenced by the fact that in Maqrizi's time only twenty-seven of the forty-eight baths listed were active.[32] Raymond notes that the concentration of baths in al-Qahira in Maqrizi's time suggests that the majority of the population was still domiciled within the Fatimid enceinte.[33] Given the location of the Fatimid and Ayyubid baths, also within al-Qahira, in addition to other topographical information, the same may be said of the Cairo of two centuries earlier. The baths clustered about the mosques, administrative centers, and markets, all of which remained, at least in the Ayyubid and early Mamluk period, concentrated on the *qasaba* of Cairo.[34]

We shall proceed to study the Fatimid and Ayyubid baths of al-Qahira on a chronological basis.

Fatimid period

Hammam Ibn Abi Damm

Located between Suwayqat al-Mas'udi and Bab al-Hawa' (west central area of al-Qahira), this bath (no.1, map 1) was constructed by Ibn Abi Damm al-Yahudi, a member of the chancery (Kitab al-Insha') during the reign of al-Hakim.[35]

Hammam al-Dari

Located in Khatt al-Akfaniyin, probably to the southwest of al-Azhar, this bath (no.2 map 1) was constructed by Shihab al-Dawla Dari al-Saghir, an Armenian slave (*ghulam*) of al-Muzaffar ibn Amir al-Juyushi. Al-Dari died after 533/1138–39.[36]

Fatimid baths with documented continuation under the Ayyubids

Hammam Ibn Qarqa

This bath (no.3, map 1) was located in Khatt Suwayqat al-Mas'udi in Harat Zuwayla, near the mosque of Ibn al-Maghrabi. It was founded by Abu Sa'id ibn Qarqa al-Hakim, supervisor of operations at Dar al-Dibaj and Khizanat al-Silah under the Fatimid dynasty. He was

executed for treason by the caliph al-Hafiz in 529/1134–35. "Under
the Ayyubid dynasty, this bath was known [by the name of] Sarim al-
Din al-Mas'udi, *wali* of al-Qahira. Then it became ruined."[37]

Hammam al-Sultan

According to Maqrizi,

> This bath is reached, presently, from Suwayqat al-Mas'udi, and from
> Qantarat al-Muski. It is among the ancient baths, and it was known in the
> Fatimid dynasty as Hammam al-Awhad, and under the Ayyubid dynasty
> as Hammam ibn Yahya. He was the *qadi* al-Mufaddal Habbat Allah ibn
> Yahya al-'Adil. Then it was known as Hammam al-Taybarsi, and now as
> Hammam al-Sultan.

This bath (no.4, map 1), like Hammam Ibn Qarqa, was located in
the west-central section, near the Khalij.[38]

Hammam al-Juyushi

> This *hammam* was in Harat Barjawan, . . . It was originally among the
> properties of al-Muzaffir ibn Amir al-Juyushi. Then, after the end of the
> Fatimid dynasty, it became part of the *awqaf* of al-Malik al-'Adil, which
> he endowed upon his *ribat*, located in Khatt al-Nakhaliyin at al-Fustat
> Misr. . . . It was destroyed after 740/1339–40.[39]

This bath (no.5, map 1) was located on the *qasaba* of al-Qahira,
to the south of the mosque of al-Hakim. [40]

Hammam al-Sabat

This bath (no.6, map 1) stood near the entrance to the *maristan* of
Qalaun.

> Ibn 'Abd al-Zahir said: "One of the doors of the small palace was known
> as Bab al-Sabat. During the *'Id*, the caliph exited from this door into the
> *midan* [Bayn al-Qasrayn]. . . ." I [Maqrizi] say Hammam al-Sabat is known
> in our times as Hammam Maristan al-Mansuri, intended for the women's
> entrance at the secret door to Maristan al-Mansuri. This *hammam* [was] a
> bath of the smaller western palace, known also as Hammam al-Sanima.
> After the end of the Fatimid dynasty in al-Qahira, the *qadi* Mu'ayyad al-
> Din Abu al-Mansur Muhammad al-Ansari al-Shafi'i, manager [*wakil*] of
> the Bayt al-Mal under al-Malik al-'Aziz, . . . sold this bath to the amir 'Izz
> al-Din Aybak al-'Azizi, along with the open spaces opposite it, for 1200
> dinars in the year 590/1193–94. Then the amir 'Izz al-Din sold it to
> Shaykh Amin al-Din Qaymar ibn 'Abd Allah al-Hamawi al-Tajir for 1600
> dinars. He left the bath to his heirs, from whom the amir al-Faris Sarim

al-Din Khatalba al-Kamili purchased half of it in 637/1239–40. [Another section was taken by an amir of Baybars in 678/1279–80.][41]

Hammam Tatar

This bath (no.7, map 1) was situated in the northeastern section of al-Qahira (Jamaliya), in Khatt Dar al-Wizarat al-Kubri. It was originally intended to serve Dar al-Wizara (founded by al-Afdal ibn Badr al-Jamali, see Chapter Five), and was later possessed by Tatar, one of the *mamalik* of Asad al-Din Shirkuh.[42]

Hammam al-Kuwayk

This bath (no.8, map 1) was located between Harat Zuwayla and Darb Shams al-Dawla (west–central section of al-Qahira). It was founded by the Fatimid vizier 'Abbas, and was associated with his palace (*dar*) in Darb Shams al-Dawla. The bath was restored by a merchant—Ibn Kuwayk al-Rab'i al-Takriti—in 749/1348–49. Its use during the Ayyubid period is uncertain.[43]

Hammam Khushayba

Located to the west of Bayn al-Qasrayn, this bath (no.9, map 1) was first known as Hammam Qawam al-Dawla, and became part of the palace of the vizier al-Ma'mun ibn al-Bata'ihi. This palace in turn became part of Madrasat al-Siyufiya (see Chapter Seven), established by Saladin. The bath was sold, and was eventually endowed on the tomb of Khunad Taghay, mother of Anuk ibn al-Malik al-Nasir Muhammad ibn Qalaun.[44]

Hammam al-Rasasi

This *hammam* [no.10, map 1] was in Harat al-Daylam. The amir Sayf al-Din Husayn ibn Abi al-Hayja' al-Marwani founded it. . . . He willed this bath—and all the neighboring houses—to his sons and [other] descendants. After the end of the Fatimid dynasty, this bath took its name from the amir 'Izz al-Din Aybak al-Rasasi. It was destroyed after 740/1339–40.[45]

Hammam al-Qadi

Located southwest of the Azhar mosque and founded under the Fatimids by the eunuch Shihab al-Dawla, this bath (no.11, map 1) became the property of two *quda* successively, the *qadi* al-Sa'id Abu al-Mu'ali Hibat Allah ibn Faris and, later, the *qadi* Kamal al-Din Abi

Hamad Muhammad, son of the chief *qadi* Sadr al-Din 'Abd Allah ibn Darbas al-Marani. The heirs of Abi Hamad sold the bath in two parts to Mamluk amirs under the reign of Baybars al-Bunduqdari.[46]

Ayyubid baths

Hammama Tughrik

These two baths (nos. 12, 13, map 1) were located near Suwayqat Harat al-Wazir, in the west–central portion of al-Qahira near Qantarat al-Muski (v.i.). They were founded by the amir Husam al-Din Tughrik al-Mahrani, one of the Ayyubid amirs.[47]

Hammam 'Ujayna

Located in Khatt al-Akfaniyin, to the west of al-Azhar, this bath (no.14, map 1) was founded by Fakhr al-Din, brother of the amir 'Izz al-Din Musk. ('Izz al-Din Musk, a relative of Saladin, died at Damascus in 584/1188–89.)[48]

Hammam al-Fadil

Located just to the northeast of Bab Zuwayla, this bath (no.15, map 1) is mentioned only in passing by Maqrizi. Although no date is given, the bath could be associated with al-Qadi al-Fadil.[49]

Hammam al-Sufiya

This bath (no.16, map 1) was constructed by Saladin for the sufis of Khanqah Sa'id al-Su'ada' (v.i.), near the present *khanqah* of Baybars al-Jashankir.[50]

Hammam Kurji

Hammam Kurji (no.17, map 1) was located opposite the entrance to Khanqah al-Salahiya, in Khatt Khara'ib Tatar. "This bath . . . was named for the amir 'Alam al-Din Kurji al-Asadi, one of the Asadi amirs, in the days of the sultan Salah al-Din Yusuf ibn Ayyub."[51]

Hammam Lu'lu'

This bath (no.18, map 1) stood at the head of Rahbat Aydamuri, adjacent to Dar al-Sinani, in the east–central section of al-Qahira (southern Jamaliya). It was established by the *hajib* Husam al-Din Lu'lu' (d.594/1197–98), who served both the Fatimids and Saladin.[52]

Hammam al-Qaffasin

Hammam al-Qaffasin (no.19, map 1) was situated at the head of Harat al-Daylam, just to the southwest of al-Azhar. This bath was constructed by Najm al-Din Yusuf ibn Mujawir, vizier to al-Malik al-'Aziz.[53]

Hammam al-Juwayni

This bath (no.20, map 1) was located in the west–central section of al-Qahira, between Hammam al-Kuwayk and the Bunduqaniyin. The amir 'Izz al-Din Ibrahim ibn al-Juwayni (d. 601/1204–1205), wali of al-Qahira under al-Malik al-'Adil, founded it in the neighborhood of his house.[54]

Hammam Ibn 'Abbud

Maqrizi describes this as an early bath located between Istabl al-Jamiza and the head of Harat Zuwayla (no.21, map 1). This bath was (originally?) known as Hammam al-Falak, after Qadi Falak, a qadi during the reign of al-Malik al-'Adil. (Modern location: center of al-Qahira, to the west of the al-Ghuri mosque.) [55]

Hammama al-Sayyida al-'Amma

Hammama al-Sayyida al-'Amma (nos. 22, 23, map 1) were located at the entrance of Harat al-Rum, to the northeast of the mosque of al-Mu'ayyad Shaykh. Following Maqrizi, "Ibn 'Abd al-Zahir said that two ample baths are known as Hammama al-Sayyida al-'Amma. They were transferred to al-Kamil ibn Shawar, and then to the heirs of the sharif Ibn Tha'lib [an amir of al-Malik al-'Adil]."[56]

Hammam al-Sultan

Located in the west–central portion of al-Qahira, near Qantarat al-Muski and Hammam Ibn Qarqa, this bath (no.24, map 1) was founded by the amir Fakhr al-Din 'Uthman ibn Qizil, ustadar of al-Malik al-Kamil.[57]

Hammam Ibn 'Alkan

This bath [no.25, map 1] was located at Harat al-Judariya in the south–central section of al-Qahira. "The amir Shuja' al-Din 'Uthman ibn 'Alkan, related by marriage [sihr] to the great amir Fakhr al-Din 'Uthman ibn Qizil, founded it. Then it was transferred to the amir 'Ilm al-Din Sinjar al-Sirfi al-Salihi al-Najmi."[58]

In comparing the locations of baths founded in al-Qahira during the Fatimid and Ayyubid dynasties, this writer detects no especial pattern or layout other than that, as previously mentioned, baths tend to be associated with mosques and market areas. Under both the Fatimids and the Ayyubids, the *hammamat*, although largely concentrated in the central section (al-Azhar, Mashhad al-Husayn, the market areas surrounding Bayn al-Qasrayn), are also scattered at random through the remaining quarters. Bayn al-Qasrayn itself, fundamentally a parade ground, was probably relatively free of permanent structures until the fall of the Fatimid dynasty.

Ayyubid baths at al-Fustat

Ayyubid baths at al-Fustat were, like all other activities, limited to a relatively narrow strip of shore line to the west of the ruined areas. Al-Qada'i (d.454/1062–63) states that there were 1,170 baths at al-Fustat. Although it was the heyday of the former commercial capital, this figure cannot be taken seriously. A more realistic number is that given by Ibn al-Mutawwaj (639–730/1241–1330), as something more than seventy baths at (albeit a much truncated) al-Fustat. Ibn 'Abd al-Zahir (620–92/1223–92) states that the number of baths at al-Qahira at the end of 685/1286–87 was close to eighty. The similarity in numbers between the two districts—a somewhat expanded al-Qahira compared with a diminutive al-Fustat—is comparable a century and a half later to the almost contemporary descriptions of Ibn Duqmaq and Maqrizi, viz. some fifty-one baths described by Maqrizi at al-Qahira, and some forty-five baths noted by Ibn Duqmaq at al-Fustat. The relative disproportion could be attributed to three factors: firstly, the continuation of preexisting baths at al-Fustat, even from pre-Fatimid times; secondly, the establishment of baths around major religious centers—the mosque of 'Amr (still highly venerated), a number of *madaris* and mosques founded during the Ayyubid and early Mamluk dynasties, and the Coptic center of Qasr al-Sham'; and thirdly, the maintenance of markets, wharves, and commercial and administrative centers at al-Fustat throughout the Ayyubid and well into the Mamluk periods. It should further be noted that, in addition to the forty-five public baths listed by Ibn Duqmaq, another eleven are described as connected with palaces or large houses (*dur*). Maqrizi's narrative restricts itself to public baths or private baths having become public through endowment.[59]

As opposed to Maqrizi's description of al-Qahira, however, it is difficult, without extensive biographical research, to determine which of the al-Fustat baths were used during the Fatimid period; some, indeed, are noted as dating almost to the Islamic conquest. Their continuance, however, and even their existence, at the time of Ibn Duqmaq (750–809/1349–1406) is somewhat doubtful. Awaiting, then, a complete study of the baths of al-Fustat, we shall concentrate on those seven with definite Ayyubid associations.

Hammam *at the tomb of Imam al-Shafi'i*

According to Ibn Jubayr, who visited Cairo in 578/1183, a bath, associated with the *madrasa* of Imam al-Shafi'i, was established by Saladin in al-Qarafa.[60]

Hammam al-Dhahab

This bath was located alongside the *madrasa* of Manazil al-'Izz (v.i.), near Bab al-Qantara. It was endowed on this *madrasa* by Taqi al-Din 'Umar, Ayyubid ruler of Hama.[61]

Hammam al-Ka'ki

Hammam al-Ka'ki (no.105, map 3) was located to the northeast of Qasr al-Sham', at Dar Mahbas al-Bananat. There were two baths established here in pre-Fatimid times, known (by Ibn Duqmaq) as Hammam al-Ka'ki and Hammam Takarara, with a common wall and fountain (*fisqiya*) between them. Hammam al-Ka'ki was endowed upon Bimaristan al-Qadim al-Salahi.[62]

Hammam al-Sayyida

Ibn Duqmaq notes in one place that this bath (no.106, map 3), located near the northeast corner of Qasr al-Sham', was among the endowments on arsenals (*khaza'in al-silah*), presumably in al-Qahira. In a second notation, however, this bath is located at Habs al-Banana, almost certainly referring to the same structure. Dating from early Islamic times, the property was eventually transferred to the estate of al-Sayyida al-'Amma, a personage of either late Fatimid or early Ayyubid date, who established baths in the southern sector of al-Qahira (v.s.).[63]

Hammam *at al-Mamsusa*

"Al-Fa'izi founded it; then it was transferred after him to others."[64] Ibn Duqmaq probably refers to Sharaf al-Din al-Fa'izi, who founded al-Madrasa al-Fa'iziya at al-Fustat before he assumed the vizierate in 636/1238–39 (v.i.).[65] Khatt al-Mamsusa was located immediately to the east of Qasr al-Sham'.[66] This bath is no.107, map 3.

Hammam al-Fa'izi

According to Ibn Duqmaq, this bath was located "between the two gates of Qantara. The vizier Sharaf al-Din ibn al-Fa'izi founded it and placed it in *waqf* on his *madrasa*."[67]

Hammam Ibn Abi al-Huwafir

According to Maqrizi, "This *hammam* is outside Madinat Misr [al-Fustat] near Jami' al-Jadid al-Nasri. Its location was formerly covered by the Nile; then the water withdrew and created an island and people built upon it after 500/1106–1107. This bath was known from the *qadi* Fath al-Din ibn Abi al-Huwafir, chief of doctors in Egypt. He died in 657/1258–59, and was buried in al-Qarafa."[68] Jami' al-Jadid was located to the south of Fam al-Khalij, near the intake tower to the aqueduct of al-Ghuri.[69]

Water Sources and Usage

Drinking water for al-Qahira and al-Fustat was transported directly from the Nile, except, in the case of al-Qahira, when the Khalij was flowing (usually for some three months after its opening at high Nile). Under the Ayyubids, the only noted use of an aqueduct (or possibly conduit) running directly from the Nile is that supplying al-Malik al-Kamil's recreational ponds at al-Rumayla. However, as described above, several canals provided direct access from the Nile to alluvial ponds, and water was channeled directly from Birkat al-Habash to the tomb–*madrasa* complex of Imam al-Shafi'i. For the most part, however, drinking water was carried to al-Qahira by porters (*saqqa'un*), with and without the assistance of camels and donkeys. With the Khalij, after three months of flow, turning into a series of fetid pools, and the alluvial ponds often drying out completely, the remaining indigenous water was drawn from a series of wells, its quality brackish and saline. In short, potable water was flowing water.[70] The use of well water, especially that located within al-Qahira, was generally limited to washing (but not bathing) and the watering of gardens and animals.[71]

General Hygiene Conditions and Water Quality

The living conditions of al-Qahira and al-Fustat under the Fatimids and Ayyubids have been described in Chapters One and Three, especially in the narratives of al-Muqaddasi, Ibn Ridwan, 'Abd al-Latif, and Ibn Sa'id. The hygienic situation in both areas was generally deplorable, due to crowding, uncleared dirt and refuse, smoke and vapors, and contamination of water supplies by latrines. While both Ibn Ridwan and 'Abd al-Latif (ca. 440/1048–49 and 597/1200–1201 respectively) report that waste from latrines was channeled directly into the Nile,[72] this situation is somewhat mitigated by two factors: firstly, the distance of al-Qahira from the Nile would effectively preclude channeling of waste to that point (but not to the Khalij and the various alluvial ponds); and secondly, archaeological excavations at al-Fustat suggest that latrines emptied, in many cases, into cesspools, three to eleven meters in depth. Waste materials were gradually mixed with sands and, when full, this congealment was removed from the cesspools and the process repeated. However, contamination must have occurred: some sewage channels must have gone directly into the Nile; congealed fill from the cesspools was probably dumped in the river; and, finally, the porous bedrock of al-Fustat must have allowed cesspool sewage (often at a depth below the water table) to seep into the Nile. The water carriers of al-Qahira, drawing from the eastern shore and (when available) the Khalij, doubtless collected water already contaminated by al-Fustat. Good water at al-Qahira and al-Fustat was simply unavailable.

Famine, Pestilence, and Earthquakes

Famines and plagues in Fatimid and Ayyubid Egypt were usually associated with low Niles, especially during the 'time of troubles' of al-Mustansir and the years 597–98/1201–1202 (as described by 'Abd al-Latif, see Chapter Three). Several other instances are described by Maqrizi in his *Suluk*. In 575/1179–80

> in Safar, a wall appeared at Misr, in the middle of the Nile in front of the nilometer. Inside this wall was the tomb of Joseph and his sarcophagus.

. . . [This tomb] had never been exposed, since Moses placed him there, until that time, with the decrease in water at the base of the nilometer. The sand was removed from it, the people observed it, and most of them did not know what it was. [For the same year], death spread throughout Misr and al-Qahira and generally through the provinces of Egypt. The odor of the wind changed, and 17,000 persons died at Misr and al-Qahira in a few days.[73]

While the identification of Joseph's tomb may be open to debate, the combination of low Nile and disease is again in evidence.

In 608/1211–12 a severe earthquake, also experienced in Jordan and Syria, destroyed many houses in al-Qahira and Misr.[74] The year 633/1235–36 witnessed a violent epidemic in Egypt which lasted three months, leaving 12,000 dead in al-Qahira and al-Fustat. This epidemic, however, was not known to be associated with a low Nile.[75]

Summary

As the water resources of al-Qahira were dependent on the Nile, so was the metropolis itself. The ability to control the flow and quality of the water met with mixed results. Despite repeated attempts to control the silting of the al-Fustat shore, constant dredging was necessary throughout the later Middle Ages. Al-Maqs, gradually blocked by the sands of Jazirat al-Fil and Bulaq, was effectively nullified as a port facility in the seventh/thirteenth century.

Drinking water for the inner sections of al-Qahira was carried by porters directly from the Nile, except during the two to three months following the opening of the Khalij. Water for other purposes was supplied by wells, which were generally shallow, saline, and contaminated by neighboring latrines. The baths, the qualities of which were lauded by 'Abd al-Latif, were probably supplied by porters as well, since he notes that the cisterns of the *hammamat* were each capable of holding two to four waterbags (undoubtedly those borne by camels or donkeys).[76]

There were three major canals from the Nile at al-Qahira/al-Fustat: Khalij al-Qahira, in Ayyubid times serving primarily as a water source during high Nile; and the canals al-Dhikr and Bani Wa'il, which fed alluvial ponds. Alluvial ponds—some of which were fed only by ground water—were, at high Nile, not only reservoirs, but sites for numerous promenades and pavilions. As the Nile receded in late autumn and winter, the ponds were reduced to stagnant pools and in some cases—specifically Birkat al-Azbakiya and Birkat al-Habash—were dessicated sufficiently to allow the planting of crops.

Although at least one piping system (of minimal capacity) has been unearthed at al-Fustat, it can be assumed that most drinking water was transported to that city by porters. By the time of the Ayyubids, the effective truncation of al-Fustat to an area west of the mosque of 'Amr left relatively little distance for transportation of water from the Nile. Other conduit or aqueduct systems (presumably above ground) were extended from Birkat al-Habash to the tomb of Imam al-Shafi'i and from the Nile to al-Rumayla. These systems were the undertakings of al-Malik al-Kamil and supplied water only to minimal religious and recreational facilities. There appear to have been no other aqueducts in service under the Ayyubids; the first constructed to the citadel per se was under the reign of al-Nasir Muhammad ibn Qalaun. The Ayyubids constructed no aqueducts to serve either the citadel or the public at large.

Despite extensive sewerage systems undertaken at al-Fustat under the Fatimids (and, presumably, continued under the Ayyubids), drainage of sewage into the Nile—direct or by infiltration—fostered contamination of the water supply for both al-Fustat and al-Qahira, and contributed not only to the undermining of health on a daily basis but also to the epidemics which raged during the years of unusually low Niles.

Chapter Seven

Religious Institutions

The fundamental shift in Ayyubid religious policy was the restoration of the Sunni schools of Islamic law (*madhahib*) in Egypt as a replacement of the officially prevailing Isma'ili doctrine of the Fatimids. Although the true extent of the 'Alid indoctrination of the masses of Egypt was at best a veneer, the policy of Saladin, inspired and dictated by his Syrian overlord Nur al-Din, was one of restoration of allegiance to the Abbasid caliphate of Baghdad. An important role in the implementation of his policy was played by the *madaris*. The *madrasa*—with its basic role as a teaching institution for one or more of the four *madhahib* of orthodox Islam (Hanafi, Hanbali, Maliki, Shafi'i)—originated under that name in Nishapur during the reign of Mahmud of Ghazna. Honed as a tool for the restoration of Sunni Islam by the Seljukid vizier Nizam al-Mulk, the *madaris* were augmented by Nur al-Din in Mesopotamia and Syria (especially Damascus and Aleppo) not only to counter the Ismai'li threat of the Assassins and the Fatimids, but also to promote the ideal of the Holy War against the Crusaders. It remained to Saladin to establish the *madrasa* as a permanent entity in Egypt.[1]

Despite the official Shiite doctrine of the Fatimids, as Lapidus points out,

> The Shafi'i and Maliki school continued to exist and at least at times obtained official recognition when members of the schools were appointed as qadis. Indeed the Fatimids seem to be the authors of the policy of appointing a qadi [not a *qadi al-qudah*] for each of the recognized schools.[2]

Specifically, following the death of the Fatimid caliph al-Amir (524/1130), Abu 'Ali Mansur, son of al-Afdal ibn al-Juyushi, revolted, seized the vizierate, and imprisoned the (future) caliph al-Hafiz.

He announced [the assumption of] the Imami *madhhab* and the invocation [*da'wa*] of the Imam al-Muntazir. . . . In 525/1130–31 he appointed four *qudah*. Of the first two one was Maliki, the other Shafi'i. Each passed judgment according to his *madhhab* and endowed [legacies] according to it. . . . When [Abu 'Ali] was killed in Muharram of 526/1131–32 the Isma'ili *madhhab* was resumed. This situation continued until the armies of Nur al-Din arrived from Damascus commanded by Asad al-Din Shirkuh. He [Shirkuh] assumed the vizierate of Egypt for the caliph al-'Adid. When he died his nephew Salah al-Din succeeded him as vizier in Jumada al-Akhira 564/March 1169. [Saladin] commenced with the changing of the dynasty and its elimination. He restrained al-'Adid; he overthrew the amirs of the dynasty and defeated their armies. At Misr he established a *madrasa* for the Shafi'i legists [*fuqaha'*] and one for the Maliki legists. He dismissed all the Shiites and entrusted the judiciary to Sadr al-Din 'Abd al-Malik ibn Darbas al-Marani the Shafi'ite. . . . The people [of Egypt] followed [*tazahara*] the Maliki and Shafi'i *madhahib* from that time. The Shiite, Isma'ili, and Imami *madhahib* disappeared from view until they had vanished entirely in Egypt. . . . Nur al-Din was zealously a Hanafi. He spread the Hanafi doctrine throughout Syria; because of him Hanafism increased in Egypt. Hanafism was accepted by a number of people in the eastern countries as well. Salah al-Din built al-Madrasa al-Siyufiya at al-Qahira for the Hanafis; their *madhhab* continued to spread and to be strengthened. Their jurists increased in Egypt and Syria from that time.[3]

Maqrizi continues:

As to the doctrines ['*aqa'id*], the sultan Salah al-Din brought the masses toward the doctrine of Shaykh Abi al-Hasan 'Ali ibn Isma'il al-Ash'ari. . . . He stipulated this in his Egyptian endowments [*awqaf*], such as al-Madrasa al-Nasiriya near the dome of Imam al-Shafi'i in al-Qarafa, al-Madrasa al-Nasiriya [known as al-Sharifiya] near the mosque of 'Amr at Misr, the *madrasa* known as al-Qamhiya at Misr, and the Khanqah Sa'id al-Su'ada' at al-Qahira. The situation on the Ash'ari doctrine [i.e. the propagation and extension thereof] continued in Egypt, Syria, the Hijaz, the Yemen, and the countries of the Maghrib as well because of Muhammad ibn Turmat's bringing it into them, until he established the Ash'ari doctrine in all of these countries to such an extent that whoever opposed it was decapitated. The affair remains thus until today. There was not [at first] in the Ayyubid dynasty in Egypt much mention of the Hanafite and Hanbali *madhahib*. Then the Hanbali and Hanafi *madhahib* became well known by the end of it.[4]

. The *jami'* (Friday or congregational mosque) was the central mosque of a Muslim city from which the *khutba* was invoked, by either the governing official or his proxy. The proliferation and location of this institution varied according to the specific area, the general expansion of the caliphate, and especially the prevailing school of law in a given locale. The Shafi'i *madhhab*—predominant in Egypt since Abbasid times—allowed only one *jami'* in each town (*balad*), assuming that the mosque could hold the entire community. While subject to some variation, this policy was generally true for the al-Fustat area during the Tulunid and Ikhshidid periods. Istakhri (ca. 340/951–52) notes three *jawami'*: 'Amr, Ibn Tulun, and al-Qarafa. Each of these mosques could have been regarded as servicing separate districts; indeed, al-Qarafa was regarded as a separate town. The spirit then, if not the letter of the Shafi'i law remained inviolate. This practice appears to have continued during the early years of the Fatimid dynasty. Ibn Hawqal, writing in 367–68/978, lists Friday mosques at al-Qahira (al-Azhar), al-Roda, and Giza (in addition to those previously mentioned). His list is corroborated by al-Muqaddasi in 375/985–86. These three mosques were, again, constructed in areas qualifying as separate towns. By the reign of al-Hakim three additional congregational mosques were constructed: Jami' al-Hakim (begun by al-'Aziz), Jami' al-Maqs, and Jami' al-Rashida.[5] The al-Hakim mosque, immediately outside the (then) north wall near Bab al-Futuh, a relatively uninhabited district, could hardly qualify as serving a separate administrative area. The same must be said for Jami' al-Rashida, lying to the south of al-Fustat between Qasr al-Sham' and Birkat al-Habash, in an area formerly occupied by Christian and Jewish cemeteries.[6] Al-Maqs, on the other hand, had long existed as a separate village and port, and qualified, therefore, as a distinct community. Nasir-i Khusraw, visiting Cairo in 439/1047, mentions the *jawami'* of al-Qahira, seven at al-Fustat, and fifteen for the entire area.[7] While both his count and his identification of specific mosques is somewhat questionable, it is nonetheless clear that the Fatimids, in several instances, established at least two Friday mosques within a given quarter. Ibn 'Abd al-Zahir states that although the *khutba* was initially read (at al-Qahira) in the Azhar mosque, ". . . the *khutba* continued in it [al-Azhar] until the mosque of al-Hakim was built, and the invoking of the *khutba* was transferred to it. Then, indeed, the caliph read the *khutba* in it and Jami' al-Azhar, Jami' Ibn Tulun, and Jami' Misr ['Amr] as well."[8] The Friday procession, in which the caliph rode to each of these mosques in turn, was, no doubt, one of considerable ceremony and splendor.

Upon the accession of Saladin to the sultanate, however, the Shafi'i principle of one Friday mosque per town was, at least in theory, honored. Ibn 'Abd al-Zahir continues:

> The *khutba* was terminated at the Azhar mosque when the sultan Salah al-Din Yusuf ibn Ayyub assumed the sultanate. He appointed Sadr al-Din 'Abd al-Malik ibn Darbas as chief *qadi*, who worked in conformity with his *madhhab*. As a Shafi'ite, Ibn Darbas forbade the reading of two *khutba*s in one town. Therefore the *khutba* was terminated at Jami' al-Azhar and was [instead] read at Jami' al-Hakim, since the latter mosque was larger. The Friday service was not celebrated at al-Azhar for a century, [i.e.] from the time of the accession of the sultan Salah al-Din Yusuf ibn Ayyub until the *khutba* returned in the days of al-Malik al-Zahir Baybars.[9]

Several mitigating factors must be considered here. While the Shafi'i *madhhab* (predominant throughout the Ayyubid dynasty) did indeed prohibit the reading of the *khutba* in more than one mosque per town, this assumed, as previously stated, that this *jami'* could hold the entire community. In moving the *khutba* from the mosque of al-Azhar to the mosque of al-Hakim, Saladin's purpose was probably twofold: firstly, to remove the religious center of al-Qahira away from that of the deposed Fatimid regime, and secondly, to use the largest mosque available. Still, Ibn Jubayr (578/1183) states that there were four congregational mosques in al-Qahira, exclusive of those of Ibn Tulun, 'Amr, and al-Roda, suggesting simultaneous usage of *jawami'* within al-Qahira.[10] Other mosques must have been used, then, to accommodate a growing population in al-Qahira, with the influx of 'commoners' begun under Badr al-Jamali and accelerated by Saladin.

Madaris

According to Lapidus,

> After centuries of Fatimid rule, with but the rump of Sunni schools still active in Egypt and lagging far behind the rest of the Muslim world in institutional organization and cultural vitality, the first Ayyubid task was to establish the cadres of viable religious institutions. Ayyubid policy was not aimed at the sponsorship of the whole Sunni religious activity, but was aimed at the creation of the organizational forms and teaching cadres of the madhahib. Ayyubid madrasas were so few in number, and

were so much the creation of Sultans (but not of all Sultans), emirs and officials because they were intended to be a stimulus and a framework for school development. The madrasas did not employ all the ulama but only the cadres upon whom the schools would be based. The Ayyubids worked out the precedents of school organization and school relations to the state.[11]

Lapidus further notes that while Saladin did indeed found *madaris* of the Shafi'i, Maliki, and Hanafi schools, the prevailing *madhhab* was definitively Shafi'i and that the chief *qudah* were consistently drawn from this school. Of the twelve chief *qudah* under the Ayyubids (at least eight of whom were non-Egyptian),

five had formerly been professors in the various Shafi'i madrasas. The Ayyubids drew many of their qadis from the ranks of leading professors, creating a career pattern which led from study and teaching to judicial administration—that is, a career pattern integrating the position of qadi with the schools of law. The qadi as chief of his madhhab was a corner stone of the Ayyubid conception of the relationship between the schools and judicial administration. In this sense the Ayyubid judicial policy sponsored the evolution of the madhahib in Egypt.[12]

In terms of Fatimid precedent for *madaris* within Egypt, Maqrizi's introduction is somewhat illuminating:

The first known establishment of study before the sultan [Saladin] was in learning which deviated from the sect [*ta'ifa*] of the people of Egypt [Isma'ilism as opposed to Sunnism] during the caliphate of al-'Aziz and the vizierate of Ya'qub ibn Killis. This was conducted at the Azhar mosque. . . . Then meetings were held at the house of the vizier Ya'qub ibn Killis, which were attended by *fuqaha'* where they read jurisprudence [*fiqh*] according to their *madhhab*. A meeting was also held at the mosque of 'Amr ibn al-'As at al-Fustat for the reading of the book of the vizier [*kitab al-wazir*]. Then [the caliph] al-Hakim built Dar al-'Ilm at al-Qahira. . . .

When the sultan Salah al-Din . . . ended the Fatimid dynasty, he terminated the Shiite *madhahib* in Egypt, and installed there [instead] the Shafi'i and Maliki *madhahib*. He emulated Nur al-Din, who built a number of *madaris*—Shafi'i and Hanafi—in Damascus, Aleppo, and their associated districts. He [Saladin] built a *madrasa* for each of the two sects [Shafi'i and Maliki] at Misr [al-Fustat]. The first *madrasa* established in Egypt was al-Madrasa al-Nasiriya near the mosque of 'Amr at al-Fustat. Later, al-Madrasa al-Qamhiya was founded near the same mosque; then al-Madrasa al-Suyufiya was founded at al-Qahira. The sons and amirs of sultan Salah al-Din emulated him by building *madaris* in al-Qahira and Misr and other districts of Egypt, as well as in Syria and the Jazira. . . .[13]

The Ayyubid *madrasa* then, while fundamentally a Syrian import, was not without precedent in Fatimid Cairo, albeit for the propagation of the Isma'ili *da'wa*. Under the impetus of Saladin, it provided a vehicle for Sunni revival, a center for the rejuvenation and/or propagation of the schools themselves, and a source for *qudah* and other officials of the *'ulama'*. We will examine them on an individual basis, with particular regard to their topographical location, their founders and terms of foundations, and particulars of their *madhahib*, instructors, and teaching practices.

Al-Madrasa al-Nasiriya (at al-Fustat)

The site of al-Madrasa al-Nasiriya, allegedly the first *madrasa* founded in Egypt,[14] had been occupied by a prison, Habs al-Ma'una (see Chapter Five), which was, according to Maqrizi, in the neighborhood of the mosque of 'Amr to its south, or, following Ibn Duqmaq, to its east. The prison was destroyed by Saladin on the first of Muharram 566/September 14 1170, and the *madrasa* constructed for the Shafi'i *madhhab*. The first professor was Ibn Zayn al-Tajir (d. 591/1194–95), from whom the *madrasa* took its name (subsequent to al-Nasiriya). Later professors included Ibn Qatita ibn al-Wazzan, Kamal al-Din Ahmad ibn Shaykh al-Shuyukh, and the *sharif* al-Qadi Shams al-Din Abu 'Abd Allah Muhammad al-Hanafi Qadi al-'Ar al-Armawi. Presumably these professors were immediately successive, and all within the Ayyubid period or shortly thereafter. It was from the last, the *sharif* al-Armawi, that the *madrasa* took its final name, al-Madrasa al-Sharifiya. As *awqaf*, Saladin had endowed on it both al-Sagha (the goldsmiths' bazaar at al-Fustat) and an unnamed village.[15]

Al-Madrasa al-Qamhiya

Al-Madrasa al-Qamhiya was constructed near the mosque of 'Amr, on the site of Dar al-Ghazl, a thread market. This *qaysariya* was destroyed by Saladin, who then founded the Maliki *madrasa* during the second half of Muharram 566/early October 1170. According to Maqrizi, Saladin placed four professors there, each having his own following of students. Ibn Duqmaq discusses the establishment of four *zawaya* (singular *zawiya*, literally 'corner'). This suggests the conducting of lessons in individual sections of the building, perhaps simultaneously, as was often the case in mosques and other *madaris*. Maqrizi and Ibn Duqmaq are lavish in their praises of both the quality of instruction and the quality of students at this *madrasa*. Its *awqaf* (the endowments of Saladin) included a *qaysariya* in Suq al-Warraqin (at al-Fustat) and a hamlet in the Fayyum, al-Hanbushiya. Funding for both professors and students was dispersed in wheat (*qamh*) from this hamlet, hence the name of the *madrasa*.[16]

It should be noted here that Maqrizi, in almost identical descriptions, notes that both al-Madrasa al-Nasiriya (at al-Fustat) and al-Madrasa al-Qamhiya were surrounded by ruins and that they themselves, were it not for the quality of instruction, would have become ruinous, suggesting that the *kharab* areas encroached upon the mosque of 'Amr from Saladin's time to that of Maqrizi.[17]

Al-Madrasa al-Nasiriya (at al-Qarafa)

Maqrizi states:

> This *madrasa* is near the dome [over the tomb] of the Imam al-Shafi'i at al-Qarafa or Misr. . . . Salah al-Din . . . founded it, and appointed there a professor to teach the Shafi'i *fiqh*. [Saladin] granted him a fixed monthly sum—for teaching—of forty dinars. Each dinar was equal to thirteen and one third dirhams. He also allotted a fixed [monthly?] sum of ten dinars for the supervision of the *awqaf* of the *madrasa*. He further allotted him a daily supply of sixty Egyptian *artal* of bread and two bags of Nile water. [Saladin] placed [in this *madrasa*] tutors [*mu'idin*] and a number of students. He endowed on it a bath in its neighborhood and the shops [*hawanit*] outside of [the *madrasa*], in addition to the island known as Jazirat al-Fil in the Nile outside of al-Qahira [see Chapter Three]. A group of leading notables administered the courses of study; then it lacked a professor for thirty years, and studies were conducted by ten tutors.[18]

Ibn Jubayr adds, in his description of the tomb of Imam al-Shafi'i (v.i.):

> [O]pposite from [the tomb] was built a madrasah the like of which has not been built in this country; there is nothing more spacious or finely built. One who walks around [the *madrasa*] might consider it a separate town. Opposite [the *madrasa*] are a bath and other conveniences, and building continues on the complex at this time. The measureless expenditure on it is controlled by the shaykh, imam, ascetic, and man of learning called Najm al-Din al-Khubushani.[19]

Intimately connected with the founder of Saladin's preferred *madhhab*, it is highly likely that this *madrasa*, above all others in Egypt, enjoyed the special beneficence and personal attention of the sultan.

Al-Madrasa al-Qutbiya (in Khatt Suwayqat al-Sahib)

Following Maqrizi,

> This *madrasa* is in al-Qahira in Khatt Suwayqat al-Sahib at the entrance to Darb al-Hariri. It and al-Madrasa al-Sayfiya [v.i.] were [formerly] among the properties of Dar al-Dibaj, earlier mentioned. The amir Qutb al-Din Balbal ibn Shuja' al-Hadbani founded this *madrasa* in 570/1174–75, as a *waqf* on the Shafi'i *fuqaha'*. [Qutb al-Din] was an amir of the sultan Salah al-Din.[20]

The approximate position of Suwayqat al-Sahib was almost due west of al-Azhar near the east bank of the Khalij. Dar al-Dibaj, in the same area, had been the residence of the Fatimid vizier Ya'qub ibn Killis, and the residence of subsequent viziers until the construction of Dar al-Wizara by Badr al-Jamali (v.s.). This structure then became a manufactory for silken brocade (*al-harir al-dibaj*), and was destroyed following the end of the Fatimid dynasty.[21] The Qutbiya Madrasa (no.26, map 1), constructed on or near its site, was probably the first non-sultanal *madrasa* established in Egypt.

The madrasa established at Mashhad al-Husayn

The Husayni mosque (no.28, map 1) was established in its present location under the caliphate of al-Fa'iz in 549/1154–55. It holds, allegedly, the head of Husayn ibn 'Ali ibn Abu Talib, transported to Cairo from Ascalon by the vizier al-Salih Tala'i' ibn Ruzayk, who feared that the relic would fall into Crusader hands. Originally intended for al-Salih's mosque, just outside Bab Zuwayla, the palace establishment insisted on the head's transferral to its current site, where the *mashhad* was constructed for that specific purpose.[22]

Maqrizi states:

> When [Saladin] assumed rule, he placed [in this *mashhad*] a circle of teaching faculty [*tadris*] and *fuqaha'*. [This group] was entrusted to the *faqih* al-Baha' al-Dimashqi, who sat with the study group at the *mihrab* in front of the tomb. When Mu'in al-Din Husayn ibn Shaykh al-Shuyukh ibn Hamwiya assumed the vizierate, and the running of this *madrasa* reverted to him after his associates [*ukhuwa*], he appropriated funds from the *awqaf* of the *mashhad* to the construction of the present study hall [*iwan al-tadris*] and the building of houses for the most important *fuqaha'*. This *mashhad* was burned at the time of [al-Malik] al-Salih in the 640s [A.H.], when the amir Jamal al-Din ibn Yaghmur was al-Malik al-Salih's deputy at al-Qahira. The reason for this was that one of the storekeepers of candles dropped a torch. The afore-mentioned Jamal al-Din himself remained on the scene until the fire was extinguished. . . . In *Kitab al-durr al-nazim,*

among the descriptions of al-Qadi al-Fadil 'Abd al-Rahim, it is noted that among the buildings [of al-Qadi al-Fadil] was an ablution fountain near the *mashhad* of imam Husayn at al-Qahira, and the mosque and *saqiya* [the reference of the latter two is uncertain]. He endowed on them lands near al-Khandaq outside of al-Qahira, as well as a neighboring house [to the *mashhad*?]; the profits from this recompense were great.[23]

Ibn Jubayr's description of the Husayni *mashhad* concentrates on its lavish embellishments and the excessive emotions displayed by those visiting the martyr's tomb. No mention is made of a *madrasa*. Of some interest, however, is his notation that the mausoleum (presumably domed) was flanked by two like chambers, and that it was entered through a mosque of similar marble decoration.[24] Classes were probably held in this mosque, thus rendering the complex the triple function of mosque, *madrasa*, and tomb, as was often the case in later Mamluk *madaris* (e.g. that of Sultan Hasan). It must immediately be stressed that the cases of the Husayni *mashhad* and the tomb of Imam al-Shafi'i are exceptional as these *madaris* were founded at centers of adulation of saints revered throughout—at least orthodox—Islam. Centers of pilgrimage for generations past, these tombs provided formidable nuclei in Saladin's quest to re-espouse Shafi'ism as the paramount *madhhab* in Egypt.

Finally, a minaret, still extant, was contructed at the Husayni mosque by Abu al-Qasim al-Sukkari in 634/1236–37. This, in addition to the almost adjacent Bab al-Akhdar (dating from 549/1154–55) are all remaining from the late Fatimid-Ayyubid structure.[25]

Madrasat Ibn al-Arsufi

Maqrizi states:

> This *madrasa* was in the area of the clothmakers [*al-bazzazin*] neighboring Khatt al-Nakhkhalin [rag-gatherers' quarter] at Misr. It was named for ['Afif al-Din 'Abd Allah ibn Muhammad] al-Arsufi, an Ascaloni trader, who founded it in 570/1174–75. . . . He died at Misr on 11 Rabi' al-Awwal 593/1196–97.[26]

Ibn Duqmaq adds further detail:

> Its studies were held in a suspended [*mu'allaq*] mosque, which has two doors, in al-Bazzazin. From the lower end of its covered passage [*sabat*], one enters al-Nakhkhalin. It is also known as the foundation [*insha'*] of Ibn al-Arsufi . . . [he lists several professors]. . . . There was a *waqf* covering its exigencies, and those of its imam—he was the teacher [*mudarris*] in it—and on the students who worked according to the *madhhab* of the Imam al-Shafi'i. [The *waqf* included] the shops below it

at the entrance to al-Bazzazin and at the entrance to the lane which leads to the Nakhkhalin. . . .

Further *awqaf* included the greater and lesser *qaysariyas* of Ibn al-Arsufi [v.i.] at al-Fustat.[27]

Casanova places al-Bazzazin just west of the mosque of 'Amr.[28] Madrasat Ibn al-Arsufi (no.108, map 3) was probably the first established in Egypt by a non-governmental individual.

Al-Madrasa al-Suyufiya

Following Maqrizi,

> This *madrasa* is in al-Qahira. It is part [of the former] palace [*dar*] of the vizier al-Ma'mun al-Bata'ihi. Salah al-Din endowed it on the Hanafis. He appointed Shaykh Majd al-Din Muhammad ibn Muhammad al-Jabti as professor. [Al-Jabti] was allotted eleven dinars a month [as salary]. The remainder of the profit of the *waqf* was allocated, as [Saladin] deemed appropriate, upon the Hanafi students assigned to him [al-Jabti] according to their classes [*tabaqat*]. [Saladin] placed al-Jabti as overseer, and, following him, others who had authority in Muslim affairs. It was known as al-Madrasa al-Suyufiya as Suq al-Suyufiyin was then at its gate. The *madrasa* is now facing Suq al-Sanadiqiyin. Ibn 'Abd al-Zahir erred. He said in *Kitab al-rawdat al-zahira* that "among the *khitat* of al-Qahira [as built by] al-Mu'izz is al-Madrasa al-Suyufiya. It belongs to the Hanafis. 'Izz al-Din Farihshah [sic], a relative of Salah al-Din, endowed it." I do not know how he made this error. The book of its *waqf* still exists, and I have become familiar with it. I have summarized its contents herewith. [It is stated] in it that Sultan Salah al-Din endowed [the *madrasa*]. . . . The date of this writing is 19 Sha'ban 572 [Feb. 20, 1177]. He endowed on its beneficiaries [i.e., of the *madrasa*] thirty-two shops in Khatt Suwayqat Amir al-Juyush, at Bab al-Futuh, and in Harat Barjawan. . . . This *madrasa* was the first endowed upon the Hanafis in Egypt, and it remains in their hands.[29]

Al-Madrasa al-Suyufiya (no.29, map 1), following Ravaisse, stood slightly to the north of the present mosque of al-Ashraf Barsbay which is located on Shari' Mu'izz li-Din at the intersection with Shari' al-Muski.[30]

Al-Madrasa al-Taqawiya

Al-Madrasa al-Taqawiya (no.101, map 3), formerly the Fatimid pavilion Manazil al-'Izz, stood on the Nile shore at al-Fustat, almost opposite the nilometer of al-Roda. According to Qalqashandi, this *madrasa* was relatively close to Bab al-Qantara (see Chapter Three).

Casanova argues that the term *bil-qarab* should not be taken too literally, and that other establishments between Bab al-Qantara and al-Madrasa al-Taqawiya place it farther to the north.[31]

According to Ibn Duqmaq,

This *madrasa* was [formerly] known as Manazil al-'Izz. Al-Malik al-Muzaffar Taqi al-Din 'Umar ibn Shahanshah ibn Najm al-Din Ayyub, nephew of Salah al-Din Yusuf ibn Ayyub, endowed it. . . . Al-Mu'izz al-'Ubaydi, the builder of al-Qahira, built this pavilion for his sister when she arrived from the Maghrib. There was not a finer pavilion at Misr. Nothing before it blocked its view of the Nile, the empty green spaces [presumably on al-Roda], and the nilometer. The caliphs continued to use it, after her, as a promenade until the time of al-'Adid. [The pavilion] served for both entertainment and seclusion. Al-Mu'izz also built the bath adjacent to it known as Hammam al-Dhahab. He placed a gate between the pavilion and the bath. . . . When [Saladin] had consolidated his position in Egypt following the death of al-'Adid, he requested his mother and sisters and their children from Syria. Nur al-Din considered this until he allowed them to go. When they arrived [Saladin] settled his nephew al-Malik al-Muzaffar Taqi al-Din 'Umar in this pavilion. When [Taqi al-Din] occupied it, he purchased [the pavilion] in its entirety, as well as the bath and the stable neighboring the bath, now known as Funduq al-Nakhla, from Bayt al-Mal. Following that, he bought the island of al-Roda, in Sha'ban 566 [Apr 9–May 8, 1171]. . . . Then he built two inns [*funduqayn*] at Misr in Khatt al-Malahin, known as Fanadiq al-Karim and a *rab'* neighboring the smaller *funduq* [of the two]. When al-Malik al-Nasir [Saladin] turned his attention toward Syria [sic], he deputized his nephew Taqi al-Din 'Umar, ancestor of the rulers of Hama, as administrator of Egypt. . . . [Ibn al-Mutawwaj mentioned that] al-Muzaffir endowed this *dar* [i.e. Manazil al-'Izz] on the Shafi'i *fuqaha'*. He endowed the surroundings on the *madrasa*, including the bath, and he rebuilt the stable as a *funduq*, and endowed it on the *madrasa* as well. Then he departed to serve his uncle al-Malik al-Nasir [Saladin], who made him ruler of Hama. The chief *qadi* 'Imad al-Din al-Sukkari taught in it, followed by his son, the *qadi* Fakhr al-Din. This situation continued until the time of al-Malik al-Salih Najm al-Din Ayyub, who appointed as professor the chief *qadi* Badr al-Din Abu al-Muhassin al-Sinjari, [who was also charged with] al-Madrasa al-Sharifiya neighboring Jami' Misr. Then its professorship returned to the descendants of al-Sukkari, and remains so till this day.[32]

Ibn Duqmaq's time sequence requires examination. Abu Shamah, for the year 566/1170–71 states:

Halfway through Sha'ban Taqi 'Umar ibn Shahanshah . . . bought Manazil al-'Izz at Misr and endowed it upon the Shafi'is. He bought al-Roda,

Hammam al-Dhahab, and other properties, and endowed them upon [the *madrasa*].[33]

Maqrizi, in a passage describing the *madrasa*, fundamentally agrees with Ibn Duqmaq, stating that Taqi al-Din lived there for a time, that the above-mentioned properties were indeed purchased in 566/1170–71, and that he endowed the *manazil* as a *madrasa* when he intended to leave Egypt for Syria.[34] However, Ibn al-Mutawwaj (cited by Maqrizi) relates that the island of al-Roda was purchased by Taqi al-Din in 566/1170–71. When he was replaced by al-Malik al-ʿAziz as administrator of Egypt, Taqi al-Din endowed al-Roda, in its entirety, on his *madrasa* at al-Fustat.[35]

Taqi al-Din ʿUmar served as Saladin's deputy (*naʾib*) in Egypt from 579/1183–84 to 582/1186–87, when he was recalled to Syria; he had previously served Saladin in several capacities in Egypt and Syria, and had been awarded Hama as an appanage in 574/1178–79. That he purchased Manazil al-ʿIzz and the other properties mentioned in 566/1170–71 is relatively certain; that he reestablished the *manazil* as a *madrasa* at this time, however, is not, especially since Ibn al-Mutawwaj states that al-Roda was not endowed upon the *madrasa* until Taqi al-Din was relieved of his position of *naʾib* in Egypt in 582/1186–87. While Taqi al-Din surely left Egypt for service in Syria on more than one occasion, the general sequence of both Maqrizi's and Ibn Duqmaq's narratives suggests that the date of these endowments lies within Taqi al-Din's tenure as *naʾib*. Al-Madrasa al-Taqawiya, then, despite Abu Shamah's chronology, may not have been established until 579/1183–84 to 582/1186–87, some thirteen years after its purchase (as Manazil al-ʿIzz) by Taqi al-Din ʿUmar.[36]

Al-Madrasa al-ʿAshuriya

According to Maqrizi,

This *madrasa* [no.30, map 1] is in Harat Zuwayla, al-Qahira, near the new Qutbiya *madrasa* and Rahbat Kawkay. Ibn ʿAbd al-Zahir said it was the palace [*dar*] of the Jew Ibn Jamiʿ the physician [*tabib*]. He bequeathed it to Qaraqush. The lady ʿAshuraʾ—daughter of Saruh al-Asadi and wife of the amir Yazkuj al-Asadayy—bought it from him, and endowed it upon the Hanafis. It was among the finest of palaces. This *madrasa* became ruined and permanently closed, only opening rarely [sic]. There was no one living in this lane [*zuqaq*] excepting Jews and those associated with them by marriage.[37]

Al-Madrasa al-Fadiliya

The *madrasa* of al-Qadi al-Fadil (no.31, map 1) was established in Darb al-Mulukhiya, in Harat Qa'id al-Quwwad, to the northeast of the eastern Fatimid palace in what is now al-Jamaliya.[38]

Following Maqrizi,

This *madrasa* is in Darb al-Mulukhiya in al-Qahira. Al-Qadi al-Fadil . . . built it near his palace in 580/1184–85. He endowed it upon two sects of *fuqaha'*, Shafi'i and Maliki. He placed there a hall for readers. The imam Abu Muhammad al-Shatbayy, organizer of the Shatbiya, taught recitation there; his student Abu 'Abd Allah Muhammad ibn 'Umar al-Qurtubayy succeeded him. Then followed Shaykh 'Ali ibn Musa al-Dihan and others. [Al-Qadi al-Fadil] appointed the *faqih* Abu'l Qasim 'Abd al-Rahman ibn Salama al-Iskandarani as professor of *fiqh* for both *madhahib*. [Al-Qadi al-Fadil] endowed a large collection of books—covering all the sciences—on this *madrasa* [see Khizanat al-Kutub, Chapter Four]. . . . This was one of the largest and most majestic of the Cairene *madaris*. Much of its neighborhood became ruinous.[39]

Al-Madrasa al-Sahibiya

Maqrizi states:

This *madrasa* is in al-Qahira in Suwayqat al-Sahib. Its location was part of the site of the *dar* of the vizier Ya'qub ibn Killis [later known as] Dar al-Dibaj. Al-Sahib Safi al-Din 'Abd Allah ibn 'Ali ibn Shukr founded it. He endowed it upon the Malikis. Its functions included the study of grammar and a library. [The *madrasa*] continued in the hands of his descendants. In Sha'ban of 758 [July 20–August 17, 1357] the *qadi* 'Ilm al-Din Ibrahim ibn 'Abd al-Latif ibn Ibrahim—known as Ibn Zubayr Nazir al-Dawla—restored it, during the [reign of] al-Malik al-Nasir Hasan ibn Muhammad ibn Qalaun. He added a pulpit [*minbar*] to it, and Friday prayers have been held there until our times. Before that there was no *minbar* and the Friday prayer was not celebrated [in the *madrasa*].[40]

Safayy al-Din ibn Shukr (548/1148–49 to 622/1225–26), vizier to al-'Adil, had previously (from 580/1185–86 onwards) served as head of the navy (Diwan al-Ustul) under Saladin, and was joined in this position by al-Malik al-'Adil in 587/1191–92. Although exiled in 609/1212–13 under the instigation of al-Malik al-Kamil, he was returned to favor during the Fifth Crusade to resolve Egypt's financial crisis.[41] The date of the founding of his *madrasa* (no.32, map 1) is uncertain, but given Ibn Shukr's career, ca. 590–600/1193–1204 is not unreasonable.

Suwayqat al-Sahib, in modern terms, was located near the junction of Shari' al-Azhar and Shari' Bayn al-Surayn just east of the Khalij.[42]

Al-Madrasa al-Uzkushiya

Maqrizi relates:

This *madrasa* [no.33, map 1] is in al-Qahira at the head of the *suq* formerly known as al-Kharuqiyin which is known today as Suwayqat Amir al-Juyush. It was built by the Amir Sayf al-Din Ayazkuj al-Asadi—a *mamluk* of Asad al-Din Shirkuh and one of the amirs of sultan Salah al-Din ibn Ayyub. He placed it in *waqf* on the Hanafi *fuqaha'* in 592/1195–96. Ayazkuj was head of the Asadiya amirs in Egypt during the time of Sultan Salah al-Din and the days of his son al-Malik al-'Aziz 'Uthman. The amir Fakhr al-Din Jaharkas was head of the Salahiya. This state of affairs continued until [Ayazkuj] died on Friday 18 Rabi' al-Akhir 599/1202–1203. He was buried at the foot of the Muqattam near the *ribat* of the amir Fakhr al-Din ibn Qizil.[43]

Suwayqat Amir al-Juyush was located to the south of Bab al-Futuh, on Shari' Amir al-Juyush, just west of Shari' Mu'izz li-Din Allah.[44]

Al-Madrasa al-Sayfiya

Following Maqrizi,

This *madrasa* is in al-Qahira between Khatt al-Bundaqaniyin and Khatt al-Malhiyin. Its location was formerly part of Dar al-Dibaj. Ibn 'Abd al-Zahir said that it was formerly a palace and that it was part of al-Madrasa al-Qutbiya. The Shaykh al-Shuyukh—i.e. Sadr al-Din Muhammad ibn Hamwiya—lived in al-Madrasa al-Sayfiya. It was built during the vizierate of Safi al-Din 'Abd Allah ibn 'Ali ibn Shukr [by] Sayf al-Islam, who endowed it. 'Imad al-Din, son of the *qadi* Sadr al-Din—i.e. Ibn Darbas—administered it. The full name of this Sayf al-Islam [was] Tughtakin ibn Ayyub.[45]

Al-Madrasa al-Sayfiya (no.34, map 1), in addition to al-Madrasa al-Qutbiya and al-Madrasa al-Sahibiya (v.s.), was founded on the site of Dar al-Dibaj. Its approximate site was the modern junction of Shari' al-Azhar and Shari' Bayn al-Surayn, just east of the former Khalij. The foundation of this *madrasa* preceded Shawwal 593 (Aug. 17–Sep. 15, 1197), the date of Sayf al-Din's death.[46]

Madrasa of 'Izz al-Din 'Abd al-Wahhab

This *madrasa* is not mentioned by Maqrizi, and is of special importance as the first Hanbali *madrasa* established at Cairo.[47] 'Abd al-Wahhab, a Hanbalite doctor of Damascus and descendant of Abu al-Faraj al-Shirazi, had accompanied Asad al-Din Shirkuh to Cairo.[48] We do not know either the location or foundation date of this *madrasa*; Lapidus places it after the death of Saladin.[49]

Al-Madrasa al-Ghaznawiya

Maqrizi states:

> This *madrasa* is at the head of the place known as Suwayqat Amir al-Juyush, facing al-Madrasa al-Yazkujiya [read: Uzkushiya]. The amir Husam al-Din Qaymaz al-Najmi—a *mamluk* of Najm al-Din Ayyub, father of the kings—built it. He installed there the Shaykh Shihab al-Din Abu al-Fadil Ahmad ibn Yusuf ibn ʿAli ibn Muhammad al-Ghaznawi al-Baghdadi, reciter of the Quʾran [*muqriʾ*] and Hanafi *faqih*. He taught in it. He was one of the foremost scholars of *fiqh*, and had studied under [lit. heard] ʿAli al-Hafiz al-Sulafi. He recited personally. He lived in Egypt at the end of his life. . . . [Al-Ghaznawi] was born at Baghdad in Rabiʿ al-Awwal 522 (Mar. 5–Apr. 4, 1128) and died at al-Qahira . . . during Rabiʿ al-Awwal 599 (Nov. 18–Dec. 17, 1202). It was among the Hanafi *madaris*.[50]

Lane–Poole dates the founding of this *madrasa* (no.35, map 1) to the reign of al-Malik al-Mansur ibn al-ʿAziz (595–96/1198–1200); Creswell dates it as before 595/1198–99.[51] While their sources are uncertain, these dates are not unreasonable, given Maqrizi's statement that al-Ghaznawi resided in Egypt in his later years. It is worthwhile to note the similarities in foundation between al-Madrasa al-Ghaznawiya and al-Madrasa al-Uzkushiya. Both were established by early Ayyubid *mamalik*, serving, respectively, Najm al-Din Ayyub and Asad al-Din Shirkuh. Both were founded in the same period, ca. 592–99/1195–1203, in the same location, and espoused the same *madhhab*, Hanafism.

Madrasat al-ʿAdil

Following Maqrizi,

> This *madrasa* is in Khatt al-Sahil near al-Rabʿ al-ʿAdili in Misr. [The *rabʿ*] is endowed upon the Shafiʿi [tomb]. Al-Malik al-ʿAdil built [the *madrasa*]. The chief *qadi* Taqi al-Din ibn Shas taught in it, and it became known by his name. It is called Madrasat Ibn Shas at this time. [The *madrasa*] is thriving. It is located in Khatt al-Qashshashin ['trash-collectors'] and is Maliki.[52]

Ibn Duqmaq adds that al-Rabʿ al-ʿAdili was endowed on the exigencies (*masalih*) of the tomb (lit. dome) of the Imam al-Shafiʿi.

Whether this *rab'* was also the foundation of al-Malik al-'Adil is unsure, but certainly possible. He continues:

> There was originally no instruction in [the *madrasa*]. However, it was the mosque of the chief *qadi* Taqi al-Din ibn Shas. His son—chief *qadi* Sharaf al-Din Muhammad—built a *rab'* in Khatt Jami' al-Tuluni, near the *masjid* where he sat in judgment. [The *rab'*] consisted of a mill [*tahun*] and a *funduq*; there were storehouses within it and shops on the south side, and stories above it. The *amir silar*, deputy of the sultanate, and the amir Baybars, before his rule, asked Sharaf al-Din for [the *rab'*], offering him a large sum of money. He did not accept this offer and, instead, endowed [the *rab'*] on the professor teaching in this mosque [i.e. Masjid Ibn Shas]. The students were Maliki. The first who taught in it was the chief *qadi* Muhi al-Din, son of the chief *qadi* Zayn al-Din ibn Makhluf al-Maliki.[53]

Given Maqrizi's statement that the chief *qadi* Ibn Shas taught in this *madrasa* compared with Ibn Duqmaq's attestation that it was only a mosque under his jurisdiction, the precise definition of *madrasa*—as opposed to *masjid*—is open to some question, as well as the possibility of a simple contradiction in the two narratives. It is conceivable, however, that Ibn Shas conducted some teaching in the mosque and as Ibn Duqmaq suggests, that it only became a full-fledged *madrasa* after its endowment on the Malikis by his son.

In modern terms, Madrasat al-'Adil (no.109, map 3) stood almost directly west of Jami' 'Amr, and to the southwest of the monastery of Abu al-Sayfayn. Casanova believed al-Qashshashin (the local quarter) to be an error; he suggests either al-Shashiyin or al-Khashshabiyin.[54]

Al-Madrasa al-Masruriya

Maqrizi relates:

> This *madrasa* is in al-Qahira inside Darb Shams al-Dawla. It was the [*dar*] of Shams al-Khawass Masrur, one of the servants of the [Fatimid] palace. It became a *madrasa* after his death by his direction. The small *funduq* [see Chapter Eight] is endowed upon it. The building of the *madrasa* was the price of a landed estate [*day'a*] in Syria, which was sold by his direction after his death. The *qadi* Kamal al-Din Khadr supervised that transaction, and taught in [the *madrasa*]. Masrur was among those distinguished by Salah al-Din Yusuf ibn Ayyub. [Saladin] gave him priority over [Masrur's] circle [*halqa*] [of servants?]. [Masrur] continued in the forefront of affairs until the days of the Kamiliya. He was devoted to God. He remained in his palace until he died, and was buried next to

his mosque in al-Qarafa. . . . Among his buildings in al-Qahira is the *funduq* known today as Khan Masrur al-Safadi.[55]

Darb Shams al-Dawla was known, under the Fatimids, as Harat al-Umara' and was located immediately south of the smaller western palace. Following the Ayyubid takeover, this quarter became the residence of Shams al-Dawla Turan Shah, hence its latter name.[56] Since the *madrasa* (no.36, map 1) assumed its role following Masrur's death "in the days of the Kamiliya," one may assume that this post-dated al-Kamil's appointment as *na'ib* of Egypt in 604/1207. Creswell dates the foundation to 610/1213–14; his source, again, is not apparent.[57]

Al-Madrasa al-Sharifiya

Maqrizi states:

> This *madrasa* is in Darb Karkama at the head of Harat al-Judariya in al-Qahira. The *amir kabir* and *sharif* Fakhr al-Din ibn Tha'lib . . . amir of the Hajj and visitors to the holy sites [*amir al-hajj wal-za'irin*] and one of the amirs of Egypt during the Ayyubid dynasty—endowed it. He died in 612/1215–16. It is among the *madaris* of the Shafi'i *fuqaha'*.[58]

Maqrizi further notes that the *madrasa* (no.37, map 1) had formerly been Ibn Tha'lib's house.[59] The foundation date, then, is probably during the latter part of the reign of al-Malik al-'Adil. Harat al-Judariya was located to the south of Harat al-Umara' and, in modern terms, just west of the Ashrafiya *madrasa*.[60]

The Dar al-Hadith of al-Malik al-Kamil

Following Maqrizi,

> This *madrasa* is in Khatt Bayn al-Qasrayn in al-Qahira. It is known as Dar al-Hadith al-Kamiliya. The sultan al-Malik al-Kamil . . . founded it in 622/1225–26. It is the second *dar* established for *hadith*. The first who built a *dar* [for *hadith*] on the face of the earth was al-Malik al-'Adil Nur al-Din Mahmud ibn Zangi at Damascus. Then al-Kamil built this *dar* and endowed it upon those occupied in [the study of] the prophetic *hadith* [*al-hadith al-nabawi*]; then, after them, [the *madrasa*] was endowed upon the Shafi'i *fuqaha'*. He endowed on it the *rab'* which is nearby at Bab al-Kharanshaf. [The *rab'*] extends to the *darb* facing Jami' al-Aqmar. This *rab'* was founded by al-Malik al-Kamil. Its place was part of the site of the western palace, following which it was occupied by grain merchants. The site of the *madrasa* had been occupied by a slave market, as well as a palace [*dar*] known as [Dar] Ibn Kastul. The first professor at the Kamiliya was al-Hafiz ibn Dahiya, succeeded by his brother, Abu 'Amr ibn Dahiya

. . . [the succession continues]. . . . [The *madrasa*] remained under the leading *fuqaha'* until the events and calamities of the year 803/1400–1401, when it disappeared as other [structures] disappeared. . . . For a long time no studies were conducted in it, until its studies were forgotten, or almost forgotten.[61]

One ruined *iwan* of the Dar al-Hadith (no.38, map 1) stands just to the north of the mosque of Sultan Barquq on Shari' Mu'izz li-Din Allah.

Al-Madrasa al-Sirmiya

This *madrasa* [no.39, map 1] is inside the small Bab al-Jamlun near the head of Suwayqat Amir al-Juyush, between it and the Hakim mosque, near the *ziyada* [of the mosque]. The amir Jamal al-Din Shuwaykh ibn Sirm— one of the amirs of al-Malik al-Kamil—built it. Jamal al-Din died on 19 Safar 636 (Oct. 2, 1238).[62]

Suwayqat Amir al-Juyush corresponds to the current Shari' Amir al-Juyush, southwest of the mosque of al-Hakim.

Al-Madrasa al-Fakhriya

Maqrizi states:

This *madrasa* [no.40, map 1] is in al-Qahira between Suwayqat al-Sahib and Darb al-'Addas. It was built by the *amir kabir* Fakhr al-Din Abu al-Fath 'Uthman ibn Qizil al-Barumi, *ustadar* of al-Malik al-Kamil. Its cession [*faragh*] was in the year 622/1225–26. Its site had been lastly known as the *dar* of the amir Husam al-Din Saruj ibn Artuq. The amir Fakhr al-Din was born in 551/1156–57 at Aleppo. . . . He died at Harran in 629/1231–32. . . . Other than this *madrasa*, his buildings include the mosque which faces it, a *ribat* in al-Qarafa with an adjoining *sabil*, and a *ribat* at Mecca.[63]

Suwayqat al-Sahib and Darb al-'Addas were within Harat al-Waziriya. In modern terms, this lay near the junction of Shari' al-Azhar and Shari' Bayn al-Surayn, just east of the former Khalij.[64]

Al-Madrasa al-Fa'iziya

Following Maqrizi,

This *madrasa* is at Misr in Khatt [blank]. Al-Sahib Sharaf al-Din Hibat Allah ibn Sa'd ibn Wahib al-Fa'izi founded it before his vizierate in the year 636/1238–39. The *qadi* Muhi al-Din 'Abd Allah—son of the chief *qadi* Sharaf al-Din Muhammad ibn 'Ayn al-Dawla—taught in it. Then the chief *qadi* Sadr al-Din Mawhub al-Jazari [succeeded him]. The *madrasa* was Shafi'ite.[65]

Ibn Duqmaq, who gives the foundation date as 637/1239–40, continues the professorial list, no doubt well into Mamluk times. Among the endowments on this *madrasa* were a neighboring bath, two *manzils* (which included shops), six additional shops, a *funduq*, a monopoly (*hikr*) of land, and a cattle pen (*zariba*). As near as can be determined, all of these *awqaf* were in or near al-Fustat. The location of the *madrasa*, however, is not given by either source.[66]

Al-Madrasa al-Salihiya

The façade of the *madrasa* of al-Malik al-Salih (no.41, map 1)—the first *madrasa* established in Egypt for all four Sunni *madhahib*—still remains, as well as his tomb, on Shari' Mu'izz al-Din Allah opposite the *madrasa* of Qalaun. Maqrizi, in the *Khitat*, relates:

This *madrasa* is in Khatt Bayn al-Qasrayn in al-Qahira. Its location was part of the site of the great eastern palace. Al-Malik al-Salih built two *madrasas* [*madrasatayn*] there. He began the destruction of a section of the palace—as a site for these *madrasas*—on 13 Dhu al-Hijja 639 [June 15, 1242]; the foundations of the *madrasas* were leveled [*dukka*] on 14 Rabi' al-Akhir 640 [Oct. 12, 1242]. [Al-Salih] established in them four courses of study for the *fuqaha'* corresponding to their four *madhahib* [Shafi'i, Hanafi, Hanbali, Maliki] in 641/1243–44. He was the first in Egypt to establish four courses of study [*durus*] in one place. The site of these *madrasas* included a gate of the palace known as Bab al-Zuhuma. Its location is now the *qa'a* of the Hanbali Shaykh. The area outside these *madrasas* was delineated in the year 65[.] and made a monopoly on the Salihiya *madrasa*. The first Hanbali who taught there was the chief *qadi* Shams al-Din ibn Surur al-Maqdisi al-Hanbali al-Salihi. In . . . 648/1250–51, al-Malik al-Mu'izz al-Din Aybak al-Turkmani appointed the amir 'Ala' al-Din Aidkin al-Bunduqdari al-Salihi as sultanal deputy in Egypt. ['Ala' al-Din] persevered in the establishment [*julus*, lit. 'sitting'] of deputies of the Dar al-'Adil at the Salihiya *madrasa* where he oversaw the investigation of wrongdoings. He conducted this session for a period of time. . . . [Qubbat al-Salih]. This *qubba* was near al-Madrasa al-Salihiya. Its site had been occupied by the *qa'a* of the Maliki Shaykh. . . . Shajarat al-Durr built it for her lord al-Malik al-Salih when he died while fighting the Franks in the district of Mansura in 647/1249.[67]

Maqrizi adds that pending the arrival of al-Malik al-Mu'azzam Turan Shah from Hisn Kayfa, the body of al-Malik al-Salih was secretly deposited in a *qa'a* of the al-Roda citadel. In 648/1250–51, following Shajarat al-Durr's marriage to al-Malik al-Mu'izz Aybak and his assumption of the sultanate, the body was interred, with considerable ceremony, in the new tomb at Bayn al-Qasrayn.[68]

In the *Suluk* for the year 638/1240–41, Maqrizi states that Frankish prisoners were used as laborers on both the al-Roda citadel and Salihiya *madrasa*.[69] On the foundation of the *madrasa*, Ibn Laqlaq states (in the *History of the Patriarchs*):

> Then the sultan ordered that a madrasah should be built at al-Qahirah in front of the goldsmiths' bazaar, in the place of the farriers, in front of the palace [*qasr*]. [The sultan] began on this, and he transferred the farriers from there. They were removed to the neighborhood of Bab al-Bahr, in the direction of Rukn al-Muhalak. He demolished that side of the palace which comes after the Bab al-Zuhumah, towards the north, for a length of a hundred cubits, doing the same in width. . . .[70]

Some elucidation is required on these commentaries. Maqrizi, in his *Khitat*, discussed the building of two *madrasas*. Creswell's reconstruction, based on Maqrizi, shows the Salihiya *madrasa* as divided into two sections, both sections springing at almost right angles (towards the *qibla*) from the main façade on Bayn al-Qasrayn. These sections (the northern of which remains) each consists of a courtyard between two *iwans*. An *iwan* was assigned to each of the four *madhahib*, the two northernmost to the Malikis and Shafi'is; the two southern to the Hanbalis and Hanafis. Hence, Maqrizi's *madrasatayn*.[71] As to the construction of al-Malik al-Salih's tomb on the site of the Maliki *qa'a* (which still remains), Maqrizi contradicts himself at the end of the passage by stating that the tomb was neighboring this structure.[72] It is noteworthy that at least a major section of the eastern Fatimid palace remained standing in 638/1240–41, despite the vicissitudes of the Ayyubid takeover of al-Qahira.

Madrasat Ibn Rashiq

Following Maqrizi,

> This *madrasa* is Maliki. It is located in Khatt Hammam al-Ra'is in Misr [al-Fustat]. He was secretary [*katim*] of the groups of Sudanese who arrived at Misr in the year 64[.] while traveling on the hajj. They paid the *qadi* 'Ilm al-Din ibn Rashiq money to build [the *madrasa*]. He taught in it, and it took his name. The [*madrasa*] established a great reputation in the Sudan. They were sending money to it almost every year.[73]

Ibn Duqmaq adds that this *madrasa* (no.110, map 3) had a great name in the Sudan among the Bani Rashiq and that they supported it annually as its endowments were limited.

The shaykh al-Imam 'Ilm al-Din ibn Rashiq taught in it until his death, . . . Then his son, the chief *qadi* Zayn al-Din, succeeded him. Before the building [of the *madrasa*] the Sudanese, when they arrived from their countries en route to the Hijaz, stopped at the house of the *qadi* 'Ilm al-Din ibn Rashiq, near Hammam al-Ra'is. They paid him money, and he built this *madrasa* and taught in it.[74]

According to Casanova, Hammam al-Ra'is was located about halfway between Suq Wardan and the mosque of Abu al-Su'ud.[75] It is remarkable that the Sudanese pilgrims traveled to the holy cities by the circuitous land route rather than a direct crossing of the Red Sea (e.g. the crossing of Ibn Jubayr from Aydhab to Jidda in 578/1183).[76]

Al-Madrasa al-Qutbiya (in Harat Zuwayla)

Maqrizi states:

This *madrasa* [no.42, map 1] is in the first part of Harat Zuwayla in Rahbat Kawkay. It was known from the very noble lady 'Ismat al-Din Mu'nisa Khatun . . . known as the daughter of al-Malik al-'Adil Abu Bakr ibn Ayyub and the sister of al-Malik al-Afdal Qutb al-Din Ahmad—hence the attribution [*nisba*]. She was born in 603/1206–1207 and died in . . . 693/1293–94 . . . [he lists her pious and intellectual attributes]. . . . She bequeathed much wealth. She ordered the building of [this] *madrasa* and appointed *fuqaha'* and readers for it. A productive *waqf* was purchased for it. She built this *madrasa*. There was established in it a class for the Shafi'is and a class for the Hanafis and readers. [The *madrasa*] is prosperous to this day.[77]

Harat Zuwayla (originally associated with the gate of that name) was located in the southern section of al-Qahira, to the north of the mosque of al-Mu'ayyad Shaykh.

Summary

Of the twenty-five *madaris* established in al-Qahira/al-Fustat under the Ayyubids, seventeen were located within al-Qahira, seven at al-Fustat, and one in al-Qarafa. During the rule of Saladin (565–89/1169–93) ten *madaris* were founded, five within al-Qahira, four at al-Fustat, and one at the tomb of the Imam al-Shafi'i. Of these ten *madaris*, six were Shafi'i, one Shafi'i and Maliki, one Maliki, and two Hanafi. Of the five established by Saladin himself, three were Shafi'i, one Maliki, and one Hanafi. The early Ayyubid *madaris*, then, while rendering at least lip service to the Maliki and Hanafi *madhahib*, predominantly favored the Shafi'is.

Under Saladin's reign, five *madaris* were founded by the sultan himself, one by Taqi al-Din 'Umar, one by an amir, one by the wife of an amir, one by al-Qadi al-Fadil, and one by an Ascaloni trader. With the exception of the last, these donors were intimately connected with the administration. In terms of endowments, these *madaris* were provided with direct allotments by Saladin and/or *waqf* properties, including land tracts, villages, commercial properties, and baths, as stipulated by the donors.

The location of these earlier *madaris* bears close examination. The first two, al-Nasiriya and al-Qamhiya, were constructed by Saladin in the vicinity of the mosque of 'Amr at al-Fustat, demonstrating the importance and veneration that structure still maintained as a religious and administrative center, as well as the emphasis Saladin placed on restoring al-Fustat as a major commercial and maritime center following the devastations at the end of the Fatimid dynasty. Both were constructed in market areas on the sites of earlier buildings of no especial consequence. Two other *madaris* were established by Saladin at major shrines, the tombs of Husayn and the Imam al-Shafi'i. The fifth and last *madrasa* founded by Saladin was located centrally in al-Qahira on the site of a palace of a former Fatimid vizier. Saladin's foundations, then, concentrated on already revered—especially Sunni—sites, as well as areas of commercial rejuvenation in al-Qahira and al-Fustat.

The establishment of the non-sultanal *madaris* during the reign of Saladin followed a somewhat different pattern. With the exception of the *madrasa* of Ibn al-Arsufi at al-Fustat, which, again, was founded near the mosque of 'Amr in a commercial area, these *madaris* were associated with current or former residences: the Qutbiya on the site of Dar al-Dibaj (which was also a commercial site under the late Fatimids); the Taqawiya at Manazil al-'Izz, a Fatimid pavilion; the 'Ashuriya, a reused *dar*; and the Fadiliya, built in the vicinity of al-Qadi al-Fadil's palace.

Turning to the fifteen *madaris* of the later Ayyubid period (589–648/1193–1250), twelve were established at al-Qahira and three at al-Fustat. Of these fifteen *madaris*, three were Maliki, two Hanafi, one Hanbali, one Dar al-Hadith (although ultimately Shafi'i), two Shafi'i and Hanafi, one serving all four Sunni *madhahib*, and four of unknown allegiance, suggesting a move towards a general acceptance of the four major schools of Sunni Islam. The founders of these *madaris* included three sultans (al-'Adil, al-Kamil, and al-Salih), two viziers and an *ustadar*, three amirs, one *mamluk*, a palace servant, a Damascene doctor, and a group of Sudanese pilgrims. Thus, while we find fewer sultanal foundations in this later period, the preponderance of *madaris* was, again, directly related to the ruling elite. The endowments are noted for only seven of these *madaris*; they included local commercial institutions, landed estates, direct sultanal support, and, in the case of Madrasat Ibn Rashiq, contributions from Sudanese adherents.

The locations of these *madaris* include three on or near the site of Dar al-Dibaj (a Fatimid palace reused as a market) in west central Cairo near the Khalij. These *madaris* were established by Ibn Shukr (vizier to al-Malik al-'Adil and al-Malik al-Kamil), Sayf al-Islam Tughtikin, and an *ustadar* of al-Kamil, in addition to al-Madrasa al-Qutbiya, founded by an amir of Saladin. We have then, a major concentration of *madaris* in a market area, all constructed by major political figures. The same phenomenon is repeated at Suwayqat Amir al-Juyush in the northern section of al-Qahira, where three *madaris* were founded by a *mamluk* of Najm al-Din Ayyub and amirs of Saladin and al-Malik al-Kamil. The three sultanal foundings were also in primarily commercial areas, but in addition, were connected with former religious and/or administrative centers. The *madrasa* of al-Malik al-'Adil was established, like others, near the mosque of 'Amr at al-Fustat, while those of al-Malik al-Kamil and al-Malik al-Salih were constructed in market areas of Bayn al-Qasrayn, at least partly on the sites of the western and eastern Fatimid palaces respectively. The reasoning for the provenance of the latter two must be approached with caution, however. While it would be tempting to think that these sultans built their *madaris* at this location to erase yet further vestiges of the previous dynasty, it would hardly have been necessary at this juncture. The Fatimids had been eclipsed (although not extinguished) for well over fifty years; there was no fear of an Isma'ili resurgence. The centers of administration had been moved by al-Malik al-Kamil to the citadel, and under al-Malik al-Salih to al-Roda. Bayn al-Qasrayn, although largely occupied by shops and markets (as it was to some extent under the late Fatimids), was still a relatively open space at the time of Ibn Sa'id's visit (ca. 640/1242–43, v.s.). The center of al-Qahira's commercial activity on its main thoroughfare was the ideal place for a sultan to build a religious monument. On a more mundane note, building materials were readily available from the destruction of remaining portions of the palaces, at least in the case of al-Madrasa al-Salihiya.

Other sites included the *madrasa* of Masrur and that of the *sharif* Ibn Tha'lib, both south of the western palace, and both the reused palaces of these personages. The locations of two *madaris*, one at al-Qahira and one at al-Fustat, have not been identified. The final two, one near Kawm al-Jarih at al-Fustat and the second in Harat Zuwayla, cannot be ascribed to any topographical patterns, although they were both relatively close to market areas.

In conclusion, Ayyubid *madaris* were founded by sultans, other family and/or government officials, private donors, and, in one case, a group of Sudanese pilgrims. The preponderance of those of the Shafi'i school under Saladin gradually gave way to a more general (although not equal) acceptance of the other *madhahib* by the end of the dynasty. The fact that Saladin built five out of the eight sultanal *madaris* suggests his urgent need to reestablish the official Sunni doctrine following the Isma'ili heresy. *Madaris* were founded, under Saladin, around centers of religious veneration and/or administration (especially those earmarked for rehabilitation), some of which were located in major commercial areas. Non-sultanal establishments were often former Fatimid mansions or palaces, a practice which continued, although to a lesser extent, during the later Ayyubid dynasty. The reuse of these former palaces was, as Creswell points out, eminently practical. Classes were often conducted in individual halls or *iwanat*. In late Ayyubid and Mamluk times the number of *iwanat* frequently corresponded to the number of *madhahib* and/or religious skills taught within a given *madrasa*, e.g. the *madaris* of the sultans al-Malik al-Salih, Baybars al-Bunduqdari (al-Zahiriya), al-Nasir Muhammad, and Sultan Hasan. A standard feature in the palaces of the late Fatimids, Ayyubids, and Mamluks, was the *qa'a*—two *iwans* facing each other across a central court or fountain. Such structures could readily be transformed into *madaris*, comprising classroom space as well, no doubt, as ample quarters for the lodging of students.[78]

The majority of the later Ayyubid *madaris* were original buildings, albeit constructed in the midst of remains of earlier Fatimid foundations such as Dar al-Dibaj and the eastern and western Fatimid palaces. Concentrations of *madaris* appeared at Dar al-Dibaj and Suwayqat Amir al-Juyush (major commercial areas), established by amirs and other officials who were, perhaps, attempting to outdo each other in benevolence. Finally, the last two sultanal foundings graced Bayn al-Qasrayn, center of the *qasaba* of al-Qahira.

A School for Children

Ibn Jubayr States:

> Among the beneficent acts that proclaim his [Saladin's] care for all of the affairs of the Muslims was his ordering the building of a school which he assigned to those preachers of the *Book of Great and Glorious God* who teach exclusively the children of the poor and orphans. For their needs he grants an annual allowance.[75]

No location is named.

Mosques

As stated above, despite Saladin's early attempt to follow the Shafi'i principle of one *jami'* per town, there were, during Ibn Jubayr's visit, four congregational mosques in al-Qahira specifically exclusive of those of Ibn Tulun, 'Amr, and al-Roda. Indeed, by the end of the Ayyubid regime, there were nine functional *jawami'* in greater Cairo (al-Qahira, al-Fustat, al-Roda, and their immediate surroundings) exclusive of the Azhar mosque and that of Ibn Tulun—both of which were demoted, at least temporarily, from their former status. The distinction, however, between *jami'* and *masjid* prevailed, although by Maqrizi's time it becomes very blurred, and in modern Cairene vernacular *jami'* is the standard word for any mosque.

Ayyubid mosque construction was minimal. Attention was concentrated on the doctrinal realignment, refurbishment, and rebuilding of Fatimid and pre-Fatimid mosques. Ten foundations fall under this category, all of which held (although not consistently) the title of *jami'* between the end of the Fatimid and the end of the Ayyubid dynasties and were recipients of either direct sultanal support or that of others who were closely associated with the administration. Seven new mosques were founded under the Ayyubids, six *masajid* and one *jami'*. Two of these were founded by members of the Ayyubid family, and the others by political and religious figures of varying degrees of eminence.

Ayyubid mosque policy: reconstruction, refurbishment, and reassignment of existing institutions

Jami' al-Azhar

The Azhar mosque (no.43, map 1) was relieved of its status as *jami'* by Saladin, and remained so until the *khutba* was reestablished under the reign of Baybars al-Bunduqdari. Saladin removed a silver band, attesting to the Fatimids, from the *mihrab* of al-Azhar, along with similar silver bands from other *jawami'*. In addition, he extended the height of the minaret, suggesting continuous use of al-Azhar as a *masjid* during the Ayyubid period.[80]

Jami' al-Hakim

Founded by the Fatimid caliph al-'Aziz and completed by al-Hakim, this mosque (no.44, map 1) was instituted as the primary mosque of al-Qahira by Saladin (v.s.). Following Maqrizi,

> [Ibn 'Abd al-Zahir] said: "The *fisqiya* in the middle of the *jami'* was built by the *sahib* 'Abd Allah ibn 'Ali ibn Shukr. He channeled water to it. The *qadi* Taj al-Din ibn Shukr put an end to it. He was chief *qadi* in the year 660/1261–62. As to the *ziyada* on its side—it is said that it was built by [al-Hakim's] son al-Zahir 'Ali. He did not finish it. It became a prison for the Franks [Crusaders] who built churches in it. [The churches] were destroyed by al-Malik al-Nasir Salah al-Din. . . . Stables were built there, and it reached me that in preceding days there were also granaries. In the days of the Salihiya and the vizierate of Mu'in al-Din Hasan ibn Shaykh al-Shuyukh to al-Malik al-Salih Ayyub son of al-Kamil, it was established that [the *ziyada*] of al-Hakim was part of the mosque, and that there was a *mihrab* in it. Those residing within it were removed, as well as the horses. Its present construction dates from al-Mu'izz Aybak, the work of al-Rukn al-Sayrafi was not roofed."[81]

The *ziyada* to the mosque of al-Hakim stood, at least in part, on its southwestern side. Its entrance, which remains, is now known as Zawiyat Abu al-Khayr al-Kulaybati.[82]

Jami' 'Amr

The first mosque established in Egypt, Jami' 'Amr, has remained the true nucleus of al-Fustat throughout its history. Following the burning of al-Fustat in 564/1168, this mosque and its surrounding area were restored and/or rebuilt as a vital commercial and religious center. As part of his policy of Sunni revival, Saladin carried out major reconstruction and restoration on Jami' 'Amr and constructed his first two *madrasas* in its immediate vicinity.

There was, apparently, minor fire damage to Jami' 'Amr during the 564/1168 conflagration, although Maqrizi does not mention it in his description of the mosque itself. However, in his discussion of Jami' al-Qarafa (v.i.), he states that it and Jami' 'Amr were burned by Ibn Samaqah, acting under the orders of Jawhar, a confidant to the Fatimid caliphate. When questioned about his actions, Jawhar stated that he burned the mosques lest the Abbasid *khutba* be recited within them.[83] Given the lack of Maqrizi's testimony elsewhere, Ibn Duqmaq's silence on the matter, and the lack of archaeological evidence, the burning of Jami' 'Amr, if a reality, must have been very minimal indeed.

Following the al-Fustat fire of 564/1168, Maqrizi relates:

> The people of Misr returned there, little by little. The mosque [of 'Amr] had fallen into disrepair. When Sultan Salah al-Din assumed the rule of Egypt, after the death of al-'Adid, he restored al-Jami' al-'Atiq at Misr in the year 568. He restored the heart [*sadr*] of the mosque, and the great *mihrab* and its marble. He inscribed his name on [the *mihrab*]. In the water tank of the hall of the *khutba* [*qa'at al-khitaba*], he placed a pipe to the roof-terrace [*sath*]. The people of the roof-terrace use it. He built a pavilion beneath the great minaret, and a water tank for it. On the northern side of the small house [*dar*] of 'Amr—running towards the west—[Saladin] constructed another pipe parallel to the roof-terrace, and a walkway allowing the people of the roof-terrace to use it. He built a water clock [*ghurfat al-sa'at*] and it was formulated precisely [*hurrarat*]. [The *ghurfat al-sa'at*] lasted until the time of al-Malik al-Mu'izz al-Din Aybak al-Turkmani, first of the Mamluk rulers. [Mu'izz al-Din] renewed the whiteness of the mosque, and ended its disheveledness. He cleaned its columns and restored its marble until the entire mosque was covered with marble; there was nothing in its entire area uncovered by marble except under the enclosure [*hasr*].[84]

Ibn Jubayr, in his discussion of Saladin's religious endowments, states: "It was told us that the mosque of 'Amr Ibn al-'As has a daily income of about thirty Egyptian dinars, which is spent on benefits connected with it and the stipends of its officials, custodians, imams, and readers."[85]

Several *zawaya* were established within Jami' 'Amr. A *zawiya* in this context was a section reserved for the teaching of one or more *fuqaha'*, serving in effect the function of a *madrasa*. Of the eight *zawaya* listed by Maqrizi, two were endowed during the Ayyubid period, the remainder appear to be Mamluk foundations. Maqrizi:

> . . . the *zawiya* of the Imam al-Shafi'i. . . . It is said that al-Shafi'i taught in it, and it is known from him. Land[s] in the area of Sandbis are endowed upon it. The sultan al-Malik al-'Aziz 'Uthman, son of Sultan al-Malik al-Nasir Salah al-Din Yusuf ibn Ayyub, endowed it. The instruction [in this *zawiya*] has been consistently supervised by leading *fuqaha'* and *'ulama'*.
> . . . Al-Zawiya al-Majdiya is in the heart of the mosque between the great *mihrab* and *mihrab al-khams* [sic], inside the central *maqsura* near the great *mihrab*. It was built by Majd al-Din Abu al-Ashbal al-Harith al-Azdi al-Bahnasi al-Shafi'i, vizier to al-Malik al-Ashraf Musa ibn al-'Adil Abi Bakr ibn Ayyub at Harran. [Majd al-Din] appointed his relative, the chief *qadi* Wajih al-Din 'Abd al-Wahhab al-Bahnasi, as its professor. He endowed this *zawiya* with a number of properties in Misr and al-Qahira, and its professorship is considered among the highest ranking. Al-Majd died at Damascus in Safar 628 (Dec. 9, 1230–Jan. 6, 1231) at the age of sixty-three.[86]

The refurbishment of Jami' 'Amr was relatively shortlived. Ibn Sa'id al-Maghribi, in his description of ca. 637/1239 states:

> Finally I arrived at the Friday mosque [i.e. of 'Amr] and I noticed, because of the narrowness of the markets which surround it, the opposite of what I have described at the mosques of Seville and Marrakech. I entered there and I saw a great mosque, of ancient construction, without embellishment [*ghayr muzakhrif*] with badly kept mats covering part of the walls. I saw the populace—both men and women—who had made [the mosque] a passage by tracking their feet from door to door in order to regain their route. Merchants sell there all sorts of sweets, cakes, and similar delicacies, and the people eat in several places, shamelessly, as is their habit. A great number of men carrying vases of water circulate among the eaters, who nourish themselves upon what they have bought and throw the remains of their food into the courtyard and the *zawaya*. Spiders multiply their webs in the ceilings, the corners, and on the walls. Children play in the courtyard. The walls are smeared, in ugly lines of red and charcoal, with various graffiti written by poor people. However, in spite of all this, there is in this mosque splendor, attraction, and freedom of spirit, that you will not find in the mosque of Seville, in spite of its decoration and the garden of its courtyard. I thought over what I had seen there of pleasure and intimacy, without knowing the reason. Then I realized that it was a mysterious grace, conferred upon it by the companions of the prophet . . . when they arrived at the site [where Jami' 'Amr] was built. I approved of the circles of students which I observed, where the reading of the Qur'an, jurisprudence, and grammar were taught in several locations [within the mosque]. I asked about the source of its

revenues, and was informed that they included endowments [*furud, zakat,*] and similar sources. Then, I was informed that the collection of its revenues was difficult, except by compulsion and severity.[87]

Under the Ayyubids, then, the mosque of 'Amr went full cycle from disrepair into squalor. The reconstruction and refurbishment of Saladin were unapparent by the reign of al-Malik al-Salih. A constant factor, however, was the reverence attached to Jami' 'Amr as the first mosque of Egypt and a bulwark of Sunni Islam.

Jami' Ibn Tulun

Ibn Jubayr states:

> Between Misr and Cairo is the great mosque which takes its name from Abu al-Abbas Ahmad Ibn Tulun. It is one of the old congregational mosques, of elegant architecture and of large proportions The sultan [Saladin] made it a retreat for the strangers from the Maghrib, where they might live and receive lectures; and for their support he granted a monthly allowance. A curious thing, told us by one of their prominent men, was that the sultan had entrusted to them their own management, and allows no other hand over them. They themselves produce their own leader, whose orders they obey and to whom they appeal in sudden contingency. They live in peace and satisfaction, devoted exclusively to the worship of their lord and finding, in the favour of the sultan, the greatest help to the good on whose path they are set.[88]

Jami' al-Maqs

Jami' al-Maqs was founded by the Fatimid caliph al-Hakim, near the present mosque of Awlad 'Inan (just south of Midan Ramses).

Maqrizi's testimony on Jami' al-Maqs is somewhat confusing, and is given chronologically herewith:

> When Sultan Salah al-Din Yusuf ibn Ayyub built this wall which is on [around] al-Qahira, he wished to connect it with the wall of Misr, from outside Bab al-Bahr to al-Kawm al-Ahmar where Minsha'at al-Mahrani is today. The supervisor of that construction was the amir Baha' al-Din Qaraqush al-Asadi. He built a large tower, known as Qal'at al-Maqs.[89]

> When Sultan Salah al-Din ordered Misr and al-Qahira encircled by a wall, he entrusted Baha' al-Din Qaraqush with that project. He placed the end of the al-Qahira segment at al-Maqs, where he built a tower rising above the Nile, as well as a Friday mosque. Tne construction extended from [al-Maqs] to the city [al-Qahira]. Friday services were celebrated in [the mosque].[90]

In Ramadan 587 (Sep. 21–Oct. 21, 1191) an enclosure [*zariba*] of this mosque collapsed because of the Nile flooding. It was feared that the mosque would collapse, and rebuilding [of the *zariba*] was ordered.[91]

In the year 770/1368–69 the vizier al-Sahib Shams al-Din 'Abd Allah al-Maqsi rebuilt this mosque. He destroyed the *qal'a* and replaced it with a garden.[92]

The first passage suggests that the tower was constructed near Jami' al-Maqs, but not on its site. The second, stating that Qaraqush built the tower and a Friday mosque bears close scrutiny. It is highly improbable that Qaraqush built a second *jami'* in the same area. Any construction, therefore, must have been either refurbishment or, as Casanova suggests, the mosque was destroyed and supplanted by the tower, and then reconstructed at a nearby site.[93] Lacking further textual evidence, the question remains open.

Jami' Qidan

Maqrizi states:

This *jami'* is outside of al-Qahira, on the east side of the Khalij, outside of Bab al-Futuh, following Qanatir al-Awz, and facing Ard al-Ba'l. It was a *masjid*, ancient in structure. The eunuch Baha' al-Din Qaraqush al-Asadi restored it in Muharram of the year 597 (Oct. 12–Nov. 10, 1200). He rebuilt the basin of the *sabil* which is in it. Then the amir Mazaffar al-Din Qidan al-Rumi built a *minbar* in it, in order to read the *khutba* on Fridays. He built the constructions in its area.[94]

The jami' near the tomb of al-Shafi'i in al-Qarafa

Following Maqrizi,

This *jami'* was a small *masjid*. The population of the smaller Qarafa increased when Sultan Salah al-Din Yusuf ibn Ayyub built the *madrasa* neighboring the tomb of Imam al-Shafi'i . . . and appointed a professor and students [to the *madrasa*]. Al-Malik al-Kamil Muhammad ibn al-'Adil . . . enlarged the above-mentioned *masjid*. He erected a *minbar* in it and he preached [*khataba*] in it. The Friday prayer was performed there in the year 607/1210–11.[95]

Jami' al-Qarafa

Maqrizi states:

This mosque is now known as Jami' al-Awwaliya. It is in the greater Qarafa. Its site was known formerly—at the time of the conquest of Egypt—as Khitat al-Ma'afir. It was a *masjid* built by 'Abd Allah ibn Mana' ibn Mawri', and it was known as Masjid al-Qubba. Al-Qada'i said that readers [of the Qur'an] were assigned to it. Then a new Friday mosque was built on its site. It was built by the wife of the caliph al-Mu'izz in the year 366/976–77.[96]

As noted above in the description of Jami' 'Amr, it and Jami' al-Qarafa were ordered burned in 564/1168 to prevent the Abbasid *khutba* from being recited therein. That substantial damage was inflicted upon Jami' al-Qarafa is more certain, however, as Maqrizi states that only its green *mihrab* remained intact. He further asserts that the mosque was reconstructed "in the days of al-Mustansir." While it is uncertain whether this reference is to the Abbasid caliph of Baghdad (623–40/1226–42), or to his brother, also Mustansir, appointed as 'puppet' caliph in Egypt by Baybars in 659/1260–61, it was probably the former, since Ibn Sa'id mentions a Friday mosque in his description of al-Qarafa.[97]

Friday mosques on al-Roda: Jami' Ghayn and Jami' al-Miqyas

Ibn Hawqal notes a Friday mosque on al-Roda (ca. 368/978).[98] The testimony of Maqrizi and Ibn Duqmaq is somewhat contradictory and examined herewith. Following Maqrizi,

Ibn al-Mutawwaj said, "As to the Friday mosque on al-Roda . . . known as Jami' Ghayn, it is an old mosque. The *khutba* was performed there until Jami' Miqyas was built. Then the *khutba* was not performed [at Jami' Ghayn] until it was resumed in the Zahiriya dynasty [i.e. Baybars al-Bunduqdari]. . . . Ghayn was one of the servants of the caliph al-Hakim bi-Amr Allah, dismissed from office in . . . the year 402/1011–12.[99]

Ibn Duqmaq's evidence is similar except for biographical particulars of Ghayn, irrelevant here.

The texts vary considerably, however, in their descriptions of Jami' al-Miqyas (no.111, map 3). According to Ibn Duqmaq,

Al-Afdal ibn Amir al-Juyush built [Jami' al-Miqyas] in the year [blank]. Then the sultan al-Malik al-Salih Najm al-Din Ayyub restored it. There was, in front of its door, a church known as that of Ibn Laqlaq, the Jacobite patriarch [A.D. 1216–43].[100]

Maqrizi's description of Jami' al-Miqyas stops short (the original manuscript is blank, according to the Bulaq edition) after stating that the mosque is near the nilometer. In another passage, however, on Jami' al-Roda at the citadel of al-Roda, Maqrizi states: "Ibn al-Mutawwaj said that this mosque was built by the sultan al-Malik al-Salih Najm al-Din Ayyub." The remainder of the text parallels Ibn Duqmaq's description of Jami' al-Miqyas.[101]

Ibn Laqlaq, in the *History of the Patriarchs*, states that during the building of the citadel of al-Roda (ca. 640/1242–43)

... then [the sultan] ordered the vacating of the church of the island and the mosque [*jami'*] of the nilometer [al-Miqyas], and [that] those at them should go out. There was at the church a man, a priest, advanced in age and weak in eyesight called Afraham, who had been in the mentioned church for sixty years. He was sent out of it, and its door was nailed shut, and Ibn Abu al-Radad was sent out of Jami' al-Miqyas. The reason for this was not known. Some people said that the sultan desired to make from the side of the church a way to the towers he had built at the nilometer; others said that he disliked the people passing the door of his palace.[102]

Later, for the same year, "The church of the island was demolished to the ground, as were other structures than it among the buildings [enclosed within] the citadel."[103]

Maqrizi notes that the mosque (presumably from the time of al-Malik al-Salih) remained constantly under the supervision of the Bani Raddad.[104]

In sum, Jami' Ghayn was, at least from the time of al-Hakim, the only congregational mosque on al-Roda. It was succeeded by Jami' al-Miqyas, constructed by al-Afdal ibn al-Juyushi, and probably assumed the function of an ordinary *masjid*. Jami' al-Miqyas was either restored or reconstructed by al-Malik al-Salih; the evidence is confusing. Ibn Duqmaq asserts that the mosque was built by al-Afdal and restored (*jadada*) by al-Salih. Maqrizi simply states that al-Malik al-Salih built (*'amara*) the mosque. The latter term, as Casanova points out, has, in certain mediaeval contexts, assumed the meaning 'restore'.[105] The text of Ibn Laqlaq asserts that Jami' al-Miqyas and the Jacobite church were evacuated by al-Malik al-Salih, thus establishing the preexistence of the mosque. However, he adds that the church and other buildings were destroyed, raising the question of whether Jami' Miqyas was among them, and then rebuilt elsewhere. This would, perhaps, explain Maqrizi's incomplete description of Jami' al-Miqyas and his separate description of the *jami'* at the citadel of al-Roda (i.e. that the former was destroyed by al-Salih and supplanted by the latter).

This theory, on balance, is unlikely. Ibn Duqmaq's Jami' al-Miqyas is demonstrably the same structure as Maqrizi's *jami'* at the al-Roda citadel. Ibn Duqmaq specifically mentions its restoration; had the mosque been demolished and reconstructed, it would hardly have escaped his narrative. In addition, had Jami' al-Miqyas been destroyed in the general demolition which included the Jacobite church, it is more likely that Ibn Laqlaq would have mentioned it specifically. The probability remains that the mosque was restored by al-Malik al-Salih and stood relatively close to his palace at the southern end of the island.[106]

Jami' Ghayn, assuming Creswell's belief that the citadel complex encompassed the southern half of the island to be correct, would have been located in the northern segment of al-Roda outside the citadel enclosure. The *khutba* was reestablished there in 660/1261–62 as "the buildings increased around [Jami' Ghayn] on al-Roda, and the population of the citadel decreased, and the walk from the upper parts of al-Roda to Jami' Miqyas presented a hardship."[107]

Jami' Mahmud at al-Qarafa

Located at the smaller Qarafa at the foot of the Muqattam, this mosque dated from ca. 200/815. According to Ibn al-Mutawwaj, the first to preach the *khutba* therein was al-Sayyid al-Sharif Shihab al-Din al-Husayn ibn Muhammad, military judge [*qadi al-'askar*], and professor at the Nasiriya *madrasa* (established by Saladin) near Jami' 'Amr. He died in 655/1257–58.[108]

Ayyubid mosques: original foundations

Masjid Najm al-Din

This mosque was founded by Najm al-Din Ayyub, father of Saladin, in 566/1170–71 and was located outside Bab al-Nasr. He placed at its side a water basin for public drinking, from which animals were barred.[109]

Masjid Raslan

According to Maqrizi:

> This mosque is in Harat al-Yanisiya. It took its name from Shaykh al-Salih Raslan, who preached in it. He was spoken of honorably. He died in the year 591/1194–95. He supported himself from the fees from his sewing in cloth.[110]

Harat al-Yanisiya was located southeast of Bab Zuwayla, between it and the citadel.

The jami' at Minsha'at al-Mahrani

Minsha'at al-Mahrani was alluvial land to the north of Fam al-Khalij, between it and Bustan al-Khashshab (see Chapter Three). Al-Qadi al-

Fadil founded a garden there, with a mosque on the garden's edge, and buildings were constructed around it. The garden, mosque, and associated constructions were undermined by the Nile after 660/1261–62. The mosque was rebuilt at the request of its *khatib* (preacher of the *khutba*), al-Muwaffaq al-Dabbaji, by the *sahib* Baha' al-Din ibn Huna.[111]

A mosque of al-Malik al-Kamil on the citadel

A mosque had existed on the citadel during the reign of al-Zahir Baybars, in which the Abbasid caliph al-Hakim had preached. Casanova believes this mosque to have dated from the time of al-Malik al-Kamil, and that it stood on the site of the mosque of al-Nasir Muhammad ibn Qalaun.[112]

Masjid of Fakhr al-Din ibn Qizil

This mosque (no.45, map 1) was founded by Fakhr al-Din Abu al-Fath 'Uthman ibn Qizil al-Barumi, *ustadar* of al-Malik al-Kamil, opposite his *madrasa* (al-Fakhriya, v.s.) between Suwayqat al-Sahib and Darb al-'Addas. This mosque is not mentioned individually by Maqrizi, but only in passing in his description of al-Madrasa al-Fakhriya. The *madrasa* dates from 622/1225–26; Fakhr al-Din died in 629/1231–32, suggesting the founding of the mosque between the two dates.[113]

Suwayqat al-Sahib and Darb al-'Addas were within Harat al-Waziriya. In modern terms, this lay near the junction of Shari' al-Azhar and Shari' Bayn al-Surayn, just east of the former Khalij.

Masjid Sawab

After Maqrizi:

> This *masjid* is outside al-Qahira in Khatt al-Saliba. It was known from al-Tawashi [the eunuch] Shams al-Din Sawab, overseer [*muqaddam*] of the sultan's *mamalik*. He died in 642/1244–45 and was buried in [his mosque].[114]

Khatt al-Saliba was near the intersection of Shari' al-'Azam and the *saliba*, northeast of the mosque of Ibn Tulun.

Masjid at Hawd Ibn Hanas

Hawd Ibn Hanas was located slightly to the east of Birkat al-Fil, adjoining Harat Halab (see Chapter Six). Both *hawd* and *masjid* were the *waqf* of Sa'd al-Din Mas'ud ibn Hanas, one of the special chamberlains (*hujjab khass*) of al-Malik al-Salih. Ibn Hanas built a tall mosque "above" the *hawd* meaning, no doubt, in its immediate vicinity. This *waqf* was established in 647/1249–50, the year of Sa'd al-Din's death. He was buried in the vicinity of the *hawd*.[115]

Summary

In terms of *jawami*', under Saladin, the *khutba* was discontinued at al-Azhar, and the mosque of al-Hakim became the primary Friday mosque of al-Qahira. The mosque of 'Amr at al-Fustat was restored, both as a major center of Sunni Islam and as a staging point for the rejuvenation of al-Fustat. The mosque of Ibn Tulun was apparently disused as a *jami*' and relegated to Maghribi visitors, and Jami' al-Maqs was either restored or rebuilt, not so much to serve the needs of the now little used port, but with a view to the metropolitan expansion fostered by the extension of the wall of al-Qahira and the construction of Qal'at Qaraqush.

The six *jawami*' which figure in the later Ayyubid period conform not so much to the reestablishment of Cairo as a mainstay of Sunnism and as a major political center, but to population movements resulting from the physical ramifications of these factors. In the case of al-Qarafa, two *masajid* were raised to the status of *jawami*', and Jami' al-Qarafa was rebuilt, largely the result of an increase in population of al-Qarafa due to the foundations of Saladin and al-Malik al-Kamil at the tomb of the Imam al-Shafi'i. Jami' Qidan, outside Bab al-Futuh, was also elevated to the status of *jami*', undoubtedly due to the concentration of population in this area following the extension of the enceinte to al-Maqs. The restoration or rebuilding of Jami' al-Miqyas was the direct result of al-Malik al-Salih's construction of his citadel thereat. Finally, Jami' Minsha'at al-Mahrani, the only Friday mosque constructed as such under the Ayyubids, was constructed by al-Qadi al-Fadil to service those attracted by his establishment on the west bank of the Khalij, a precursor of the *ahkar* established northward at al-Luq.

Of the six *masajid* founded by the Ayyubids, only one was built within al-Qahira itself, reflecting two factors: firstly, the continuous use of preexisting mosques within the Fatimid city; and secondly, population shifts to the suburbs. The mosque of Najm al-Din Ayyub reflects development in the Husayniya district. Of three mosques located between al-Qahira and al-Fustat, Masjid Raslan, in Harat al-Yanisiya, represents a foundation in a Fatimid military district deserted, according to 'Abd al-Latif al-Baghdadi, during the famine of 597–98/1200–1202. Masjid Sawab and the *masjid* at Hawd Ibn Hanas, both established during the reign of al-Malik al-Salih were located on the *saliba* of Ibn Tulun and the eastern bank of Birkat al-Fil, respectively. Ibn Sa'id al-Maghribi describes these areas as populated during his time; the extent, however, is debatable, as argued in Chapter Three. Finally, the mosque of the citadel, presumably founded by al-Malik al-Kamil, served the needs of the palace establishment.

Khawaniq, Ribatat, Zawaya

Maqrizi defines a *khanqah* as a monastery for sufis, while a *ribat* houses a group (*qawm*) of sufis following a specific use of rules.[116] While his distinction somewhat eludes this writer, Casanova's glossary defines a *khanqah* as a large convent for sufis, and a *ribat* as a convent, or hospice, suggesting a simple delimitation in size.[117] A *zawiya* (literally, 'corner') implies a small mosque or *madrasa*, or (especially in the case of Jami' 'Amr), a section of a larger mosque specifically used for teaching purposes. Qalqashandi states that no *ribatat* or *khawaniq* existed in Egypt prior to the Ayyubids; this appears to be true for *zawaya* as well, at least those independent of earlier foundations.[118]

Al-Khanqah al-Salahiya

Following Maqrizi,

> This *khanqah* is in Khatt Rahbat Bab al-'Id in al-Qahira. It was originally a *dar*, known in the Fatimid dynasty as Dar Sa'id al-Su'ada'. [Sa'id al-Su'ada'] was the professor Qunbur—also said 'Unbur. Ibn Muyassar mentioned that his name was Bayan and that his nickname [*laqab*] was Sa'id al-Su'ada', one of the sophisticated teachers in the service of the great palace under the caliph al-Mustansir. . . . This *dar* was located in front of Dar al-Wizara. When al-'Adil Ruzayk, son of al-Salih Tala'i' ibn Ruzayk, was vizier, he lived in it. He dug a basement [*sirdab*] beneath the ground from the Dar al-Wizara to it, so that he could pass in it. Then the vizier Shawar ibn Mujir lived in it in the days of his vizierate, and then his son al-Kamil. When al-Nasir Salah al-Din . . . assumed the rule of Egypt following the death of the caliph al-'Adid, and changed the designs of the Fatimid dynasty, he humbled the caliphal palace and allocated it as living quarters to the Kurdish amirs of his state. He assigned this *dar* to newcoming sufi dervishes, arriving from distant lands. He endowed [the *dar*] on them in the year 569/1173–74, and

appointed a shaykh to administer them. He endowed on them Bustan al-Habaniya, near Birkat al-Fil outside of al-Qahira, as well as Qaysariyat al-Sharab in al-Qahira, and a section of Dahmar[?] and of Bahnasa. He stipulated that if one of the sufis died and bequeathed twenty dinars to the poor, the *diwan* of the sultan could not interfere with it. Those among them who wished to travel received travel allowance. He supplied the sufis a daily allotment of meat and bread, and built a bath for them nearby. It was the first *khanqah* built in Egypt. It was known as Duwayrat al-Sufiya, and its shaykh was titled Shaykh al-Shuyukh. This situation continued until the events and ordeals of 806/1403–1404, when the circumstances [of the *khanqah*] became debased, and its arrangement ended.[119]

Khanqah al-Salahiya (no.46, map 1) stood on Shari' Jamaliya, almost opposite the *madrasa* of Qarasunqur.[120]

A ribat *at al-Maqs*

According to Ibn Khallikan, Qaraqush constructed a *ribat* at al-Maqs. No further information is available.[121]

Ribat *of Safi al-Din ibn Shukr*

Safi al-Din ibn Shukr founded a *ribat* (no.47, map 1) and bath near his *madrasa* (al-Sahibiya, v.s.). Al-Madrasa al-Sahibiya was located at Suwayqat al-Sahib, near the junction of Shari' al-Azhar and Shari' Bayn al-Surayn, just east of the Khalij.[122]

Ribat *of Fakhr al-Din ibn Qizil*

Fakhr al-Din ibn Qizil, *ustadar* to al-Malik al-Kamil, founded a *ribat* in al-Qarafa, with a *kitab sabil* beside it. Fakhr al-Din died in 629/1231–32.[123]

Zawiyat al-Qasri

According to Maqrizi,

> This *zawiya* is in Khatt al-Maqs outside of al-Qahira. It was known from the shaykh Abu 'Abd Allah Muhammad ibn Musa 'Abd Allah ibn Hasan al-Qasri, . . . the Maliki *faqih* from the Maghrib, who came to al-Qahira from Qasr al-Kitama in the Maghrib. At this *zawiya*, he devoted himself to the exalted path of worship, and the quest for knowledge, until he died . . . in the year 633/1235–36.[124]

Zawiyat al-Shaykh Abu al-Khayr

Ibn Duqmaq states that this *zawiya* was in Khatt Dar al-Nahhas facing Bustan al-'Alima, stretching along the Nile. Al-Malik al-Salih built it for the Shaykh Abu al-Khayr, who remained there until his death and was succeeded by his sons.[125] Khatt Dar al-Nahhas was located on the Nile shore at al-Fustat just south of Fam al-Khalij.[126]

Zawiyat al-Khaddam

Maqrizi states that this *zawiya* was located in Husayniya outside Bab al-Nasr, halfway between that gate and Bab al-Futuh. "The eunuch Bilal al-Faraji founded it. . . . He placed it in *waqf* on the Ethiopian slave–soldiers in the year 647/1249–50."[127]

Summary

One *khanqah*, three *ribatat*, and three *zawaya* were established in the al-Qahira/al-Fustat area under the Ayyubids. The *khanqah*, founded by Saladin, represented yet another of his pious/political works in the reestablishment of Sunnism, this one in the heart of the Fatimid city. Its foundation, according to Lapidus, "created a position for Sufi organization corresponding to the state appointed qadi at the head of the Shafi'i madhhab."[128] The *ribatat* were the work of major political figures; that of Qaraqush at al-Maqs, an area in fact revitalized by him; of Ibn Shukr near his *madrasa*; and Fakhr al-Din's in al-Qarafa, an area replete with religious endowments (v.i.). In the case of the *zawaya* established in the later Ayyubid period, all three were located in suburban areas of current repopulation (viz: Zawiyat al-Qasri at al-Maqs; Zawiyat al-Shaykh Abu al-Khayr, established by al-Malik al-Salih on recent alluvial land at al-Fustat and relatively close to his new citadel of al-Roda; and Zawiyat al-Khaddam, in Husayniya). These *zawaya* seem generally to have been established for relatively minor religious figures. Those of Jami' 'Amr are distinct phenomena, and are discussed above.

Khawaniq, *ribatat*, and *zawaya* (as separate entities) all appear to have been introduced to al-Qahira/al-Fustat under the Ayyubids. While their numbers were small, they were nonetheless the touchstones to considerable emulation under the Mamluks.

Hospitals

Saladin built a hospital (*maristan* or *bimaristan*) in al-Qahira and a similar one at al-Fustat. Our main sources on these foundations are the texts of Maqrizi, Qalqashandi, and Ibn Jubayr, examined herewith. According to Maqrizi:

Al-Qadi al-Fadil said, in the *Mutajaddadat* for the year 577/1182: "On 9 Dhu al-Qa'da [March 17] the sultan—i.e. Salah al-Din Yusuf ibn Ayyub—ordered the opening of a *maristan* for the sick and the weak. As its site, he selected a part of the [Fatimid] palace. For its maintenance, he set aside a monthly amount of two hundred dinars from rent [*riba*] of houses belonging to the *diwan*, as well as crop revenues from sections of the Fayyum. He hired doctors, natural scientists, surgeons, superintendents, administrators, and attendants. The people approached it in a spirit of friendliness; it was considered a resting place and a place of benefit. Similarly, [Saladin] ordered the [re]opening of the old *maristan* at Misr. He allotted [the *maristan*] an increase of twenty dinars in its assessment from the *diwan* of endowments, and he assigned it a doctor, an administrator, and supervisors. The weak profited by it, and the invocation of God [*du'a*] increased because of it." Ibn 'Abd al-Zahir said: "There was a *qa'a*; al-'Aziz bi-Allah built it in the year 384/994–95. It is said that a Qur'an was written within its walls, and that among its peculiarities was that an ant would not enter because of the talisman within it. When that was told to Salah al-Din . . . , he decided that this was the proper place for a *maristan*. . . . The *maristan* was formerly—according to what reached me—in al-Qashshashin [*suq* of the rag gatherers], and I think it is the site of Dar al-Daylam." End [of Ibn 'Abd al-Zahir's narrative]. Al-Qashshashin is known today as al-Kharratin [wood-turners' bazaar]. One passes through it to the tent sellers and to Jami' al-Azhar.[129]

Qalqashandi gives a slightly different—and far more lucid—version of Ibn 'Abd al-Zahir's text.

It reached me that the *bimaristan* was first in al-Qashshashin, i.e. the place known now as al-Kharratin—near al-Jami' al-Azhar. There was [also] Dar al-Darb, built by Ma'mun ibn al-Bata'ihi vizier to al-Amir, facing the mentioned *bimaristan*. . . . Then, when Sultan Salah al-Din assumed power in Egypt and took over the palace, there was a *qa'a* of the palace built by al-'Aziz ibn al-Mu'izz. . . . Salah al-Din made it a *bimaristan*. It is the old *bimaristan* [*al-bimaristan al-'atiq*] which is inside the *qasr*. It is remaining in its appearance until now.[130]

Ibn Jubayr states:

Another of the things we saw, doing honor to the sultan [Saladin] was the maristan in the city of Cairo. It is a palace, goodly for its beauty and spaciousness. This benefaction he made so that he might deserve a heavenly reward, and to acquire merit. He appointed as intendant a man of science with whom he placed a store of drugs and whom he empowered to use the potions and apply them in their various forms. In the rooms of this palace were placed beds, fully appointed for lying patients. At the disposal of the intendant are servants whose duty it is, morning and evening, to examine the conditions of the sick, and to bring them the food and potions that befit them.

Facing this establishment is another specially for women, and they also have persons to attend them. A third which adjoins them—a large place—has rooms with iron windows, and it has been taken as a place of confinement for the insane. They also have persons who daily examine their condition and give them what is fitting for them. All these matters the sultan oversees, examining and questioning, and demanding the greatest care and attention to them. In Misr there is another hospital of precisely the same model.[131]

The hospital foundations of Saladin in al-Qahira and al-Fustat appear in both cases to have supplanted pre-Ayyubid establishments. In the case of al-Maristan al-'Atiq (Saladin's foundation in al-Qahira), a Fatimid hospital in Suq al-Kharratin (according to Ravaisse, roughly opposite Madrasat al-Ashraf on Shari' Mu'izz li-Din Allah) was succeeded by a refurbished *iwan* of the Fatimid palace. As to the opening of the "old" *maristan* at al-Fustat, the identification is questionable, but the probable reference is to the *maristan* of Kafur (al-Ikhshidi).[132]

Cemetery Areas

The original Muslim cemetery for al-Fustat and al-Qahira was al-Qarafa, the massive 'city of the dead,' now extending southeast from the *mashhad* of Sayyida Nafisa, with the Muqattam on its east and the mounds of al-Fustat to its west. Maqrizi states:

> The people of Misr and al-Qahira had numerous tombs. This area is known as al-Qarafa. The area near the foot of the mountain [al-Muqattam] was known as the lesser Qarafa, while the area to the east of the inhabited section of Misr [al-Fustat] was known as the greater Qarafa. In the greater Qarafa were the graves of the Muslims since the conquest of Egypt and the Arab division of the city of al-Fustat. They had no other cemetery, except it. When the military commander [*qa'id*] Jawhar arrived preceding al-Mu'izz li-Din Allah—he built al-Qahira. The caliphs who lived in it used a tomb known as Turbat al-Za'faran where they buried their dead. The burial place of their dead subjects was in al-Qarafa until

the *harat* were planned outside Bab Zuwayla. The residents [of these *harat*] interred their dead outside Bab Zuwayla . . . between Jami' al-Salih and Qal'at al-Jabal. The tombs increased in this area with the events of the great calamity of the days of al-Mustansir. Then when the Amir al-Juyush Badr al-Jamali died he was buried outside Bab al-Nasr, and the people used that place as tombs for their dead. The tombs of the people of Husayniya [also] increased in this area. Then the people buried their dead outside of al-Qahira in the place known as Midan al-Qubuq between Qal'at al-Jabal and Qubbat al-Nasr. They built fine tombs there. The people were also buried outside al-Qahira between Bab al-Futuh and al-Khandaq.[133]

He continues in a passage on al-Qarafa:

Know that the people were formerly burying their dead between Masjid al-Fath and the foot of the Muqattam. They also built fine tombs between Musalla Khulan and Khatt al-Mu'afir, which are now mounds of earth. The area is known as al-Qarafa al-Kubra. When al-Malik al-Kamil . . . buried his son in the year 608/1211–12 near the tomb of the imam Muhammad ibn Idris al-Shafi'i, he built the great dome over al-Shafi'i's grave He channeled water to it from Birkat al-Habash by *qanatir* extending from it. Then the people moved the buildings from the greater Qarafa to [the area] around al-Shafi'i. They founded tombs there. It became known as the lesser Qarafa, and its buildings increased. . . . As for the section which follows Qal'at al-Jabal, it was extended after 700/1300–1301.[134]

Al-Qarafa, a major center of visitations and pilgrimages replete with shrines, mosques, villas (*jawasiq* or *manazil*), and a *suq*, was, even in Ayyubid times, a functioning subdivision unto itself. Such was the pilgrimage traffic that special guides and routes were established to facilitate the movement of visitors. It was, in addition, a popular promenade of the people of al-Qahira and al-Fustat. Before analyzing the significance of al-Qarafa under the Ayyubids we shall examine contemporary descriptions of the cemetery and its major shrines, the 'officialization' of the visiting patterns to the major shrines under al-Malik al-Kamil, and the tombs and shrines established by the Ayyubids themselves.

Ibn Jubayr's description

The night of that day [Wednesday 11 Dhu al-Hijja 578/April 8, 1183] we passed in the cemetery known as al-Qarafa. This also is one of the wonders of the world for the tombs it contains of prophets . . . of the kindred of Muhammad . . . of his companions, of the followers of the companions, of learned men and ascetics, and of saintly men renowned for their miracles and of wonderful report. . . .

The names of the occupants of these venerable tombs we discovered from the records engraved over them and the unbroken oral traditions which confirm them, but God best knows. Over each of these is a splendid edifice, all being exquisite monuments of wondrous construction. For their care, persons have been appointed who live in them and receive a monthly stipend. It is indeed a sight to marvel on. . . .

The tomb of the Shafi'i imam . . . a shrine superb in beauty and size. Over against it was built a school the like of which has not been made in this country, there being nothing more spacious or more finely built. He who walks around it will conceive it to be itself a separate town. Beside it is a bath and other conveniences, and building continues to this day. The measureless expenditure on it is controlled by the sheik, imam, ascetic, and man of learning called Najm al-Din al-Khubushani. The Sultan of these lands, Saladin, bounteously pays all for this purpose saying: "Be lavish in splendour and elegance; ours it will be to provide all." Glory to Him who made him Salah Dinihi . . . like his name. We visited this man Khabushani, to be blessed by his prayers, for we had heard of him in Andalusia. We came upon him at his mosque in Cairo in the closet in which he lives inside the mosque; and a narrow closet it is. He prayed for us and we departed. Of all the men in Egypt, we saw none like him. . . .

Al-Qarafa is remarkable for being all built with mosques and inhabited shrines in which lodge strangers, learned men, the good and the poor. The subsidy for each place comes monthly from the sultan, and likewise is it for the theological colleges [mudaris] in Misr and Cairo. We were assured that the cost of all this exceeds two thousand Egyptian dinars, or four thousand mu'mini, a month.[135]

Yaqut's description

[Al-Qarafa] is now the cemetery of the people of Misr. In it are fine buildings and wide places [mahall wasi'a], an imposing market, the tombs [mashahid] of the pious and graves [turab] of leaders such as Ibn Tulun and al-Madhara'i indicating majesty and splendor. In it is the tomb of the Imam . . . al-Shafi'i in a madrasa belonging to the Shafi'i legists. The [Qarafa] is among the promenades and excursion spots of the people of al-Qahira and Misr, especially during religious holidays.[136]

Ibn Sa'id's description

Ibn Sa'id al-Maghribi (ca. 638/1240–41) states:

I spent many nights in al-Qarafa of al-Fustat. It was to its east. In it were the manazil of the nobles of al-Fustat and al-Qahira, and tombs with structures built above them. Among them is the great decorated dome which covers the grave of the Imam al-Shafi'i. . . . In [al-Qarafa] is a Friday mosque and many tombs, which are endowed with readers of the Qur'an, and a great Shafi'i *madrasa*. The [Qarafa] was almost always delightful, especially on moonlit nights. It is revered as a meeting place of the people of Misr, and the most famous of their promenades.[137]

Visitations

Although pilgrimages to al-Qarafa were often made on an individual basis, attempts were made to channel the visitors to the principal tombs of veneration on specific nights and on specific routes. The starting (and finishing) point of these visitations was established under the Ayyubids at the *mashhad* of Sayyida Nafisa. Maqrizi relates:

[T]he visit to al-Qarafa was first on Wednesday. Then it became Friday night. As for the Saturday visit—it is said that it was earlier, and it is said later. The first who visited on Wednesday—and who began the visit from the *mashhad* of Sayyida Nafisa—was the shaykh al-Salih Abu Muhammad 'Abd Allah ibn Rafi' ibn Yazham ibn Rafi' al-Sar'i al-Shafi'i al-Maghafiri al-Zuwwar [the visitor] known as 'Abid. He was born in the year 561/1165–66, and he died in al-Hilaliya, outside Bab Zuwayla . . . in the year 638/1240–41. He was buried at the foot of the Muqattam at the tomb of the Bani Nahar, north of the tomb of al-Radayni. The first who [officially performed] the visit on Friday night was the pious shaykh and reader Abu al-Hasan 'Ali ibn Ahmad ibn Jawshan, known as Ibn al-Jabbas, the father of Sharaf al-Din Muhammad ibn 'Ali ibn Ahmad ibn al-Jabbas. The people gathered together, and he made the visit with them on Friday night each week. On some nights the sultan al-Malik al-Kamil . . . performed the visit with him. Dignitaries of the *'ulama'* walked with him. . . . Al-Muwaffaq ibn 'Uthman related, after al-Qada'i, that Ibn al-Jabbas had urged the visit to seven [specific] tombs.[138]

The tombs of seven shaykhs are listed by Maqrizi, viz: Dinawari, 'Abd al-Samad Baghdadi, Mazani, Mufaddal, Qumani, Dhu al-Nun, and Bakar. He gives, in addition, two rival lists.[139]

Massignon adds the following, gleaned from various sources:

It is under the Ayyubid al-Malik al-Kamil . . . that the weekly circuit was first 'officialized' for early Friday evening; this was under the impetus of Ibn al-Jabbas . . . and encouraged by the spiritual director of the sovereign—Fakhr Farisi—and previously, perhaps, by the queen mother Shamsah.

There were a *naqib* of pilgrims, *shuyukh al-ziyara,* and a *sahib al-shurta lil-Qarafa.*

This organization, unique in the Islamic world, had been rendered necessary by the number of private pilgrimages, female and mixed, which took place in al-Qarafa daily and nightly, without supervision, among the tombs.[140]

Specific Ayyubid funerary monuments

With the exception of the tomb of al-Malik al-Salih at his *madrasa* in al-Qahira (v.s.) the major Ayyubid funerary monuments were located in al-Qarafa. They are noted chronologically herewith.

Musalla of Ibn al-Arsufi (Musalla al-Sharifiya)

Following Maqrizi, "it was in Darb al-Qarafa, near the Jabbasin and Khittat Sadaf. Abu Muhammad 'Abd Allah ibn al-Arsufi, the Syrian trader, built it in the year 577/1181–82."[141] Ibn al-Arsufi, an Ascaloni merchant who founded a *madrasa* at al-Fustat in 570/1174–75 (v.s.), died at al-Fustat in 593/1196–97. It is quite likely that he was buried in or near his *musalla* (oratory).

Tomb of Ibn Firroh Shatibi

According to Massignon, the tomb of Ibn Firroh (sic) Shatibi, "the great reader," was located at the southeast of al-Qarafa, bordering the Muqattam and joining, allegedly, the tomb of al-Qadi al-Fadil. Shatibi died in 595/1198–99.[142]

Tomb of Shihab al-Din Tusi

Located to the southeast of the tomb of Imam al-Shafi'i. Massignon states that Shihab al-Din Tusi (d.596/1199–1200) was

> a Shafi'i canonist and audacious preacher, of great independence of character, who had provoked violent reactions [from Shiites as much as Hanbalites] in Baghdad. Then Saladin invited him to come to Cairo and direct first the Khanqah al-Su'ada', then Manazil al-'Izz [579/1183–84]; he was a reformer of morals.[143]

Tomb of Imam al-Shafi'i

As noted above, Ayyubid attention to this major shrine initially focused on the construction of Saladin's *madrasa* adjacent to it. The great dome over the tomb (still extant) was constructed by al-Malik al-Kamil in 608/1211–12, wherein were included the graves of his son, his mother Shamsah, and al-Malik al-'Aziz. According to Maqrizi, the cost of the dome was 50,000 Egyptian dinars. Al-Kamil channeled water to the tomb from Birkat al-Habash; Qur'an readers and the distribution of alms were established at his mother's grave. (How this was differentiated from the functions of the mausoleum of al-Shafi'i himself is questionable.) In the process of the dome's construction, many local graves were removed elsewhere in al-Qarafa. The attraction of the new monument, however, soon fostered new building and population in the area of the Shafi'i complex (the lesser Qarafa), resulting in the decline and the eventual abandonment of the greater Qarafa to the east and southeast.[144]

Mausoleum of Abu Mansur Isma'il Fakhr al-Din ibn Tha'lib

The remains of the mausoleum of the *sharif* Ibn Tha'lib (no.112, map 3) stand on the west side of Shari' Imam al-Shafi'i, shortly to the south of the Shafi'i tomb. Ibn Tha'lib, *amir al-hajj* in 591/1194–95, was an amir of al-Malik al-'Adil, and founded al-Madrasa al-Sharifiya in al-Qahira (v.s.). The mausoleum dates from his death in 612/1215–16. Creswell believed, because of the combination of the mausoleum and *iwan*, that this tomb may have been part of a two-*iwan madrasa*.[145]

Mausoleum of Fakhr al-Farisi

The tomb (no.103, map 3) of Fakhr al-Farisi (d. 622/1225–26) lies at the southern end of al-Qarafa (in modern terms) on Shari' Sidi 'Uqba, and southeast of the tomb of Imam al-Layth.[146]

Tomb of Abu al-'Abbas Ahmad Harrar

According to Massignon, this tomb was located in the greater Qarafa near Masjid al-Fath. Harrar, a Sevillian mystic, died ca. 630/1232–33.[147]

Tomb of the Abbasid caliphs

The 'tomb of the Abbasid caliphs' (no.113, map 3) stands adjacent to the *mashhad* of Sayyida Nafisa. The oldest cenotaph is that of Abu Nadla, ambassador of the Abbasid caliph of Baghdad (d. 640/1242–43), suggesting that the mausoleum was his undertaking. Later burials include sons of Sultan Baybars al-Bunduqdari and various descendants of the Abbasid caliphs of Baghdad, transferred by Baybars to Egypt to lend credence to his sultanate.[148]

Tomb of Abu al-Su'ud al-Wasiti

The tomb of Abu al-Su'ud al-Wasiti, a mystic who died in 644/1246–47, lies at the edge of the Muqattam to the south of the tomb of Shatibi.[149]

Tomb of Shajarat al-Durr

Constructed in 648-49/1250, the tomb of al-Malik al-Salih's widow (no.114, map 3) lies on Shari' al-Khalifa at the extreme northern end of al-Qarafa.

Christian and Jewish cemeteries

The Christian cemeteries of al-Qahira/al-Fustat, as described by Abu Salih the Armenian, are located in that section of al-Fustat formerly known as al-Hamra', and to the south of al-Fustat in the environs of Birkat al-Habash. They are usually, but not always, associated with churches and/or monasteries (v.i.). Specifically noted are the cemetery outside the great church of al-Hamra', that outside the church/monastery of Abu Mina (west of Mashhad Zayn al-'Abidin, near Fam al-Khalij) and the burying ground and the church of St. Onuphrius, which stood, according to Ibn Duqmaq, in the middle Hamra' on the street of al-Kibara.[150] While there were several churches and monasteries in the area of Birkat al-Habash, the cemeteries noted by Abu Salih appear to be unassociated with them. His description is illuminating:

> There is also a burying place for the Coptic Jacobite Christians and the Bishops of Misr, in the district of al-Habash; and the body of Anba Zacharias, the sixty-fourth patriarch is buried there, and the people receive blessings from it. . . . In [the burying ground] also are the tombs of the bishops of Misr; and near it are two wells of running water; one constructed by Abu al-Hasan Sayyid Ibn Mansur, the scribe, and the second by Nasir, the grave-digger. In this burying-ground there is a conspicuous monument of syenite, sculptured with a cross of points. . . . At the upper end of this ground, there is a cemetery of the Jews and Samaritans. . . . The Malkites, however, have no cemetery in the district of al-Habash, but their burying-places are within their churches, and on the hill where the monastery of al-Qusayr stands. The Armenians and the Nestorians likewise [bury] in their churches.[151]

Summary

Al-Qarafa under the Ayyubids was, as a tomb city, unique in the Islamic world. It combined several paradoxical aspects: a center of religious veneration and of promenades and entertainments; of individual pilgrimages and of the attempted channelization of visitations; of imposing tombs and *mashahid* together with palaces and markets; of nobility and *'ulama'* with the poverty-stricken who lived among the graves. The major Ayyubid benefactors to al-Qarafa were Saladin and al-Malik al-Kamil; Saladin through his establishment of a *madrasa* at the tomb of Imam al-Shafi'i and his general financial support of cemetery foundations, and al-Kamil through his attention to the visitations and his construction of the dome over the Shafi'i grave. This latter construction fostered a new concentration of both tombs and population in the smaller Qarafa, leaving the greater Qarafa to its eventual abandonment.

Of the known major tombs established under the Ayyubids, all save that of al-Malik al-Salih were founded in al-Qarafa. While cemeteries existed—at least in late Fatimid times—in the area of Darb al-Ahmar and Husayniya, these did not figure in Ayyubid chronicles, and the former, indeed, was probably removed by the Ayyubids during the construction of the citadel. Christian and Jewish burying grounds, some of which were centers of veneration, were located in the area of al-Fustat and Birkat al-Habash, and usually, but not always, associated with churches and monasteries.

Churches and Monasteries under the Early Ayyubids

The primary source on al-Qahira/al-Fustat churches and monasteries under Saladin is Abu Salih the Armenian. His narrative, however, concentrates on those establishments to the south and southwest of al-Qahira, and does not provide in any sense a complete list of the Christian institutions in the greater Cairo area. While it is true that the largest concentration of churches and monasteries was located in the general area of al-Hamra', al-Fustat, and Birkat al-Habash, Abu Salih virtually ignores churches within al-Qahira itself, and, indeed, the churches and monasteries located within Qasr al-Sham' at al-Fustat. His interest, rather, lies in the vicissitudes of those churches and monasteries in more exposed areas, especially in relation to anti-Christian sentiment—whether perpetrated by indigenous Islam, anti-Crusader sentiment, or mob desire to loot these relatively unprotected buildings—and the eventual restoration of these institutions under Saladin's reign.

The location of the relevant Christian institutions of al-Hamra'—in respect to the burning of al-Fustat in 564/1168—has been discussed above (see Chapter Three). Of interest here is the succession of attacks upon and discrimination against the churches and monasteries, together with the dates of their restorations and/or reopenings. The great church of al-Hamra', the church of the angel Gabriel, and the monastery of St. Menas were burned by the Ghuzz and the Kurds, in or about the year 559/1164. They were restored, respectively, in 560/1164–65; under the caliphate of al-'Adid; and during the vizierate of Shawar (i.e. all within eight years following their destruction). Two other churches, those of St. Onuphrius and Abu al-Sayfayn, were burned in the al-Fustat fire of 564/1168 and in mob violence shortly thereafter, and restored in 578–79/1183 and 570–71/1174–76 respectively. Other restorations included two smaller churches or chapels variously related to the great church of al-Hamra' and the church of Abu al-Sayfayn. These restorations took place in 568/1172–73, 571–72/1175–77, and 576–77/1180–82, and probably replaced damage from burning.[152]

Four churches in the Cairo area were pillaged, with no mention of burning. These include the churches of St. Victor and St. Mark in Giza, both of which were attacked by "the Ghuzz and Kurds" (no date); an unnamed church in al-Hamra', overlooking the Khalij, which was pillaged at the time of the al-Fustat fire of 564/1168; and a church of St. John at Birkat al-Habash, attacked by the "blacks" (no date), and restored in 579–80/1184. Of these four, only the last church was definitely restored.[153]

In addition, two churches were closed and reopened by Muslim authorities. That of al-Zuhri was closed because of a Muslim–Christian confrontation in 572–73/1177; it was reopened by order of Saladin shortly thereafter. Secondly, the Armenian—later Coptic—church of Basatin was closed by the *faqih* al-Tusi in 581/1185, but reopened by order of al-Malik al-'Adil the following year. Other restorations and reopenings included the church of the Four Living Creatures in al-Hamra' (571–72/1176), the church of St. Menas at Birkat al-Habash (573/1178), and a kitchen in al-Hamra' rebuilt as a church and dedicated to "our lady the pure virgin" in 582/1187.[154]

Despite the burnings, pillagings, and closings of churches and monasteries in the Cairo area, the administration of Saladin allowed not only the restoration of damaged buildings and the reopening of officially closed churches, but also the refurbishment and even extension of some institutions undamaged by Muslim harassment.

Churches under the Later Ayyubids

Information on churches under the later Ayyubids—gleaned, primarily, from the *History of the Patriarchs*—is sparse, sporadic, and relatively insignificant. In 634–65/1236–37, the enclosure (*zariba*) of the church of al-Roda (at the nilometer) collapsed, allowing the river to undermine its garden and part of the structure. It was also feared that the water would damage Jami' al-Miqyas nearby. Al-Malik al-Kamil authorized the patriarch to undertake the necessary restorations, resulting in a major reconstruction at the cost of a thousand dinars. The restoration was short-lived, however, as the church was closed by al-Malik al-Salih in 640/1242–43, making way for the construction of his citadel. As a passing note, the church of St. Mercurius (Abu al-Sayfayn) at al-Fustat was used to house the Frankish prisoners engaged in the construction of the citadel of al-Roda.[155]

Synagogues

Benjamin of Tudela, writing during the caliphate of al-'Adid, states that al-Fustat contained two thousand Jews and two synagogues. It is probable, but not certain, that his visit occurred after the al-Fustat fire of 564/1168.[156]

Summary

The religious institutions have been individually summarized within this chapter. It would, however, be worthwhile to note the variations in sponsorship of these foundations by the four mainstays of the Ayyubid regime, Saladin, al-Malik al-'Adil, al-Malik al-Kamil, and al-Malik al-Salih. Saladin introduced both the first *madrasa* and the first *khanqah* to Egypt. The former was a means for reestablishment of the Sunni *madhahib*, and the latter created "a position for Sufi organization corresponding to the state-appointed qadi at the head of the Shafi'i madhhab."[157] He proceeded with major mosque restorations, and established hospitals, a school for the poor, and a retreat for Maghribi travelers. The maintenance of the venerated tombs and shrines of al-Qarafa was, according to Ibn Jubayr, largely supported by regular stipends allotted by the sultan as were, indeed, all the Muslim institutions of al-Qahira and al-Fustat.[158]

Saladin's largesse was a combination of the need to root out Isma'ilism combined, no doubt, with some genuine religious charity. His was the spearhead that uprooted the Fatimid heresy; it was eclipsed in his lifetime. The later Ayyubid sultans, while not indifferent to pious works, lacked the political urgency of Saladin for their foundation. Although their numbers are less, as religious establishments they are no less significant. Al-Malik al-'Adil, admittedly, founded only one relatively inconsequential *madrasa*, although he probably endowed a *rab'* on the tomb of the Imam al-Shafi'i. Al-Malik al-Kamil, however, founded the first Dar al-Hadith in Egypt, spent lavishly on the tomb of Imam al-Shafi'i, and sponsored the first officially conducted visitations to al-Qarafa on Friday evenings. Al-Malik al-Salih, in addition to founding the first four-rite *madrasa* in Egypt, spent lavishly on the repair and rebuilding of the mosques of al-Qahira and al-Fustat.[159] Religious building activity spawned by the Sunni restoration of Saladin continued—albeit at a slightly reduced pace—throughout the remainder of the dynasty, fostered not only by the sultans but by their family, religious and lay officials, and wealthy private individuals.

Chapter Eight

Commercial Institutions

The favorable commercial climate established under the Ayyubids (see Chapter Two) fostered the continued development of the industrial and trading facilities of al-Qahira and al-Fustat upon a pattern which, in large part, continued a topographical pattern already established by the Fatimids. The markets (aswaq, singular suq) of al-Qahira were established, initially, to serve the immediate needs of the caliphate: the palace complex, the administration, and the military. During the 'vulgarization' of al-Qahira which was initiated by Badr al-Jamali and completed by Saladin, new markets were established to serve the general needs of newcomers, military and otherwise, who built in al-Qahira with the remnants of the derelict areas of al-Qata'i' and al-'Askar.[1] The primary commercial center of the Qahira–Fustat area remained the qasaba of al-Qahira, the grand artery extending from Bab al-Futuh to Bab Zuwayla and south—although to a limited extent—to the saliba of Ibn Tulun. Despite the movement of the center of power to the citadel and later to the island of al-Roda, choice products continued to be sold in the qasaba. Basic staples for the general populace continued to be supplied at al-Fustat and the general area of the saliba, while certain markets and storehouses, especially germane to the sultan and his military supporters, were moved to the area of the citadel and, under the reign of al-Malik al-Salih, to the al-Fustat shore and to Giza.[2]

Al-Qahira

The major commercial institutions of al-Qahira have been described in detail by Maqrizi, whose narrative is translated and annotated by Raymond and Wiet.[3] These institutions include the *suq*, the *qaysariya*, the *khan*, and the *funduq*. Those attributable to the Fatimid and Ayyubid periods are discussed herewith.

Aswaq and *suwayqat*

In the context of mediaeval Cairo, a *suq* refers to a market—or a group of markets on a given street—which caters to a specific merchandise or service. *Suwayqa*, a diminutive, represents a smaller market although, following Maqrizi's descriptions, the difference in size is not readily apparent. It is impossible to attain a complete picture of the markets of al-Qahira under the Fatimids and Ayyubids for two reasons. Firstly, as Maqrizi points out,

> There were at Misr [al-Fustat], al-Qahira, and the immediate surroundings of the two cities a considerable number of markets, most of which have ceased to exist. As an example, it is enough to know that between the lands of al-Luq and Bab al-Bahr at al-Maqs, fifty-two *aswaq* have disappeared which I have known and patronized; some of them contained as many as sixty shops. This is only the western suburb of al-Qahira; what could one say of the three other directions, along with al-Qahira and Misr?[4]

Secondly, Maqrizi's description does not, in all cases, give the dates of relevant markets. Those which are dated, however, render us a reasonably accurate picture of the topographical pattern and specialized wares and trades of the Cairene markets under the late Fatimids and Ayyubids.

Suq al-Shawwaiyin

Suq al-Shawwaiyin (meat roasters; no.48, map 1)—according to Maqrizi, the first market established in al-Qahira—was founded in 365/975–76 during the caliphate of al-Mu'izz. This market was originally Suq al-Sharayhiyin (butchers), who were transferred after 700/1300–1301. Extending between the entrance to Harat al-Rum and Suq al-Halawiyin, Suq al-Shawwaiyin was located, in modern terms, on the eastern side of the *qasaba* (Shari' Mu'izz li-Din Allah) near the mosque of al-Fakahani.[5]

Suwayqat al-Sahib

Located almost due west of al-Azhar near the east bank of the Khalij, Suwayqat al-Sahib (no.49, map 1) was first known as Suwayqat al-Wazir, established at the doorway to the house of Ya'qub ibn Killis, vizier to the Fatimid caliph al-'Aziz. This palace later became known as Dar al-Dibaj, a manufactory of silk brocade.

> At the end of the Fatimid dynasty, this market became known as the great *suq* [al-Suq al-Kabir]. When Safi al-Din ibn Shukr became vizier to al-Malik al-'Adil Abu Bakr ibn Ayyub, he lived in this street [Khatt Dar al-Dibaj], founding there a *madrasa* known today as al-Madrasa al-Sahibiya, as well as a *ribat* and a bath near this *madrasa*. From that time it was known as Suwayqat al-Sahib.[6]

Maqrizi adds that this market maintained a considerable variety of foodstuffs, largely due to the notables who dwelt in the immediate area.[7]

Suq al-Shamma'in

Suq al-Shamma'in (sellers of candles; no.50, map 1) was located on the *qasaba* near the mosque of al-Aqmar. It was, under the Fatimids, a market for grain merchants (*qammahin*), and apparently predated the founding of the mosque (519/1125–26); its precise status under the Ayyubids is uncertain. Maqrizi's description—somewhat vague—suggests the establishment of shops on both sides of the *qasaba* as well as along the northern façade of the mosque.[8]

Suq Bab al-Zuhuma and its environs

Known from a gate at the southwest corner of the eastern Fatimid palace, Suq Bab al-Zuhuma (no.51, map 1) was, under the Fatimids, occupied by money changers. Several other markets were in its immediate vicinity, not all of which are described individually by Maqrizi; his narrative, therefore, is given in full here.

> Under the Fatimid dynasty, the emplacement [of Suq Bab al-Zuhuma] served as a market of money changers, which faced Suq al-Suyufiyin [swordmakers], whence [one proceeded to] the barrier [al-Khushayba], in the direction of the entrance to the present Suq al-Haririyin [silk merchants] and the Suq al-'Anbar [grey amber] which was then a prison known as al-Ma'una. Facing Suq al-Suyufiyin there was, at the same time, Suq al-Zujjajin [glassmakers], which abutted Suq al-Qashshashin [rag-dealers], now known as al-Kharratin [turners]. After the fall of the Fatimid dynasty, all of this changed. Suq al-Suyufiyin extended from al-Sagha [the

goldsmiths' bazaar] to Darb al-Silsila. Between al-Madrasa al-Salihiya and al-Sagha a *suq* was founded with shops selling combs, Suq al-Amshatiyin, extending [southward] from that *madrasa*. Between the shops where the combs were sold and al-Sagha were shops partly occupied by money changers and partly by sellers of dried fruits [*nuqaliyin*]. . . . In the center of these buildings stood Suq al-Kutubiyin [booksellers], surrounded by Suq al-Amshatiyin and Suq al-Nuqaliyin; all of this group was made part of the *awqaf* of al-Maristan al-Mansuri. Suq Bab al-Zuhuma was one of the best known and most reputed markets of al-Qahira; people spoke of the excellent quality of the goods sold there.[9]

Following the breakup of the Fatimid dynasty, then, a series of markets was established in or removed to the area of Bab al-Zuhuma at the southern end of Bayn al-Qasrayn. With the exception of the goldsmiths' bazaar (al-Sagha, v.i.) and Suq al-Kutubiyin (the latter probably founded after 700/1300–1301), it is uncertain which of these *aswaq* were built under the Ayyubids and which under the Bahri Mamluks. It can be assumed, however, that the process began soon after Saladin's accession to the sultanate.[10]

Suq al-Muhayriyin

Suq al-Muhayriyin (makers of palanquins; no.52, map 1) was located just to the north of and probably abutted the mosque of al-Aqmar. An unconfirmed story, related by Maqrizi, suggests the existence of this market during the caliphate of al-Hakim.[11]

Suq al-Bunduqaniyin

Suq al-Bunduqaniyin (manufacturers of crossbows; no.53, map 1) stood directly west of al-Azhar, about halfway between it and the Khalij. Following Maqrizi,

> It was formerly known as Suq Bi'r Zuwayla, since there was an old well there which served Istabl al-Jummayza, where the horses of the Fatimid caliphs were kept. . . . After the fall of the [Fatimid] dynasty, Istabl al-Jummayza was parceled out, and several houses and other buildings were constructed there; the place of the stable took the name 'al-Bunduqaniyin,' and this name passed to the *suq*.[12]

He states in another passage that "when the [Fatimid] dynasty ended, the stable was parceled out, and houses and a *suq* were built. Within the *suq* were a number of shops in which were made crossbows; hence the name Khatt al-Bunduqaniyin."[13]

Suq Harat Barjawan

Known under the Fatimids as Suq Amir al-Juyush (as opposed to Suwayqat Amir al-Juyush, v.i.), this market (no.54, map 1) was founded by Badr al-Jamali at the entrance to Harat Barjawan (slightly to the north of the mosque of al-Aqmar on Shari' al-Mu'izz li-Din Allah). During Maqrizi's youth this was the largest market in al-Qahira, dealing primarily in foodstuffs, vegetables, and meats; it was, however, abandoned in 806/1403–1404.[14]

Suq Bab al-Futuh

This *suq* (no.55, map 1), again on the present Shari' Mu'izz li-Din Allah (the *qasaba*), stood at the entrance of Harat Baha' al-Din (to the west of the *qasaba*). It was founded at the time Baha' al-Din Qaraqush established his residence in the neighboring quarter. This market again, in Maqrizi's time, dealt primarily in meats and vegetables.[15]

Suq al-Silah

Suq al-Silah (weapons; no.56, map 1) was located in the center of Bayn al-Qasrayn, between the *madrasa* of Baybars al-Bunduqdari and the entrance to Qasr Bishtak. Founded after the fall of the Fatimids, this market sold "bows, arrows, armor, and weapons of war in general."[16]

Suwayqat Amir al-Juyush

This market (no.57, map 1) stood on the present Shari' Amir al-Juyush, an east–west thoroughfare which runs from Shari' al-Mu'izz li-Din Allah to Shari' Port Said in the northwest section of al-Qahira. In a mediaeval context, this street ran from the *qasaba* to Bab al-Qantara on the Khalij, and between Harat Baha' al-Din and Harat Barjawan. "After the fall of the Fatimid dynasty, it was called Suq al-Khuruqiyin [sellers of cloaks]. It is in this market that the amir Ayazkuj al-Asadi founded al-Madrasa al-Uzkushiya [see Chapter Seven]."[17]

Suq al-Mahamiziyin

Suq al-Mahamiziyin (manufacturers of spurs; no.58, map 1) stood on the *qasaba*, west of the Azhar mosque and opposite Dar al-Darb. It was founded following the end of the Fatimid dynasty.[18]

Suq al-Sharabishiyin

Also established after the end of the Fatimid dynasty, this *suq* (no.59, map 1) sold the robes of honor designated by the sultan to "amirs, viziers, *qudah*, and other functionaries." The *sharbush*, an honorary medallion worn in a turban (awarded by the sultan), gave its name to the market. This was a distinction conferred under the Bahri Mamluks. The precise circumstances of the market under the Ayyubids is uncertain, but it may be assumed that it catered strictly to the sale of honorary robes. Suq al-Sharabishiyin was located on the *qasaba*, on or near the present site of the mosque of al-Ghuri.[19]

Suq Bayn al-Qasrayn

The northern section of the parade ground between the two Fatimid palaces became, following the end of that dynasty and the reassignment of the palaces, a food market (no.60, map 1).[20]

Suwayqat al-Balashun

Following Maqrizi,

> This market [no.61, map 1], outside Bab al-Futuh, carries the name of Sabiq al-Din Sunqur al-Balashun, *mamluk* and sword-bearer [*silahdar*] of the sultan Salah al-Din Yusuf ibn Ayyub. He was also owner of a garden in al-Maqs, outside of al-Qahira near al-Dikka [see Chapter Three] known as Bustan al-Balashun.[21]

Suq al-Jamalun al-Saghir

Suq al-Jamalun al-Saghir (market of the small ridged roof; no.62, map 1) stood to the east of the *qasaba* on the present Shari' al-Dibbiya, west of Wikalat Qawsun and south of the *ziyada* of the mosque of al-Hakim. It was established by the amir Jamal al-Din Shuwaykh ibn Sirm, one of the amirs of al-Malik al-Kamil. Ibn Sirm also founded al-Madrasa al-Sirmiya in or near this *suq* (see Chapter Seven), as well as Bustan Ibn Sirm outside Bab al-Futuh. In Maqrizi's time this market was occupied by sellers and manufacturers of cloth.[22]

Suwayqat al-Mas'udi

Maqrizi states:

> This market is part of Harat Zuwayla in al-Qahira. It was named after the amir Sarim al-Din Qaymaz al-Mas'udi, *mamluk* of al-Malik al-Mas'ud

Aqsisi, son of al-Malik al-Kamil. This Mas'udi had been *wali* of al-Qahira; he was a tyrannical, violent, and cruel man.[23]

Mas'udi was assassinated in 664/1265–66, and the date of the market is questionable. Raymond locates Suwayqat al-Mas'udi (no.63, map 1) in the west central portion of al-Qahira, north of Suwayqat al-Sahib.[24]

Al-Sagha

Al-Sagha (the goldsmiths' bazaar; no.64, map 1) was located opposite al-Madrasa al-Salihiya and immediately south of the *madrasa* of Qalaun. Occupying the site of the palace kitchens (the southeast corner of the western Fatimid palace), al-Sagha predated al-Malik al-Salih's *madrasa*, demonstrating the destruction of that section of the western palace prior to 639/1241–42.[25]

Farriers

A *suq* of farriers (al-Bayatira; no.65, map 1), between al-Sagha and the eastern palace, was transferred to Rukn al-Muhalaq at the time of the building of the Salihiya *madrasa*. Rukn al-Muhalaq was located immediately to the rear of the mosque of al-Aqmar; Maqrizi makes no mention of this *suq*.[26]

Summary

Eighteen principal markets noted by Maqrizi and Ibn Laqlaq existed during the Ayyubid period. Seven of these were founded under the Fatimids; the remaining eleven under specific Ayyubids or "following the end of the Fatimid dynasty." Eleven markets were established on the *qasaba*, four in the west and northwest of the city, two in the northeast quarter, and one outside Bab al-Futuh. Of the four known to be established by individuals, one was established by Badr al-Jamali and three by Ayyubid *mamalik* and/or amirs.

No specific pattern can be drawn between the locations of the markets and the products or services provided therein. The sole exception to this is Suq al-Silah, the weapons market established in Bayn al-Qasrayn. The importance of this *suq* is suggested by its foundation in such a central area, close to the center of administration; it was later (probably under the early Mamluks) transferred to al-Rumayla, beneath the citadel.[27] The opening of Bayn al-Qasrayn to the general populace fostered a new concentration of markets in that area especially near Bab al-Zuhuma. These *aswaq*, of no particular genre, took advantage of a massive open square, centrally located and suddenly liberated. It must be reiterated, however, that our list of markets is far from complete, and barring the discovery of new texts, our survey remains cursory at best.

Qayasir

Qaysariya (plural qayasir), a word derived from Greek, is only an urban establishment which applies to a covered market of a certain size, a square building in the form of a cloister which includes bedrooms, storerooms, and shops for merchants. "Qayasir are larger than markets [aswaq] and consist of several covered galleries [as opposed to markets which have only one]; qayasir include manufactories and works, while aswaq only display merchandise for sale. Finally, each type of artisan or merchant is concentrated in the same qaysariya or the same suq; otherwise, if a single qaysariya includes several groups of crafts, each type occupies a particular gallery."[28]

While there are certainly exceptions to DeSacy's statement that "aswaq only display merchandise for sale," his basic hypothesis is probably correct. Eight qayasir were established under the Fatimids and Ayyubids and are examined herewith.

Qaysariyat Ibn Quraysh

This qaysariya (no.66, map 1) was located at the entrance to Suq al-Jamalun al-Kabir, just to the west of the qasaba and north of Madrasat al-Ghuri. According to Ibn 'Abd al-Zahir,

> It was renewed [astajadda] by the qadi al-Murtada ibn Quraysh, under the reign of al-Malik al-Nasir Salah al-Din, on the site of a stable. The qadi al-Murtada Safi al-Din ibn Quraysh al-Makhzumi was one of the secretaries of the chancellery under the reign of Salah al-Din Yusuf ibn Ayyub. This Ibn Quraysh died on the battlefield before Acre, Friday 10 Jumada 586 [June 16, 1190], and was buried at Jerusalem. He was born in 524/1129–30 and had followed, among others, the course of al-Silafi."[29]

Qaysariyat Ibn Abi Usama

Located on the western side of the qasaba just north of Madrasat al-Ghuri, this qaysariya (no.67, map 1) was constituted as waqf (and presumably founded by) the shaykh Abu al-Hasan ibn Abi Usama, secretary of the chancellery under the reign of the Fatimid caliph al-Amir. The act of waqf was dated 518/1124. Its disposition under the

Ayyubids is uncertain; in Maqrizi's time it was occupied by ironmongers.[30]

Qaysariyat Ibn Yahya

Qaysariyat Ibn Yahya (no.68, map 1) was located slightly south of Madrasat al-Ghuri on the west of the *qasaba*. Maqrizi:

> It was founded by the *qadi* al-Mufaddal Hibat Allah ibn Yahya al-Tamimi the notary, confidential secretary for the drafting of notarized acts, about 540/1145–46, under the Fatimids. He continued to take part in the corps of notaries until 580/1184–85. . . . This *qaysariya* was demolished and no trace remains.[31]

Qaysariya *near Madrasat al-Ghuri*

An unnamed *qaysariya* (no.69, map 1) stood on the west of the *qasaba*, slightly north of Madrasat al-Ghuri. Maqrizi states:

> A part was constituted as *waqf* by the *qadi* al-Ashraf, son of al-Qadi al-Fadil 'Abd al-Rahim ibn 'Ali al-Baysani, for the expenses of filling the cistern in Darb al-Mulukhiya, and a part was attached to the *waqf* of al-Salih Tala'i' ibn Ruzayk.[32]

Qaysariyat al-Sharb

Located on the *qasaba* immediately south of the Ghuri *madrasa*, Qaysariyat al-Sharb (fabrics; no.70, map 1) was endowed by Saladin on the sufis of Khanqah Sa'id al-Su'ada'. It was formerly a stable.[33]

Qaysariyat al-Fadil

Located on the *qasaba* opposite the mosque of al-Mu'ayyad Shaykh, this *qaysariya* (no.71, map 1) was named after al-Qadi al-Fadil. It was, allegedly, endowed as *waqf* on more than ten different occasions, and was, in Maqrizi's time, the *waqf* of al-Maristan al-Mansuri.[34]

Qaysariyat Jaharkas

Built by the amir Fakhr al-Din Jaharkas in 592/1195–96, this *qaysariya* (no.72, map 1) stood on the eastern side of the *qasaba* to the south of the mausoleum of al-Ghuri.[35] A *mamluk* of Saladin, Fakhr al-Din became *ustadar* under al-Malik al-'Aziz 'Uthman and, as head of the Salahiya, played an important and diverse role in the succession to al-'Aziz and the ultimate installation of al-Malik al-'Adil.[36] Maqrizi gives two versions of its disposition under the Ayyubids.

Formerly the site was known as Funduq al-Firakh. The *qaysariya* passed to his [Jaharkas'] heirs, and then in part to the amir 'Alam al-Din Aytmish [through his wife's legacy] and in part to Bint Shuman of Damascus. Then it was bought by Umm Khalil, known as Shajar al-Durr al-Salihiya, in 655/1257–58. . . . However, according to certain historians, its founder Jaharkas sold it at auction when it was completed, and it was awarded to the *sharif* Fakhr al-Din Isma'il ibn Tha'lib for 95,000 dinars.[37]

Further on, citing Ibn Khallikan:

> [Fakhr al-Din Jaharkas] was the founder, in al-Qahira, of the great *qaysariya* which bears his name. According to a group of merchants that I met who had traveled throughout the world, they had never encountered a construction so beautiful, large, and solidly built. In the upper section a large mosque and *rab'* were constructed. [Fakhr al-Din] died at Damascus in one of the months of 608/1211–12.[38]

Qaysariyat al-Fa'izi

Qaysariyat al-Fa'izi (no.73, map 1) stood on the eastern side of the *qasaba* to the south of the present junction with Shari' Jawhar al-Qa'id. Later known as Qaysariyat al-Nushshab (arrow makers), it stood at the entrance to Suq al-Kharratin, near Suq al-Mahamiziyin, with a door facing each of these markets.[39] Its founder, al-As'ad Sharaf al-Din Abu al-Qasim Hibat Allah ibn Sa'id Wuhayb al-Farisi, was by origin a Christian from Asyut who had come to Cairo and converted to Islam under the reign of al-Malik al-Kamil,

> where he entered the the service of al-Malik al-Fa'iz Ibrahim, son of al-Malik al-'Adil, hence his surname [Fa'izi]. He served as administrator of the *diwan* for a short period of time under the reign of al-Malik al-Salih . . ., and he became *wali* of an Egyptian province.[40]

Having been recalled from this position for alleged misappropriation of lands, al-Fa'izi was jailed, released, and entered the service of the governor of Damascus, Jamal al-Din (Musa ibn) Yaghmur. Returning to Egypt with al-Mu'azzam Turan Shah in 647/1249–50, he later served as vizier to al-Malik al-Mu'izz Aybak. Shortly after the installation of al-Malik al-Mansur 'Ali (655/1257–58), al-Fa'izi, suspected of plotting to supplant the young sultan by the Ayyubid al-Nasir Yusuf of Damascus, was summarily strangled.[41]

Summary

Of the eight *qayasir* founded by the Fatimids and Ayyubids, seven were established on or near the *qasaba* in an area west of the Azhar mosque, six of which were in the immediate environs of the (later) *madrasa*/mausoleum complex of al-Ghuri. These took advantage, presumably, of their central location. The eighth, also on the *qasaba*, was founded opposite the present mosque of al-Mu'ayyad Shaykh. Five of these *qayasir* were apparently founded by chancellery figures of religious background; the remaining three by Saladin, an *ustadar*, and a vizier. Four were endowed as *waqf* properties.

Khanat and *fanadiq*

These two institutions were, in Maqrizi's time, effectively synonymous. Four *fanadiq* (singular *funduq*) and *khanat* (singular *khan*) were established at al-Qahira under the Ayyubids. A general description would suggest a square enclosure with a courtyard surrounded on the ground level by storerooms and/or stables for traveling merchants, with sleeping accommodations on the upper (usually single) story. While the term *funduq*—especially in Alexandria—often applied to hostels and storehouses for foreign merchants, this discrimination cannot be categorically applied to Cairo during the Ayyubid period.[42]

Although according to Nasir-i Khusraw *khanat* certainly existed at al-Qahira under the Fatimids, none are specifically mentioned by Maqrizi.

Khan Mankuwirish

Following Maqrizi, this *khan* (no.74, map 1) was located in Khatt Suq al-Khiyamiyin, near the mosque of al-Azhar. This stood, in modern terms, about halfway between Jami' al-Azhar and the *qasaba*.

Ibn 'Abd al-Zahir wrote: it was founded by the amir Rukn al-Din Mankuwirish, second husband of the mother of [al-Malik] al-Awhad, son of [al-Malik] al-'Adil. The property passed to his heirs, then to the amir Salah al-Din Ahmad ibn Sha'ban al-Irbili, who endowed it as *waqf.* By intrigues, his son succeeded in annulling the *waqf* and sold this property to al-Malik al-Salih [Ayyub] for 10,000 Egyptian dinars. [Al-Salih] entrusted the administration to Umm Khalil [Shajar al-Durr]; it was then reneged from her. This Mankuwirish, adds the same author, was one of the *mamalik* of Sultan Salah al-Din Yusuf ibn Ayyub; he ultimately became one of Salah al-Din's amirs. Following his death, in Shawwal 577 (Feb. 7–March 7, 1182), the amir Yazkuj al-Asadi took over his *iqta*.[43]

Khan al-Sabil

Following Maqrizi,

> This *khan* [no.75, map 1] is situated outside Bab al-Futuh. Ibn 'Abd al-Zahir said, "This Khan al-Sabil was founded by the amir Baha' al-Din Abu Sa'id Qaraqush ibn 'Abd Allah al-Asadi; . . . for people of the road [*ibna' al-sabil*] and travelers [*musafirin*], free of charge. In it are a well with water scoops [*bi'r saqiya*] and a trough."[44]

Khan Masrur

Maqrizi states:

> Khan Masrur consists of two establishments [nos. 76, 77, map 1], one large and one small. The larger is situated on the left when one passes from Suq Bab al-Zuhuma to [Suq] al-Haririyin. Its site was formerly Khizanat al-Daraq [storehouse of shields], of which we have spoken in the chapter on the storehouses of the [Fatimid] palace. The smaller is located on the right when one passes from Suq Bab al-Zuhuma to the mosque of al-Azhar; it was formerly an open space where slaves were sold, replacing the slave market on the site of al-Madrasa al-Kamiliya. According to Ibn Tuwayr, Khizanat al-Daraq is on the site of Khan Masrur.[45]

Maqrizi continues, citing Ibn 'Abd al-Zahir:

> This Masrur was one of the palace slaves serving the Egyptian [Fatimid] dynasty. He attached himself to Salah al-Din . . . who made him a commander in his guard. He continued to advance in grade. He was a pious man, generous and obliging, and devoted himself to good works and pious acts. He left [government] service under the reign of [al-Malik] al-Kamil and devoted himself to God, never leaving his house. Then, he built the smaller *funduq* to its side, on the site which was formerly an open space used as a slave market. He bought a third of the land from my father . . . and the other two thirds from the heirs of Ibn 'Antar. The larger *funduq* was owned by one of [Masrur's] slaves, Rihan. Masrur had bequeathed it to him; then after him, as a *waqf* for the prisoners of war, and the poor of the holy cities [*haramayn*]. It consisted of ninety-nine chambers, and included a mosque in which Friday prayers were celebrated. Masrur established many pious endowments in Syria and Egypt. He stipulated that his house be converted into a *madrasa*, and he endowed the small *funduq* upon it. He owned property at Damascus which he sold for a large price to the amir Sayf al-Din Abu al-Hasan al-Qaymari. The aforementioned *madrasa* was constructed after his death.[46]

Raymond and Wiet, following Ravaisse, place the larger Khan Masrur at the east of the *qasaba* near the intersection of the present

Shari' Jawhar al-Qa'id. The smaller—located "on the right when one passes from Suq Bab al-Zuhuma to the mosque of al-Azhar"—is somewhat more vague. Since, however, Maqrizi states that al-Madrasa al-Masruriya was located in Darb Shams al-Dawla (immediately south of the western palace; see Chapter Seven), we can assume that the smaller *khan* stood in that area as well.[47]

Funduq Ibn Quraysh

Maqrizi states:

> According to Ibn 'Abd al-Zahir, Funduq Ibn Quraysh was founded by the *qadi* Sharaf al-Din Ibrahim ibn Quraysh, secretary of the chancelry; it passed to his heirs. End [of Ibn 'Abd al-Zahir's text]. [Ibrahim ibn 'Abd al-Rahman ibn 'Ali ibn 'Abd al-Rahman ibn 'Ali ibn 'Abd al-'Aziz ibn 'Ali ibn Quraysh] Abu Ishaq al-Makhzumi al-Misri al-Katib Sharaf al-Din was among the secretaries reputed for calligraphy and style. He served during the reigns of al-Malik al-'Adil Abu Bakr ibn Ayyub and his son al-Malik al-Kamil Muhammad in the administration of the chancellery [*diwan al-insha*]. He had studied hadith at Mecca and in Egypt, and he taught it as well. He was born in al-Qahira on 1 Dhu al-Qa'da 572 (May 1, 1177). He recited the Qur'an, memorized a large part of the book *al-Muhadhdhab fi al-fiqh*, according to the *madhhab* of Imam al-Shafi'i, and he excelled in the literary arts. He copied more than four hundred volumes by hand. He died on 25 Jumada 643 (Oct. 19, 1245).[48]

The location of this *funduq* is uncertain. The *qaysariya* of Sharaf al-Din's father, Safi al-Din (v.s.), was located to the north of Madrasat al-Ghuri.[49]

Summary

Of the four *khanat* and *fanadiq* of the Ayyubid period, two were located in the central area of al-Qahira on or near the *qasaba*, a third outside Bab al-Futuh, while the location of the fourth is unknown. All were founded by magnates of the Ayyubid regime, of military or religious/administrative backgrounds. At least three out of four were endowed as *waqf* properties.

A *rab'* constructed by al-Malik al-Kamil

As noted in the description of the Dar al-Hadith of al-Malik al-Kamil (v.s.), a *rab'* (no.79, map 1) was founded by al-Malik al-Kamil and endowed on this *dar*. Casanova, citing Lane, defines a *rab'* in Egyptian terms as "a row of separate lodgings situated above shops and storerooms and served by a single stairway."[50] This *rab'* was located near the *madrasa* "at Bab al-Kharanshaf and extended to the *darb* facing Jami' al-Aqmar. . . . Its site was formerly part of the western palace, following · which it was occupied by grain merchants."[51] This is the only Ayyubid *rab'*—existing as a separate entity—noted within al-Qahira.

The Citadel Area

Maqrizi states that the markets for horses, donkeys, and camels were transferred to al-Rumayla, beneath the citadel, by al-Malik al-Kamil.[52] While other markets, germane to the military needs of the citadel (such as Suq al-Silah, v.s.) were undoubtedly transferred to this area at a later date, only these *aswaq* established by al-Malik al-Kamil can definitely be assigned to the Ayyubids. There is, in addition, no evidence of any significant commercial activity on the Darb al-Ahmar during this period.

Al-Fustat and Giza

The information on the economic activities at al-Fustat under the Ayyubids is sparse, sporadic, and often contradictory. Many of the institutions described by Ibn Duqmaq (*aswaq, khanat, fanadiq*, etc.) are incompletely documented, undated, and when dated, often refer to pre-Fatimid foundations of uncertain usage under the Ayyubids. That many establishments existed, however, is certain from the few general narratives available, especially those of Ibn Laqlaq and Ibn Sa'id. We shall examine, first, the overall situation of commerce and industry at al-Fustat and Giza, then study the individual establishments whose operations were specifically relevant to the Ayyubids.

As previously noted (see Chapter Three) the al-Fustat fire of 564/1168, while a catastrophe, did not, according to archaeological evidence, considerably delimit al-Fustat's eastern boundaries. Moreover, the excavations of Bahgat and Scanlon in these eastern areas failed to reveal other than domestic architecture, with the exception of occasional (and minor) intrusive Mamluk elements.[53] The commercial and industrial center remained, as always, within a triangular area encompassed by (1) the Nile shore from Bab al-Qantara to Fam al-Khalij, (2) an east–west line from Fam al-Khalij to

Bab al-Safa', and (3) a line extending from Bab al-Safa' to Bab al-Qantara passing just to the east of the mosque of 'Amr and Qasr al-Sham'.[54] The commercial development of this area can be attributed to two factors: (1) proximity to the Nile, and (2) the early concentration of markets around the mosque of 'Amr. While the 564/1168 fire must, sporadically, have penetrated this triangle (cf. Abu Salih, v.s.), it is conceivable that the commercial activity of al-Fustat—basically riverine—remained relatively unscathed.

Benjamin of Tudela (ca. 566/1170) states that al-Fustat boasted many markets and inns. Ibn Jubayr, some thirteen years later, notes that the city was almost completely rebuilt after the fire. He does not, however, mention commercial institutions specifically.[55] Barring individual structures, little further commercial information exists on al-Fustat until the capture of Damietta by the Crusaders in 616/1219–20. Fiscally strapped, al-Malik al-Kamil summoned Safi al-Din ibn Shukr, formerly vizier to al-Malik al-'Adil, to reassume the vizierate. Among the stringent measures taken by Ibn Shukr were the closing of the *dur al-wakalat* and *fanadiq* at al-Qahira and al-Fustat, "in which there were sold goods such as linen and other than it. It was ordered that nothing should be sold, except in the *dar al-wakala* of the sultan, which was in the Dar al-Mulk [v.i.], and that the brokerage should belong to the sultan."[56]

Ibn Sa'id's description of al-Fustat's commercial activities (see Chapter Three) will be recapitulated here. On his arrival at al-Fustat (ca. 640/1242–43) he noted the profusion of dockyards, with boats arriving replete with both foreign and indigenous commodities. The markets boasted cheaper prices because of the proximity of the Nile, and had expanded due to the construction of the citadel of al-Roda. The soldiers' *suq* had been transferred from al-Qahira to a *qaysariya* constructed in front of the boat bridge to al-Roda. In terms of industry, Ibn Sa'id noted the processing and/or manufacturing of sugar, soap, glass, steel, copper, and paper, none of which took place in al-Qahira. The construction industry as well must have been somewhat spurred by the building of houses and pavilions along the al-Fustat shore (according to Ibn Sa'id) by al-Malik al-Salih's amirs.

This description is in sharp contradistinction with the narrative of Ibn Laqlaq who notes, for the year 640/1242–43, a predilection of al-Malik al-Salih to shift much of the commercial activity of al-Fustat to Giza.

> The sultan . . . ordered that some people be transferred from every market to al-Gizah and should reside there, as he intended to rebuild it

[Gizah]; it was said that he had measured for its rebuilding the extent of Alexandria in length and width. He further ordered the transfer of the storehouses [*al-shuwani*] to the district of Gizah and be constructed there, and that the amirs should build their palaces there. Thus, the residence of the sultan would be the citadel of the island [al-Roda], and the amirs' in Gizah. [He also directed] that the dockyards of the warships and the Nile ships be transferred from al-Fustat to the dockyards [*sana'a*] which he had planned at Gizah.[57]

Further on, in discussing the dredging of the al-Fustat channel, he states:

As a result of the excavations [al-Malik al-Salih] ordered the transfer of the market for corn and the dealers in corn—who owned the sites at the shore—in addition to the establishments which sold melons, squirting cucumbers, and cucumbers—to Kawm al-Ahmar south of al-Fustat. Some [of these establishments] were transferred to Gizah.[58]

No other contemporary writer or later chronicler has mentioned this projected transfer of commercial and residential properties to Giza, nor is there any evidence that such a program was carried out. Ibn Sa'id's silence is significant. Barring further evidence we can only assume this project was merely a pipe dream of al-Malik al-Salih, perhaps in the hope of yet further isolation for himself and his Bahri *mamalik* at his island citadel. Further verification of al-Fustat's continued commercial prominence can be gleaned from the description of individual establishments, below.

Aswaq

As previously stated, al-Fustat was replete with markets during the Ayyubid period, many dating from pre-Fatimid times. We can attribute only one market specifically to the Ayyubids, the soldiers' *suq* transferred from al-Qahira to the *qaysariya* constructed by al-Malik al-Salih in front of the bridge to al-Roda, where "furs, broadcloth, and similar things were sold."[59]

Khanat

The *khanat* of al-Fustat are mentioned only in passing by Ibn Sa'id, who states that they are generally smaller than those of al-Qahira. Ibn Duqmaq is silent on the matter suggesting his usage of a different term (*fanadiq*? *qayasir*?)[60]

Fanadiq

Only four *fanadiq* can be noted with definite Ayyubid associations, although Benjamin of Tudela noted "many inns" in his visit to al-Fustat.[61]

Funduq Abi al-Thana'

On Ibn Jubayr's arrival at al-Fustat, he stayed at Funduq Abi al-Thana' "in Zuqaq al-Qanadil beside the mosque of 'Amr ibn al-'As. . . . Our room was a large one at the door of the inn."[62]

Fanadiq al-Karim

The two *funduq*s constructed by Taqi al-Din 'Umar, larger (no.97, map 3) and smaller (no.96, map 3), were known as Fanadiq al-Karim. These were located in Khatt al-Malahin, on opposite sides of Suq al-Fatayiriyin, the smaller to the north and the larger to the south. In modern terms, Casanova places the smaller west of al-Masjid al-Suwaydi, and the larger to the south of it.

Subhi Labib associates these *funduq*s with the Karimi merchants and states that they were founded by Taqi al-Din in 579/1183–84. Ibn Duqmaq relates that Funduq al-Karim (not *fanadiq*) was the *waqf* of Taqi al-Din 'Umar; it can be assumed that the two terms are here identical in meaning. Although the beneficiary of the *waqf* is not given, al-Madrasa al-Taqawiya, notably endowed with other local properties (see Chapter Seven), was the probable recipient.[63]

Funduq al-Nakhla

Funduq al-Nakhla (no.102, map 3), formerly a stable, was endowed upon al-Madrasa al-Taqawiya by Taqi al-Din 'Umar. It stood at the eastern end of al-Suq al-Kabir, in the immediate neighborhood of al-Madrasa al-Taqawiya (on the Nile shore, opposite the nilometer).[64]

Qayasir

Fifteen *qayasir* are listed by Ibn Duqmaq, at least eight of which date to pre-Ayyubid times. Three *qayasir*, however, can definitely be listed as Ayyubid foundations.[65]

Two qaysariyas of Ibn al-Arsufi

The larger (no.99, map 3) and smaller (no.100, map 3) *qaysariyas* of Ibn al-Arsufi were located just northwest of the mosque of 'Amr, between al-Nahhasin and al-Bazzazin. Both were endowed upon Madrasat Ibn al-Arsufi (see Chapter Seven) nearby in al-Bazzazin. Ibn al-Arsufi, an Ascaloni trader, died in 593/1196–97.[66]

The qaysariya *of al-Malik al-Salih*

As noted above, Ibn Sa'id describes a great *qaysariya* (no.98, map 3) constructed by al-Malik al-Salih in front of the boat bridge to al-Roda. The soldiers' *suq* was moved thence from al-Qahira, where furs, broadcloth, and similar commodities were sold.[67]

Rubu'

Two Ayyubid *rab'* s are noted at al-Fustat. The first, that of Taqi al-Din 'Umar, was founded near his smaller *funduq* (v.s.).[68] The second, al-Rab' al-'Adili (no.95, map 3), founded by al-Malik al-'Adil, was located near the Nile shore southwest of Dayr Abi al-Sayfayn, and north of al-'Adil's *madrasa*, (also known as Madrasat Ibn Shash, v.s.). This *rab'* was, however, endowed upon the tomb of the Imam al-Shafi'i.[69]

Dur/Wakalat

Two commercial institutions known variously as *dar* and *dar al-wakala* existed at al-Qahira and al-Fustat during the Fatimid and Ayyubid periods. The term *wakala* apparently underwent several changes of meaning between the fifth and eighth centuries.

From its conception, a *dar al-wakala* was "a state establishment, where fiscal agents estimated imported or transitory merchandise, and imposed tolls or customs taxes."[70] By Maqrizi's time, however, the term—only rarely used—was a synonym for *funduq* or *khan*.[71] On the subject of the term *wakala*, Raymond states: "Very much used in the Fatimid epoch, possibly proscribed by their Ayyubid successors, the expression returned to favor from the eighth/fourteenth century onward."[72] With regard to al-Qahira/al-Fustat his assertion is questionable due, firstly, to evidence of but few Fatimid *wakalat*; secondly, the recording of considerable *wakala* activity under the Ayyubids; and thirdly, the fact that only three were noted by Maqrizi and none by Ibn Duqmaq (although they vastly multiplied in the late Mamluk and Ottoman periods). We shall examine these commercial *dur* on an individual basis, in an attempt to learn their function and extent under the later Fatimids and Ayyubids.

Dar al-Mulk

Dar al-Mulk (no.91, map 3), located at the southwest extremity of al-Fustat near Bab al-Qantara (in modern terms, near the mosque of 'Abdi Bey al-Shahir), was founded by the vizier al-Afdal ibn Badr al-Jamali in 501/1107–1108, whence he transferred his residence and administrative apparatus from Dar al-Wizara in al-Qahira. Upon al-Afdal's death, Dar al-Mulk became a caliphal pavilion. According to Maqrizi it became a *dar al-matjar* under al-Kamil, which Casanova believes represented a trading depot similar to a *funduq* or (in his terms) *wakala*. Maqrizi states that it became a *dar al-wakala* only under the reign of Baybars al-Bunduqdari. This is in sharp contradiction to Ibn Laqlaq's statement that, during the Damietta crusade, Ibn Shukr utilized Dar al-Mulk as a *dar al-wakala* for government brokerage, as opposed to the private *wakalat* and *fanadiq* already established at al-Qahira and al-Fustat (v.i.).[73]

Dar al-wakala *of Ibn Muyassar at al-Fustat*

This was founded by Ibn Muyassar, an immigrant from Caesarea entrusted by Badr al-Jamali with the (lessons in?) oratory (*khitaba*) at the mosque of 'Amr. Ibn Muyassar died in 515/1121–22; no further information is available on the location or usage of this establishment.[74]

Dar al-wakala *at al-Qahira*

Located near Dar al-Darb, west of al-Azhar, this *dar al-wakala* was founded by al-Ma'mun ibn al-Bata'ihi, vizier to the caliph al-Amir, in 516/1122–23. It was established for the use of merchants arriving from Syria, Iraq, and elsewhere, and was, according to Maqrizi, the first *dar al-wakala* in al-Qahira.[75]

Dar al-Tamr (al-Dar al-Fadiliya)

Also known as Sana'at al-Tamr, this foundation (no.92, map 3) was near the site of Joseph's granaries (v.i.) at the Nile shore southwest of Qasr al-Sham'.[76] From Ibn Duqmaq and Maqrizi, we learn that Dar al-Tamr was founded by al-Qadi al-Fadil on land abandoned by the Nile after 500/1106–1107, and that he placed it in *waqf* for the ransoming of Muslim prisoners from the Franks.[77] This *waqf* continued at least until the time of Ibn 'Abd al-Zahir (620–92/1223–92). According to the *qadi* Jamal al-Din ibn Shayth, al-Qadi al-Fadil owned a large *rab'*. When he left on the hajj, he endowed it for the ransoming of prisoners from the Franks.[78]

Following Ibn al-Mutawwaj, quoted by Maqrizi,

> Among the *awqaf* is al-Waqf al-Fadili. This *dar* is known as Sana'at al-Tamr, endowed for the ransom of prisoners from the enemy. [The *dar*] includes storehouses, booths of reeds [*akhsas*], granaries, raised pavilions, and shops, both within it [*bimajaziha*] and outside of it. These numbered twelve shops, five parlors [*maqa'id*], fifty-eight storehouses, fifteen booths of reeds, six halls [*qa'at*], a courtyard [*saha*], six granaries, seventy-five pavilions, and five raised parlors. The income from this ensemble was, at the end of Sha'ban 689 [1290], 136,000 silver dirhams per month.[79]

This *waqf*, although perhaps considerably enlarged by 689/1290, was no doubt of considerable extent under the later Ayyubids. It can, however, only be considered as a massive, complex trading institution functioning as a religious endowment, with no specific attachments to either foreign traders or indigenous government institutes of taxation. Its second appellation—*Sana'at* al-Tamr—is of unknown origin. *Sana'a*, as Casanova points out, generally refers to a naval shipyard, perhaps suggesting one in the immediate area prior to the withdrawal of the Nile.[80] *Al-Tamr* (dates) probably referred to one of the many commodities traded at this multifaceted institution.

Dar al-wakala of Anba Yuhanna

The seventy-fourth patriarch of the Egyptian church, prior to his consecration in 585/1189–90, was known as Abu al-Majd ibn Abi Ghalib ibn Suris. From a wealthy background, "he owned a Dar-al-Wakalah at Misr, in which he traded, buying and selling various sorts of goods; he also had a sugar factory, mills, and other property."[81] No location is given.

Later Ayyubid *wakalat*

As previously stated, the fiscal crisis brought on by the Damietta crusade of 616/1219 fostered the closing of all *dur al-wakalat* and *fanadiq* at al-Fustat and al-Qahira "selling goods such as linen and other than it."[82] Such sales were thenceforth restricted to the "Dar al-Wakalah of the sultan, which was in the Dar al-Mulk, that the brokerage should belong to the sultan."[83] This suggests that several institutions known as *dar al-wakala* existed at al-Qahira/al-Fustat in 616/1219 and that they served the same function as the *fanadiq*, i.e. private institutions not collecting government revenues. Al-Kamil's *dar al-wakala* (the Dar al-Matjar of Maqrizi) was apparently a similar institution, preempted by governmental authorities out of political and economic necessity.

Summary

Of the late Fatimid and Ayyubid *wakalat* studied, only Dar al-Mulk definitely served the function of a *wakala*—a government institution exacting customs duties. All others would appear to serve the same function as *fanadiq*, although this does not categorically rule out their occasional usage as government brokerages or the presence of fiscal agents. The "first *dar al-wakala* at al-Qahira," although established by the vizier al-Bata'ihi, may also have been simply a private *funduq*. Dar al-Tamr, the *waqf* of al-Qadi al-Fadil, was a manifold institution indulging in trade on a strictly local basis.

Granaries and Associated Storages

A customs depot?

The alluvial lands added to the al-Fustat shore after 500/1106 hosted several storehouses—probably all granaries—and, apparently, a customs house, which was established in late Fatimid times and eliminated by the Ayyubids.

The shuwan and the 'granaries of Joseph'

The *shuwan* (singular *shuna*) and the 'granaries of Joseph' (*ahra' Yusuf*; no.94, map 3) were, according to Casanova, located on the Nile near the boat bridge to al-Roda, in the immediate neighborhood of Dar al-Tamr. Following sporadic notations of Ibn Duqmaq, he suggests that the *shuwan* (storehouses, usually for grains) stretched along the Nile immediately north of Joseph's granaries. Given the information compiled, it is questionable that these were in fact separate entities; they were certainly identical by the time of Fourmont's visit (A.D. 1735).[84] Lane–Poole suggests that these were the granaries of Joseph mentioned by Benjamin of Tudela (ca. 566/1170–71).[85] This theory, on closer examination of the text, is untenable; Benjamin almost undoubtedly referred to the pyramids.[86] More convincing evidence that these granaries existed in Saladin's reign is presented by Casanova. He notes, first, that the royal granaries (*ahra' al-sultaniya*) are identical with the 'granaries of

Joseph.'[87] Secondly, Maqrizi refers to "another *sana'a*" (a word normally referring to a naval shipyard), which Casanova believes to be on the site of—or perhaps identical with—these granaries.[88] A list of *mukus*, or nuisance taxes, compiled by al-Qadi al-Fadil for Saladin, mentions this *sana'a* in ten places;[89] its function, Maqrizi states elsewhere, was that of a customs house.[90] Casanova:

> This [*sana'a*] played the role of an entrepot or dock in which various merchandise was deposited: it was, in sum, the *shuna* of the state, as opposed to the *shuwan* located in its neighborhood belonging to private individuals. It is probable that originally it was there that all were required to deposit their merchandise and pay, consequently, duties for entrance, storage, and exit by a fiscal mechanism almost similar to the banalities of our modern age. Once these duties were abolished [by Saladin], one could freely store one's merchandise and build the *shuwan* which extended along the river near the *shuwan*—or granaries of the government.[91]

It would appear, then, that at least some of these storages were established in late Fatimid times for the purpose of collecting customs duties and/or the *mukus*, most of which were abolished by Saladin in 567/1171.[92] While it is apparent that various commodities were stored there for customs purposes, the terms *ahra'* and *shuwan* suggest that these storehouses—if, perhaps, not initially—were primarily granaries and ultimately assumed that function exclusively. That these customs depots were established only in late Fatimid times can be discerned from Maqrizi's statements that 1) the Nile receded in this area only after 500/1106–1107 and 2) *mukus* were reestablished only under Fatimid decline, having been repealed by Ahmad ibn Tulun.[93] Maqrizi relates that the *mukus* were restored by al-Malik al-'Aziz; the effect, if any, this had upon these storehouses is uncertain.[94] It is noteworthy that al-Qadi al-Fadil's *dar*, which also included storehouses and *shuwan*, was in the immediate area; this, however, as *waqf* property, would not have been subject to taxation.

Granaries near Fam al-Khalij

These granaries (*shuwan*; no.93, map 3) were located on the site of al-Madrasa al-Taybarsiya, on alluvial land to the south of what is now the intake tower of al-Ghuri's acqueduct.[95] Ibn Duqmaq, in his description of this *madrasa*, states:

> Its site, during the time of [al-Malik] al-Salih Najm—in 644/1246–47—was occupied by granaries. Grains were stored in them. Then the grains were

removed from them, and it became a storehouse for the sultan's straw. Later yet, part of it was made a stable for animals of the shipyard established for the building of the citadel of the island. All of those activities ceased, and the rent of this area was assigned to al-Dar al-Qutubiya. The vacancy continued until the year 54 of the reign of al-Mu'izz.[96]

Ibn Duqmaq's post-644 (1246–47) date for the founding of the stable of al-Malik al-Salih must be considered erroneous as the construction of the Roda citadel was completed ca. 641/1243–44 (see Chapter Three). His general time sequence is, nonetheless, acceptable.

Summary

While the generally favorable commercial climate under the Ayyubids undoubtedly had significant impact on al-Qahira and al-Fustat, lack of sources prevent us from making an accurate comparison of trading and manufacturing establishments under the Fatimids and Ayyubids. The topographical mainstays remained fundamentally the same: the *qasaba* of al-Qahira, and the mosque of 'Amr and shore areas of al-Fustat. Such extension as took place was primarily limited to that associated with the construction of Qal'at al-Jabal and Qal'at al-Roda, initiated by Saladin and al-Malik al-Salih respectively. These citadels, however, attracted only those markets specifically oriented to servicing the immediate needs of the sultan's military entourage. The market areas of al-Fustat, despite the fire of 564/1168, probably remained relatively unaffected due to two factors: firstly, that they were concentrated around the mosque of 'Amr, which remained relatively unscathed; and secondly, due to the silting of al-Maqs, al-Fustat remained the only viable port for the area.

Chapter Nine

General Conclusions

The topographical history of the Qahira–Fustat complex during the later Fatimid and Ayyubid dynasties was, with few exceptions, one of contraction rather than expansion. Al-Qahira, as first constructed by Jawhar, was a walled administrative/military complex which capped the gradual sprawl of the three previous Islamic capitals of al-Fustat, al-'Askar, and al-Qata'i'. A century later, however, during the reign of al-Mustansir, this urban combination was critically delimited due to recurrent famines and ensuant social unrest. Al-'Askar and al-Qata'i' virtually disappeared; al-Fustat was severely truncated. Badr al-Jamali's rebuilding and limited extension of the al-Qahira enceinte, together with his at least partial opening of the walled city to the general populace, probably only further reduced such population as remained in the ruined areas by allowing their emigration within the city. Attempts at repopulation of the southern areas under the caliphs al-Amir and al-Hafiz were largely limited to Shari' al-A'zam and its eastern extension to al-Fustat. What little real expansion took place under the Fatimids—other than al-Qahira itself—was relegated to the soldiers' ḥarat outside the northern and southern gates of that city.

The al-Fustat fire of 564/1168—allegedly set by Shawar as an anti-Crusader measure—while a reality, was immensely exaggerated by Maqrizi and, except for spot incursions into the still active port areas of al-Fustat, probably did not greatly extend the already ruinous areas perpetrated by the famines under al-Mustansir. Saladin then decided to accept an accomplished fact and planned a quasi-triangular enceinte, based on the citadel, to enclose al-Qahira and the inhabited areas of al-Fustat, regardless of the ruined areas of the previous capitals. This enceinte, never completed, surrounded the most populous districts of the Qahira–Fustat complex, i.e. the original walled city of al-Qahira and the port area of al-Fustat. During the roughly eighty years of Ayyubid rule in Egypt, the bulk of the population remained in these areas. The end of the Ayyubid era boasted considerably less settled territory in al-Qahira/al-Fustat than at the beginning of al-Mustansir's reign. Most of al-'Askar and al-Qata'i', ruined under al-Mustansir, was not seriously repopulated under either the later Fatimids or the Ayyubids. Such destruction as took place during the 564/1168 al-Fustat fire was minimal, and probably was quickly restored. But other catastrophic events had more lasting effects. Saladin's burning of Harat al-Mansuriya and adjacent areas outside Bab Zuwayla in 564/1168 wrought considerable devastation, while what remained—or was rebuilt—of the former soldiers' *harat* north and northeast of Birkat al-Fil was effectively eclipsed during the famine years of 597–98/1201–1202. Al-Qahira and al-Fustat themselves were decimated by the famines of these years, in addition to famines and/or epidemics in 573/1177–78 and 633/1235–36. In addition, the population of al-Maqs, already reduced by the 597–98/1201–1202 famine, must have been further depleted by the effective termination of al-Maqs as a port due to alluviation.

This is not to say that no areas were resettled or newly settled under the Ayyubids. Many 'easterners'—those driven to Egypt by recurring Mongol onslaughts—settled in Husayniya, the surroundings of Birkat al-Fil, and on the banks of the Khalij (south of al-Qahira). New alluvial lands in the area of al-Luq and to the north of al-Maqs were occupied and utilized for agriculture and recreation. These alluvial areas, however, with the exception of Bulaq, remained relatively free of population until the time of the Napoleonic conquest. Other building programs and/or population shifts included a concentration of activity around the tomb of the Imam al-Shafi'i (as reconstructed by al-Malik al-Kamil), and the establishment of supporters and support services near the citadel of Saladin and that of al-Malik al-Salih on al-Roda.

The effects of these latter establishments were somewhat ephemeral. The shift in al-Qarafa toward the tomb of Imam al-Shafi'i left what remained of the greater Qarafa virtually abandoned. The establishment of al-Malik al-Kamil at Qal'at al-Jabal attracted certain markets, germane to military needs, to al-Rumayla, while the construction of the citadel of al-Roda attracted similar ventures in addition to the settlement of amirs along the al-Fustat shore. This, however, was camp following. The real development of Darb al-Ahmar only began under the Bahri Mamluks, while such augmentation as occurred at al-Fustat—in terms of both population and commercial establishments—probably disappeared with the abandonment of the Roda citadel soon after the death of al-Malik al-Salih.

Fatimid al-Qahira originally represented a royal, quasi-sacrosanct complex for the caliphs, their administration and retainers, and some military units. While the city was at least partially opened to others under Badr al-Jamali, the palace complex itself preserved the isolation of the later Fatimid caliphs. With the exception of al-Malik al-Salih, the Ayyubid rulers of Egypt did not appear to require such isolation. Understandably the Fatimid palaces, as remnants of the former regime, were sidestepped, and the Ayyubid sultans lived in Dar al-Wizara until al-Malik al-Kamil occupied the completed citadel. This citadel, however, while obviously offering isolation, was primarily constructed for purposes of defense; the Ayyubids, after all, made no claim to divinity. Only al-Malik al-Salih, in his desire for isolation for himself and his *mamalik*, coupled with a genuine attraction to the Nile, went out of his way to extend himself from the populace in the construction of his Nilotic citadel.

The lion's share of religious and commercial activity of al-Qahira/al-Fustat under the Fatimids took place on the *qasaba* of al-Qahira and in the port section of al-Fustat, districts of major population density. This remained true under the Ayyubids. In both areas markets succeeded markets; new Sunni religious institutions were introduced to obliterate the Fatimid heresy on its own turf. Al-Fustat remained the major port and manufacturing center with its markets, mosques, and *madaris* radiating from the mosque of 'Amr ibn al-'As, its epicenter from the time of the Islamic conquest.

Notes

Chapter One

1   Ravaisse, pp. 415–17.
2   Ibid., pp. 420–80.
3   al-Maqrizi. *al-Mawa'iz*, vol. 1, pp. 348, 383–90.
4   Ibid., vol. 1, pp. 465–68.
5   Nasir-i Khusraw, p. 131.
6   Clerget, pp. 141–42.
7   Ibid., vol. 1, p. 126; Nasir-i Khusraw, p. 132.
8   Lane-Poole, pp. 123–24, 137.
9   Clerget, vol. 1, pp. 114–15.
10   al-Maqrizi. *al-Mawa'iz*, vol. 2, pp. 21–22.
11   Ibid.
12   Clerget, vol. 1, p. 131.
13   al-Maqrizi. *al-Mawa'iz*, vol. 1, pp. 361, 467, 470; vol. 2, pp. 109-111; Clerget, vol. 1, p. 140.
14   al-Maqrizi. *al-Mawa'iz*, vol. 2, pp. 100–101; Salmon, pp. 50, 51, 54–63, 69.
15   al-Maqrizi. *al-Mawa'iz*, vol. 2, p. 136; Lane-Poole, p. 65.
16   Lane-Poole, p. 65.
17   Nasir-i Khusraw, pp. 147–53; al-Muqaddasi, pp. 197–200.
18   Ibn Hawqal, vol. 1, pp. 144–45.
19   al-Muqaddasi, pp. 197–200.
20   al-Maqrizi. *al-Mawa'iz*, vol. 1, pp. 339–40.
21   Nasir-i Khusraw, pp. 145–56.
22   Lane-Poole, p.96.
23   al-Maqrizi. *al-Mawa'iz*, vol. 2, pp. 181–82, 196–97.
24   Ibid., p. 181. Misr (colloquially Masr) was used as a general term for al-Fustat from the earliest Islamic period, both interchangeably and in apposition (Fustat Misr; Misr al-Fustat). In this context, however, Maqrizi refers to the conglomeration of al-Fustat, al-'Askar, and al-Qata'i'. The island of al-Roda, in the medieval period was often referred to simply as al-Jazira.
25   Nasir-i Khusraw, pp. 152–53; Clerget, vol. 1, p. 136.
26   Clerget, vol. 1, p. 135.
27   Ibid.; al-Maqrizi. *al-Mawa'iz*, vol. 2, pp. 443–63.
28   Ibn Hawqal, vol. 1, p. 145; Nasir-i Khusraw, pp. 124–35.
29   Nasir-i Khusraw, pp. 132–36.
30   al-Maqrizi. *al-Mawa'iz*, vol. 1, pp. 365–66.
31   Clerget, vol. 1, map opposite p. 26.
32   Lane-Poole, pp. 146–49; al-Maqrizi. *al-Mawa'iz*, vol. 1, pp. 335–57; Clerget, vol. 1, pp. 137–39.
33   Lane-Poole, pp. 146–49; al-Maqrizi. *al-Mawa'iz*, vol. 1, pp. 337.
34   al-Maqrizi. *al-Mawa'iz*, vol. 1, p. 337.
35   Lane-Poole, pp. 146–49; al-Maqrizi. *al-Mawa'iz*, vol. 1, p. 364; vol. 2, p. 265.
36   Creswell, vol. 1, map opposite p. 19; Ravaisse, plate 2.
37   al-Maqrizi. *al-Mawa'iz*, vol. 1, pp. 337.
38   Ibid., vol. 2, pp. 110–11.
39   Ibid., p. 109.

40   Ibid., vol. 1, p. 305.
41   Salmon, p. 74.
42   Ibid.
43   Ibid., pp. 50–65.
44   al-Maqrizi. *al-Mawa'iz*, vol. 1, p. 305; vol. 2, pp. 20, 100; Salmon, pp. 58–60.
45   al-Maqrizi. *al-Mawa'iz*, vol. 2, pp. 20, 100.
46   Ibid., p. 20; Salmon, pp. 58–59.
47   al-Maqrizi. *al-Mawa'iz*, vol. 2, p. 20.
48   Ibid., p. 100.
49   Clerget, vol. 1, p. 139.
50   Kubiak, pp. 51–64.

Chapter Two

1   Ehrenkreutz, pp. 13–18.
2   Ibid., pp. 233–38.
3   Cahen, p. 799.
4   Ibid.
5   Ibid., pp. 803–804.
6   Ibid., p. 797.
7   Ibid., p. 802.
8   Ibid., p. 798.
9   Ibid., p. 799.
10   Ibid., p. 802.
11   Ibid., p. 803.
12   Ibid., p. 800.
13   Ehrenkreutz, pp. 101–105.
14   Cahen, p. 800.
15   Ibid., p. 801.

Chapter Three

1   Casanova. "Citadelle," pp. 554–62.
2   Ibid., pp. 535–51.
3   al-Maqrizi. *al-Mawa'iz*, vol. 1, p. 364.
4   Ibid., vol. 2, pp. 2–17.
5   Ibid., pp. 2–3; Ehrenkreutz, pp. 76–79.
6   al-Maqrizi. *al-Mawa'iz*, vol. 1, p. 364.
7   Ibid., p. 496. "Ghuzz" here probably refers to the Turkish soldiery in the employ of Saladin.
8   Ibid.
9   Ibid., p. 384; Casanova. "Fatimides."
10   'Abd al-Latif al-Baghdadi, pp. 360–74.
11   Ibid., pp. 410–11, 420.
12   al-Maqrizi. *al-Mawa'iz*, vol. 1, p. 366.
13   Ibid.
14   Ibid., p. 367.
15   al-Maqrizi. *al-Mawa'iz*, vol. 2, p. 21.
16   Ibid., vol. 1, pp. 364–65; vol. 2, pp. 21, 93, 111, 197.
17   Ibid., vol. 1, pp.104–105.
18   Ibid., vol. 2, p. 124.
19   Ibid., p. 125; Ibn Sa'id al-Maghribi, p. 25.
20   al-Maqrizi. *al-Mawa'iz*, vol. 2, p. 129.
21   Ibid., p. 130–31, 185.

22   Ibid., pp. 130–31, 185.
23   Ibid., pp. 117–18.
24   Ibid., vol. 1, pp.345–46.
25   Ibid., vol. 2, pp. 117–18.
26   Ibid., p. 117.
27   Ibid., pp. 118, 147, 198.
28   Ibid., pp. 117–18, 162.
29   Ibid., p. 198.
30   Ibid., p. 118.
31   Ibid., pp. 120, 198.
32   Ibid., p. 120.
33   Ibid., pp. 120–21.
34   Ibid., p. 119.
35   Ibid.
36   Ibid., p. 120.
37   Ibid., pp. 116, 119–20.
38   al-Maqrizi. *Suluk,* Ziyadah, vol. 1, p. 120; Blochet, vol. 9, pp. 75–76.
39   al-Maqrizi. *Suluk,* Blochet, vol. 9, p. 76. On *muhtasib,* see Glossary.
40   Ibid., p. 93.
41   al-Maqrizi. *al-Mawa'iz,* vol. 2, p. 143.
42   Ibid., vol. 1, p. 368.
43   Ibid., vol. 2, pp. 19, 110.
44   Ibid., vol. 1, p. 364; Casanova. "Citadelle," pp. 594–95; Qalqashandi, vol. 3, pp. 373–74.
45   al-Maqrizi. *al-Mawa'iz,* vol. 2, p. 136.
46   Ibid.
47   Ibid., p. 110.
48   Salmon, pp. 65-69, plate 2; Maqrizi. *al-Mawa'iz,* vol. 1, pp. 364–65; vol. 2, pp. 134, 161; *History of the Patriarchs of the Egyptian Church,* vol. 4, part 2, p. 220.
49   'Abd al-Latif al-Baghdadi, pp. 373–374, 410–11.
50   al-Maqrizi. *al-Mawa'iz,* vol. 2, p. 133.
51   Ibid., vol. 1, p. 367; Ibn Sa'id al-Maghribi, p. 22.
52   al-Idrisi, vol. 1, pp. 301–304.
53   Benjamin of Tudela, vol. 1, pp. 147–53, cf. Adler edition, p. 9.
54   Casanova. "Foustat," plate 3.
55   Abu Salih al-Armani, pp. 90–91.
56   Ibid., pp. 94–95.
57   Ibid., pp. 102–106.
58   Ibid., pp. 111–12.
59   Ibid., pp. 122–24.
60   Ibid., pp. 127–35.
61   al-Maqrizi. *al-Mawa'iz,* vol. 2, pp. 159, 185.
62   Ibid., p. 153; Ibn Duqmaq, vol. 4, p. 56.
63   Ibn Jubayr. *Travels,* pp. 46–47.
64   Ibn Duqmaq, vol. 4, pp. 109–110; al-Maqrizi. *al-Mawa'iz,* vol 2, pp. 181–82.
65   al-Maqrizi. *Suluk,* Blochet, vol. 9, p. 121.
66   al-Maqrizi. *al-Mawa'iz,* vol. 1, pp. 342, 345, 367.
67   Ibid., p. 342; Ibn Duqmaq, vol. 4, p. 108.
68   al-Maqrizi. *al-Mawa'iz,* vol. 1, pp. 341–42.

Chapter Four

1   Casanova. "Citadelle;" Creswell, vol. 2.
2   Casanova. "Citadelle," pp. 535–53.

3   Creswell, vol. 1, map opposite p. 30. This Bab al-Jadid should not be confused with the free-standing gate of the same name, constructed by al-Hakim to the south of Bab Zuwayla.
4   al-Maqrizi. *al-Mawa'iz*, vol. 1, pp. 379–80. Maqrizi's statement "the joining of the wall of the citadel with that of Misr did not occur" is misleading. Maqrizi obviously meant al-Qahira rather than Misr (al-Fustat). The "tower at Kawm al-Ahmar" refers to Bab al-Qantara.
5   Casanova. "Citadelle," pp. 535–38; al-Maqrizi. *Suluk*, Blochet, vol. 8, p. 525.
6   al-Maqrizi. *al-Mawa'iz*, vol. 2, p. 123, 283–84; Casanova. "Citadelle," p. 539; Creswell, vol. 2, p. 59.
7   Casanova. "Citadelle," pp. 541–44; Creswell, vol. 1, map opposite p. 30, vol. 2, pp. 58–59.
8   Survey of Egypt, Sheet 2.
9   Casanova. "Foustat," Plan 1.
10   Ibid., pp. 51–52; Casanova. "Citadelle," pp. 545–47; Creswell, vol. 2, pp. 55–58.
11   al-Maqrizi. *al-Mawa'iz*, vol. 1, p. 347; Casanova. "Foustat," pp. 3–4, Plan 1; Creswell, vol. 2, p. 59.
12   Casanova. "Foustat," pp. 72–77, Plan 1; Ibn Duqmaq *al-Intisar*, vol. 5, p. 40; al-Maqrizi. *al-Mawa'iz*, vol. 1, pp. 344, 347.
13   A possible exception to this were the seemingly jerry-built—and unfinished—walls constructed by Shawar in 564/1168 against the impending invasion of Amalric, as described by Maqrizi in *Ittiaz al-Hunafa'*, Cairo 1947, vol 3, page 296. These walls, not completed on the river side, included eight gates, most of which had disappeared by 650/1252–53. Bab Misr was not mentioned among these gates, nor, as near as can be determined, could it have been included in these fortifications, constructed farther to the south.
14   al-Maqrizi. *al-Mawa'iz*, vol. 1, p. 380.
15   Creswell, vol. 2, pp. 58–59.
16   al-Maqrizi. *Suluk*, Ziyadah, part 1, p. 150; Blochet, vol. 9, p. 108.
17   *H.P.E.C.*, vol. 4, part 1, pp. 41, 56–57; part 2, pp. 153, 166, 174.
18   Casanova. "Citadelle," pp. 555–63.
19   al-Maqrizi. *al-Mawa'iz*, vol. 2, p. 203.
20   Creswell, vol. 2, pp. 5–6.
21   Ibid., p. 38; Casanova. "Citadelle," pp. 569–84.
22   al-Maqrizi. *al-Mawa'iz*, vol. 2, p. 204.
23   Casanova. "Citadelle," p. 586.
24   Ibid., pp. 588–89.
25   Ibid., pp. 574–75.
26   Ibid., pp. 585, 588.
27   al-Maqrizi. *al-Mawa'iz*, vol. 2, p. 204; Ibn Jubayr. *Travels*, p. 43; *Rihla*, p. 25.
28   *H.P.E.C.*, vol. 3, part 2, p. 150.
29   al-Maqrizi. *al-Mawa'iz*, vol. 1, p. 111.
30   'Abd al-Latif al-Baghdadi, pp. 171–72.
31   Ibn Jubayr. *Travels*, p. 43; *Voyages*, vol. 1, p. 63.
32   Casanova. "Citadelle," pp. 541–42.
33   Creswell, vol. 2, p. 5.
34   Casanova. "Citadelle," pp. 571–73.
35   al-Maqrizi. *Suluk*, Blochet, vol. 9, p. 141.
36   Creswell, vol. 2, p. 39; Casanova. "Citadelle," pp. 535–37, 577.
37   Creswell, vol. 2, p. 39.
38   Casanova. "Citadelle," p. 577.
39   Creswell, vol. 2, p. 38.
40   Casanova. "Citadelle," pp. 595–98; al-Maqrizi. *al-Mawa'iz*, pp. 231–32.
41   Creswell, vol. 2, pp. 14–16, 38.

42   Casanova. "Citadelle," p. 592.
43   Ibid., pp. 593–94.
44   Ibid., p. 594.
45   Ibid.
46   Ibid., p. 595.
47   al-Maqrizi. *al-Mawa'iz*, vol. 1, pp. 408–409.
48   Ibid., p. 409.
49   al-Maqrizi *Suluk*, Ziyadah, vol. 1, part 1, pp. 232–33; Casanova. "Citadelle," p. 598.
50   Casanova. "Citadelle," p. 599.
51   Ibid., p. 598–99.
52   al-Maqrizi. *al-Mawa'iz*, vol. 2, p. 366.
53   Ibid.
54   Casanova. "Citadelle," p. 598.
55   Ibid., p. 595.
56   Ibid., p. 602.
57   Ibn Jubayr. *Travels*, p. 45.
58   'Abd al-Latif al-Baghdadi, p. 172.
59   Ibid., p. 213, footnote 6.
60   al-Maqrizi. *al-Mawa'iz*, vol. 2, pp. 151–52.
61   *H.P.E.C.*, vol 4, part 1, p. 38; vol. 4, part 2, pp. 219, 279–80.
62   al-Maqrizi. *al-Mawa'iz*, vol. 2, pp. 184–85.
63   Ibid., p. 183.
64   Ibid.
65   Ibid.
66   Ibid., pp. 183–84.
67   Ibid., p. 184.
68   Ibn Duqmaq, vol. 4, p. 110.
69   al-Maqrizi. *Suluk*, Ziyadah, vol 1, part 2, p. 301.
70   Ibn Wasil, vol. 5, (Cairo: 1977), p. 278.

Chapter Five

1   al-Maqrizi. *al-Mawa'iz*, vol. 1, p. 384.
2   Ibid., p. 364.
3   Ibid., p. 381.
4   Ravaisse, plate 3.
5   al-Maqrizi. *al-Mawa'iz*, vol. 1, p. 438.
6   Ibid.
7   Ibid., p. 461.
8   Ibid., pp. 406, 407, 445; Clerget, vol. 1, map, p. 132.
9   *H.P.E.C.*, vol. 4, part 1, p. 88.
10   al-Maqrizi. *al-Mawa'iz*, vol. 1, p. 464.
11   Ibid., vol. 2, pp. 187–88.
12   Ibid., p. 188.
13   Ibid., vol. 1, pp. 423–24; vol. 2, p. 188; Clerget, vol. 1, map, p. 132.
14   al-Maqrizi. *al-Mawa'iz*, vol. 2, p. 188; Clerget, vol. 2, p. 145.
15   al-Maqrizi. *al-Mawa'iz*, vol. 2, p. 188.
16   Ibid., p. 71.
17   Ibid., vol. 1, p. 404.
18   al-Qalqashandi, vol. 3, p. 355.
19   Abu Salih, pp. 132–33.
20   Salmon, p. 67; al-Maqrizi. *al-Mawa'iz*, vol. 2, p. 134.
21   Abu Salih, p. 92; al-Maqrizi. *al-Mawa'iz*, vol. 1, p. 467; Ibn Jubayr. *Travels*, p. 46.

22 Ibn Wasil, vol. 5, p. 278.
23 Ibn Duqmaq, vol. 4, pp. 30–31; Casanova. "Foustat," p. 78.
24 al-Maqrizi. *al-Mawa'iz*, vol. 2, pp. 133–34; Salmon, pp. 79–81.

Chapter Six

1 al-Maqrizi. *al-Mawa'iz*, vol. 1, p. 343.
2 Ibid., p. 344.
3 Ibid., vol. 2, p. 124.
4 Ibid., pp. 196–97.
5 Clerget, vol. 1, p. 25.
6 'Abd al-Latif al-Baghdadi, p. 374.
7 al-Maqrizi. *al-Mawa'iz*, vol. 1, pp. 344–45.
8 Ibid., p. 345.
9 Ibid., p. 347.
10 Ibid., vol. 2, p. 283.
11 Ibid., vol. 1, pp. 345–46.
12 Clerget, vol. 1, pp. 24–31; *Description de l'Egypte: Etat Moderne*, vol. 1, plate 26.
13 al-Maqrizi. *al-Mawa'iz*, vol. 2, pp. 153, 158–59; Ibn Duqmaq, vol. 4, p. 56.
14 Clerget, vol. 2, pp. 176–78; Abu Salih, pp. 171–73; Ibn Duqmaq, vol. 4, p. 120.
15 Clerget, vol. 2, pp. 65–66.
16 al-Maqrizi. *al-Mawa'iz*, vol. 2, p. 162.
17 Ibid., pp. 144, 163.
18 *H.P.E.C.*, vol. 4, part 1, pp. 96–98.
19 al-Maqrizi. *al-Mawa'iz*, vol. 2, pp. 144, 163.
20 Ibid., p. 170.
21 *H.P.E.C.*, vol. 4, part 1, p. 38.
22 al-Maqrizi. *al-Mawa'iz*, vol. 2, p. 183; *H.P.E.C.*, vol. 4, part 2, p. 279.
23 al-Maqrizi. *al-Mawa'iz*, vol. 2, p. 170.
24 Ibid., p. 147.
25 Ibid.
26 Ibid., p. 146; al-Maqrizi. *Suluk*, Blochet, vol. 10, p. 343; *Description de l'Egypte: Etat Moderne*, vol. 1, plate 26, Y-14.
27 *Répertoire Chronologique d'Epigraphie Arabe*, vol. 9, 1937, p. 216.
28 Qalqashandi, vol. 3, pp. 373–74.
29 al-Suyuti, Jalal al-Din, vol. 2, p. 33.
30 al-Maqrizi. *al-Mawa'iz*, vol. 2, p. 133; Salmon, plate 2.
31 Raymond. "Bains," pp. 353–55.
32 Ibid.
33 Ibid., p. 356.
34 Ibid., p. 357.
35 Ibid., p. 350; al-Maqrizi. *al-Mawa'iz*, vol. 2, p. 80.
36 al-Maqrizi. *al-Mawa'iz*, vol. 2, p. 81; Raymond. "Bains," p. 348.
37 al-Maqrizi. *al-Mawa'iz*, vol. 2, p. 81.
38 Ibid.; Raymond. "Bains," p. 352.
39 al-Maqrizi. *al-Mawa'iz*, vol. 2, p. 82.
40 Raymond. "Bains," p. 349.
41 Ibid., p. 351; al-Maqrizi. *al-Mawa'iz*, vol. 2, p. 80.
42 al-Maqrizi. *al-Mawa'iz*, vol. 2, p. 80; Raymond. "Bains," p. 353.
43 al-Maqrizi. *al-Mawa'iz*, vol. 2, pp. 83–84; Raymond. "Bains," p. 350.
44 al-Maqrizi. *al-Mawa'iz*, vol. 2, pp. 83, 365; Raymond. "Bains," p. 349.
45 al-Maqrizi. *al-Mawa'iz*, vol. 2, p. 82; Raymond. "Bains," p. 351.
46 al-Maqrizi. *al-Mawa'iz*, vol. 2, p. 83; Raymond. "Bains," p. 351.
47 al-Maqrizi. *al-Mawa'iz*, vol. 2, p. 81; Raymond. "Bains," p. 353.

48 al-Maqrizi. *al-Mawa'iz*, vol. 2, pp. 81, 147; Raymond. "Bains," p. 353.
49 al-Maqrizi. *al-Mawa'iz*, vol. 1, p. 373; Raymond. "Bains," p. 349.
50 al-Maqrizi. *al-Mawa'iz*, vol. 2, p. 85; Raymond. "Bains," p. 352.
51 al-Maqrizi. *al-Mawa'iz*, vol. 2, p. 80; Raymond. "Bains," p. 350.
52 al-Maqrizi. *al-Mawa'iz*, vol. 2, pp. 85-86; Raymond. "Bains," p. 351.
53 al-Maqrizi. *al-Mawa'iz*, vol. 2, p. 84; Raymond. "Bains," p. 351.
54 al-Maqrizi. *al-Mawa'iz*, vol. 2, p. 84; Raymond. "Bains," p. 349.
55 al-Maqrizi. *al-Mawa'iz*, vol. 2, p. 81; Raymond. "Bains," p. 350.
56 al-Maqrizi. *al-Mawa'iz*, vol. 2, p. 80; Raymond. "Bains," p. 352.
57 al-Maqrizi. *al-Mawa'iz*, vol. 2, p. 81; Raymond. "Bains," p. 352.
58 al-Maqrizi. *al-Mawa'iz*, vol. 2, p. 83; Raymond. "Bains," p. 350.
59 al-Maqrizi. *al-Mawa'iz*, vol. 2, pp. 79-86; Ibn Duqmaq, vol. 4, pp. 104–107.
60 Ibn Jubayr. *Travels*, p. 40.
61 al-Maqrizi. *al-Mawa'iz*, vol. 2, p. 364; Ibn Duqmaq, vol. 4, p. 104.
62 Ibn Duqmaq, vol. 4, pp. 104, 106.
63 Ibid.; Casanova. "Foustat," pp. 20–21, 26.
64 Ibn Duqmaq, vol. 4, p. 104.
65 al-Maqrizi. *al-Mawa'iz*, vol. 2, p. 365.
66 Casanova. "Foustat," pp. 12–13.
67 Ibn Duqmaq, vol. 4, p. 104.
68 al-Maqrizi. *al-Mawa'iz*, vol. 2, p. 85.
69 Casanova. "Foustat," p. 78.
70 Raymond. "Porteurs d'Eau," pp. 183–202.
71 Ibid., p. 184.
72 al-Maqrizi. *al-Mawa'iz*, vol. 1, pp. 339–40; 'Abd al-Latif al-Baghdadi, p. 295.
73 al-Maqrizi. *al-Mawa'iz*, Ziyadah, vol. 1, part 1, pp. 69–70.
74 Ibid., p. 175.
75 Ibid., p. 250.
76 'Abd al-Latif al-Baghdadi, pp. 297–99.

Chapter Seven

1   Cresswell, vol. 2, p. 105.
2   Lapidus, original text, p. 7.
3   al-Maqrizi. *al-Mawa'iz*, vol. 2, p. 343.
4   Ibid.
5   Pedersen, pp. 327–29; al-Mawardi, pp. 215–18.
6   Ibn Duqmaq, vol. 4, p. 78.
7   Pedersen, p. 328; Nasir-i Khusraw, p. 134ff., 147.
8   al-Maqrizi. *al-Mawa'iz*, vol. 2, p. 275.
9   Ibid., pp. 275–76.
10 Ibn Jubayr. *Travels*, pp. 42–47.
11 Lapidus, p. 284 (cf. original manuscript).
12 Ibid., p. 283.
13 al-Maqrizi. *al-Mawa'iz*, vol. 2, p. 363.
14 According to Qalqashandi, the Qamhiya *madrasa* was earlier. See vol. 3, p. 343; al-Maqrizi. *al-Mawa'iz*, vol. 2, p. 363.
15 al-Maqrizi. *al-Mawa'iz*, vol. 2, pp. 363–64; Ibn Duqmaq, vol. 4, p. 93; Qalqashandi, vol. 3, p. 343.
16 al-Maqrizi. *al-Mawa'iz*, vol..2, p. 364; Ibn Duqmaq, vol. 4, p. 95; Qalqashandi, vol. 3, p. 343.
17 al-Maqrizi. *al-Mawa'iz*, vol. 2, pp. 363–64.
18 Ibid., p. 400.
19 Ibn Jubayr. *Travels*, p. 40. See also *Rihla*, pp. 22–23.

20 al-Maqrizi. *al-Mawa'iz*, vol. 2, p. 365.
21 Ibid., vol. 1, p. 464; vol. 2, p. 104; Raymond and Wiet, plan 2.
22 al-Maqrizi. *al-Mawa'iz*, vol. 1, p. 427.
23 Ibid., pp. 427–28.
24 Ibn Jubayr. *Travels*, pp. 36–37.
25 Berchem, pp. 100–102.
26 al-Maqrizi. *al-Mawa'iz*, vol. 2, p. 364.
27 Ibn Duqmaq, vol. 4, p. 98; Casanova. "Foustat," pp. 132–33, 140.
28 Casanova. "Foustat," pp. 134–35, 140–41.
29 al-Maqrizi. *al-Mawa'iz*, vol. 2, pp. 365–66.
30 Clerget, vol. 1, p. 129.
31 Qalqashandi, vol. 3, p. 343; Casanova. "Foustat," pp. 96–99.
32 Ibn Duqmaq, vol. 4, pp. 93–94.
33 Abu Shamah, part 2, p. 487.
34 al-Maqrizi. *al-Mawa'iz*, vol. 2, p. 364.
35 Ibid., pp. 184–85.
36 Humphreys, pp. 48–50.
37 al-Maqrizi. *al-Mawa'iz*, vol. 2, p. 368.
38 Ibid., p. 14.
39 Ibid., p. 366.
40 Ibid., p. 371.
41 Humphreys, pp. 140, 145, 437–38.
42 Raymond and Wiet, plan 2, K8.
43 al-Maqrizi. *al-Mawa'iz*, vol. 2, p. 367.
44 Raymond and Wiet, pp. 183–84, 230; plan 3, F6.
45 al-Maqrizi. *al-Mawa'iz*, vol. 2, p. 368.
46 Ibid.
47 Lapidus, p. 283.
48 Laoust, pp. 126–27.
49 Lapidus, p. 283.
50 al-Maqrizi. *al-Mawa'iz*, vol. 2, p. 390.
51 Creswell, vol. 2, p. 105; Lane-Poole. *Cairo*, p. 318.
52 al-Maqrizi. *al-Mawa'iz*, vol. 2, p. 365.
53 Ibn Duqmaq, vol. 4, p. 98.
54 Casanova. "Foustat," p. 211.
55 al-Maqrizi. *al-Mawa'iz*, vol. 2, p. 378.
56 Ibid., p. 37.
57 Creswell, vol. 2, p. 105.
58 al-Maqrizi. *al-Mawa'iz*, vol. 2, p. 373.
59 Ibid., p. 374.
60 Clerget, vol. 1, p. 129.
61 al-Maqrizi. *al-Mawa'iz*, vol. 2, p. 375.
62 Ibid., p. 378.
63 Ibid., pp. 367–68.
64 Ibid., p. 42; Raymond and Wiet, pp. 200–201.
65 al-Maqrizi. *al-Mawa'iz*, vol. 2, p. 365.
66 Ibn Duqmaq, vol. 4, p. 92.
67 al-Maqrizi. *al-Mawa'iz*, vol. 2, p. 374.
68 Ibid., pp. 374–75.
69 al-Maqrizi. *Suluk*, Ziyadah, vol. 1, part 2, p. 350.
70 *H.P.E.C.*, vol. 4, part 2, p. 246.
71 Creswell, vol. 2, pp. 94–100.
72 al-Maqrizi. *al-Mawa'iz*, vol. 2, p. 375.
73 Ibid., p. 365.

74 Ibn Duqmaq, vol. 4, p. 96.
75 Casanova. "Foustat," pp. 148–49
76 Ibn Jubayr. *Voyages*, part 1, pp. 78–82.
77 al-Maqrizi. *al-Mawa'iz*, vol. 2, p. 368.
78 Creswell, vol. 2, pp. 129–31.
79 Ibn Jubayr. *Travels*, p. 45.
80 al-Maqrizi. *al-Mawa'iz*, vol. 2, p. 275; Creswell, vol. 1, p. 37.
81 al-Maqrizi. *al-Mawa'iz*, vol. 2, p. 278; cf. Qalqashandi, vol. 3, pp. 360–61.
82 Survey, sheet 1, no. 477.
83 al-Maqrizi. *al-Mawa'iz*, vol. 2, pp. 319–20.
84 Ibid., p. 251; cf. Ibn Duqmaq, vol. 4, p. 69.
85 Ibn Jubayr. *Travels*, p. 42.
86 al-Maqrizi. *al-Mawa'iz*, vol. 2, pp. 255–56.
87 Ibid., vol. 1, pp. 341–42.
88 Ibn Jubayr. *Travels*, p. 44.
89 al-Maqrizi. *al-Mawa'iz*, vol. 2, p. 283.
90 Ibid., pp. 283–84.
91 Ibid., p. 283.
92 Ibid.
93 Casanova. "Citadelle," p. 539.
94 al-Maqrizi. *al-Mawa'iz*, vol. 2, pp. 312–13.
95 Ibid., p. 296.
96 Ibid., p. 318.
97 Ibid., pp. 319–20, 444.
98 Ibn Hawqal, p. 145.
99 al-Maqrizi. *al-Mawa'iz*, vol. 2, p. 297.
100 Ibn Duqmaq, vol. 4, pp. 115–116.
101 al-Maqrizi. *al-Mawa'iz*, vol. 2, pp. 290, 297.
102 *H.P.E.C.*, vol. 4, part 2, pp. 280–81.
103 Ibid., p. 287.
104 al-Maqrizi. *al-Mawa'iz*, vol. 2, p. 297.
105 Casanova. "Citadelle," p. 535.
106 Creswell, vol. 2, pp. 84–87.
107 Ibid., p. 85; al-Maqrizi. *al-Mawa'iz*, vol. 2, p. 297.
108 al-Maqrizi. *al-Mawa'iz*, vol. 2, pp. 296–97.
109 Ibid., pp. 412–13.
110 Ibid., p. 411.
111 Ibid., vol. 1, pp. 345–46; vol. 2, p. 298.
112 Casanova. "Citadelle," p. 595.
113 al-Maqrizi. *al-Mawa'iz*, vol. 2, pp. 367–68.
114 Ibid., p. 413.
115 Ibid., p. 133.
116 Ibid., pp. 414, 427.
117 Casanova. "Foustat," pp. xxxiv–xxxv.
118 Qalqashandi, vol. 3, p. 364.
119 al-Maqrizi. *al-Mawa'iz*, vol. 2, p. 415.
120 Survey, sheet 1, no. 31.
121 Ibn Khallikan, vol. 2, p. 520.
122 al-Maqrizi. *al-Mawa'iz*, vol. 2, p. 104.
123 Ibid., pp. 367–68. *Kitab sabil*, presumably the same as *sabil-kuttab*, suggests a combination of a school and public fountain. If this interpretation is correct, it is the earliest instance known to me in Cairo.
124 Ibid., p. 434.
125 Ibn Duqmaq, vol. 4, p. 103.

126   Casanova. "Foustat," pp. 78, 86.
127   al-Maqrizi. *al-Mawa'iz*, vol. 2, p. 432.
128   Lapidus, p. 20.
129   al-Maqrizi. *al-Mawa'iz*, vol. 1, p. 407.
130   Qalqashandi, vol. 3, p. 375.
131   Ibn Jubayr. *Travels*, pp. 43–44.
132   al-Maqrizi. *al-Mawa'iz*, vol. 2, p. 406; cf. Ibn Duqmaq, vol. 4, p. 99.
133   al-Maqrizi. *al-Mawa'iz*, vol. 2, pp. 442–43.
134   Ibid., p. 444.
135   Ibn Jubayr. *Travels*, pp. 39–42; *Ribla*, pp. 20–24. I have deleted from Ibn Jubayr's text an exhaustive list of notables buried at al-Qarafa, irrelevant here.
136   Yaqut al-Rumi, vol. 4, p. 48.
137   al-Maqrizi. *al-Mawa'iz*, vol. 2, p. 444.
138   Ibid., pp. 460–61.
139   Ibid.
140   Massignon, p. 43.
141   al-Maqrizi. *ai-Mawa'iz*, vol. 2, p. 454.
142   Massignon, p. 66.
143   Ibid., p. 62.
144   al-Maqrizi. *al-Mawa'iz*, vol. 2, pp. 444–45, 461–62; *Suluk*, Blochet, vol. 9, pp. 99, 149.
145   Creswell, vol. 2, p. 79.
146   Massignon, p. 61.
147   Ibid., pp. 54–55.
148   Creswell, vol. 2, pp. 88–94
149   Massignon, p. 66.
150   Abu Salih, pp. 91, 107, 114; Ibn Duqmaq, vol. 4, p. 108.
151   Abu Salih, pp. 135–36.
152   Ibid., pp. 87–91, 94–95, 104–106, 111–12, 116, 119–24.
153   Ibid., pp. 95, 127, 174–75.
154   Ibid., pp. 11–13, 25–26, 91–92, 131–32.
155   *H.P.E.C.*, vol. 4, part 2, pp. 158, 222, 280–81, 287.
156   Benjamin of Tudela, p. 147.
157   Lapidus, p. 286, footnote 10.
158   Ibn Jubayr. *Travels*, pp. 42, 44–45.
159   *H.P.E.C.*, vol. 4, part 2, p. 224.

Chapter Eight

1   al-Maqrizi. *al-Mawa'iz*, vol. 1, pp. 337, 364; vol. 2, p. 265.
2   Clerget, vol. 2, pp. 140–50; *H.P.E.C.*, vol. 4, part 2, pp. 279–80; Ibn Sa'id, p. 27.
3   Raymond, André and Gaston Wiet. *Les marchés du Caire*, Cairo: 1979.
4   al-Maqrizi. *al-Mawa'iz*, vol. 2, p. 94; Raymond and Wiet, p. 94.
5   al-Maqrizi. *al-Mawa'iz*, vol. 2, p. 100; Raymond and Wiet, pp. 177–80.
6   al-Maqrizi. *al-Mawa'iz*, vol. 2, p. 104; Raymond and Wiet, pp. 200–201.
7   al-Maqrizi. *al-Mawa'iz*, vol. 2, p. 104; Raymond and Wiet, pp. 200–201.
8   al-Maqrizi. *al-Mawa'iz*, vol. 2, p. 96; Raymond and Wiet, pp. 155–56.
9   al-Maqrizi. *al-Mawa'iz*, vol. 2, p. 297; Raymond and Wiet, pp. 163–64.
10   al-Maqrizi. *al-Mawa'iz*, vol. 2, p. 102; Raymond and Wiet, p. 189.
11   al-Maqrizi. *al-Mawa'iz*, vol. 2, pp. 101–102; Raymond and Wiet, pp. 186–87.
12   al-Maqrizi. *al-Mawa'iz*, vol. 2, pp. 104–105; Raymond and Wiet, pp. 201–202.
13   al-Maqrizi. *al-Mawa'iz*, vol. 2, p. 31.
14   Ibid., pp. 95–96; Raymond and Wiet, pp. 151–55.
15   al-Maqrizi. *al-Mawa'iz*, vol. 2, p. 95; Raymond and Wiet, pp. 149–50.

16 al-Maqrizi. *al-Mawa'iz*, vol. 2, p. 97; Raymond and Wiet, pp. 160–61.
17 al-Maqrizi. *al-Mawa'iz*, vol. 2, p. 101; Raymond and Wiet, pp. 183–84.
18 al-Maqrizi. *al-Mawa'iz*, vol. 2, pp. 97–98; Raymond and Wiet, pp. 165–66.
19 al-Maqrizi. *al-Mawa'iz*, vol. 1, p. 374; vol. 2, pp. 98–99; Raymond and Wiet, pp. 169–74.
20 al-Maqrizi. *al-Mawa'iz*, vol. 2, pp. 28–29, 97.
21 Ibid., p. 106; Raymond and Wiet, p. 208.
22 al-Maqrizi. *al-Mawa'iz*, vol. 2, pp. 101, 378; Raymond and Wiet, pp. 184–86.
23 al-Maqrizi. al-Mawa'iz, vol. 2, p. 106; Raymond and Wiet, pp. 206–207.
24 al-Maqrizi. *al-Mawa'iz*, vol. 2, p. 106; Raymond and Wiet, pp. 206–207.
25 al-Maqrizi. *al-Mawa'iz*, vol. 2, p. 102; Raymond and Wiet, pp. 187–88.
26 *H.P.E.C.*, vol. 4, part 2, p. 242.
27 Raymond and Wiet, pp. 160–61.
28 Cited by Raymond and Wiet, p. 19.
29 Ibid., p. 112; al-Maqrizi. *al-Mawa'iz*, vol. 2, p. 86.
30 Raymond and Wiet, p. 113; al-Maqrizi. *al-Mawa'iz*, vol. 2, p. 86.
31 Raymond and Wiet, p. 129; al-Maqrizi. *al-Mawa'iz*, vol. 2, pp. 90–91; *Description de l'Egypte: Etat Moderne*, vol. 1, plate 26.
32 Raymond and Wiet, p. 124; al-Maqrizi. *al-Mawa'iz*, vol. 2, p. 89.
33 Raymond and Wiet, pp. 112–13; al-Maqrizi. *al-Mawa'iz*, vol. 2, p. 86.
34 Raymond and Wiet, p. 122; al-Maqrizi. *al-Mawa'iz*, vol. 2, p. 89.
35 al-Maqrizi. *al-Mawa'iz*, vol. 2, p. 87; Raymond and Wiet, p. 115.
36 al-Maqrizi. *al-Mawa'iz*, vol. 2, pp. 87–89; Raymond and Wiet, pp. 116, 120–22; Humphreys, pp. 93, 110–11, 117–18.
37 al-Maqrizi. *al-Mawa'iz*, vol. 2, p. 87; Raymond and Wiet, p. 115.
38 al-Maqrizi. *al-Mawa'iz*, vol. 2, p. 87; Raymond and Wiet, p. 116.
39 al-Maqrizi. *al-Mawa'iz*, vol. 2, p. 89; Raymond and Wiet, p. 125.
40 al-Maqrizi. *al-Mawa'iz*, vol. 2, pp. 89–90; Raymond and Wiet, pp. 125–26.
41 al-Maqrizi. *al-Mawa'iz*, vol. 2, pp. 89–90; Raymond and Wiet, pp. 125–28.
42 Raymond and Wiet, pp. 2–15; 'Abd al-Latif al-Baghdadi, pp. 303–304.
43 al-Maqrizi. *al-Mawa'iz*, vol. 2, p. 93; Raymond and Wiet, pp. 138–39.
44 al-Maqrizi. *al-Mawa'iz*, vol. 2, p. 93; Raymond and Wiet, p. 138.
45 al-Maqrizi. *al-Mawa'iz*, vol. 2, p. 92; Raymond and Wiet, p. 133–34.
46 al-Maqrizi. *al-Mawa'iz*, vol. 2, p. 92; Raymond and Wiet, pp. 134–35; cf. Chapter Seven, al-Madrasa al-Masruriya.
47 Raymond and Wiet, p. 134, footnote 1; al-Maqrizi. *al-Mawa'iz*, vol. 2, p. 378; see Chapter Seven.
48 Raymond and Wiet, pp. 139–40; al-Maqrizi. *al-Mawa'iz*, vol. 2, p. 93.
49 Raymond and Wiet, p. 139, footnote 3.
50 al-Maqrizi. *al-Mawa'iz*, vol. 2, p. 375; Casanova. "Foustat," p. xxxv, footnote 3.
51 al-Maqrizi. *al-Mawa'iz*, vol. 2, p. 375.
52 Ibid., vol. 1, p. 364.
53 Scanlon. "Preliminary Report 1965," part 1, part 2.
54 Casanova. "Foustat," plan 1.
55 Benjamin of Tudela, vol. 1, p. 149; Ibn Jubayr. *Travels*, p. 46.
56 *H.P.E.C.*, vol. 4, part 1, p. 68.
57 Ibid., part 2, pp. 279–80.
58 Ibid., p. 280.
59 Ibn Sa'id, p. 27.
60 Ibid.
61 Benjamin of Tudela, vol. 1, p. 149.
62 Ibn Jubayr. *Travels*, p. 36.
63 Ibn Duqmaq, vol. 4, pp. 40, 93; al-Maqrizi. *al-Mawa'iz*, vol. 2, p. 364; Casanova. "Foustat," pp. 96–102; Labib, p. 640.

64   al-Maqrizi. *al-Mawa'iz,* vol. 2, p. 364; Ibn Duqmaq, vol. 4, pp. 80, 93; Casanova. "Foustat," pp. 7–10, 96–97.
65   Ibn Duqmaq, vol. 4, pp. 37–40.
66   Ibid., pp. 38, 98; Raymond and Wiet, p. 111, footnote 6; al-Maqrizi. *al-Mawa'iz,* vol. 2, p. 364; Casanova. "Foustat," pp. 132–34.
67   Ibn Sa'id, p. 27.
68   Ibn Duqmaq, vol. 4, p. 93; al-Maqrizi. *al-Mawa'iz,* vol. 2, p. 364; Casanova. "Foustat," pp. 96–97.
69   al-Maqrizi. *al-Mawa'iz,* vol. 2, p. 365; Casanova. "Foustat," pp. 212–13.
70   Raymond and Wiet, p. 16.
71   al-Maqrizi. *al-Mawa'iz,* vol. 2, p. 93.
72   Raymond and Wiet, p. 16.
73   al-Maqrizi. *al-Mawa'iz,* vol. 1, p. 483; Casanova. "Foustat," pp. 103–104, 282; Ibn Muyassar, pp. 76–77; *H.P.E.C.,* vol. 4, part 1, p. 68.
74   Ibn Muyassar, pp. 126–27, footnote 423.
75   al-Maqrizi. *al-Mawa'iz,* vol. 1, pp. 450–51.
76   Casanova. "Foustat," pp. 219–22.
77   Ibn Duqmaq, vol. 4, p. 12; al-Maqrizi. *al-Mawa'iz,* vol. 2, pp. 78–79.
78   al-Maqrizi. *al-Mawa'iz,* vol. 2, p. 79.
79   Ibid.
80   Casanova. "Foustat," p. 220.
81   *H.P.E.C.,* vol. 3, part 2, pp. 166–67.
82   Ibid., vol. 4, part 1, p. 68.
83   Ibid.
84   Casanova. "Foustat," pp. 92–94, 222–24.
85   Lane–Poole, p. 48.
86   Benjamin of Tudela, p. 150.
87   Casanova. "Foustat," p. 93.
88   Ibid., pp. 221, 223–24; al-Maqrizi. *al-Mawa'iz,* vol. 1, p. 476.
89   al-Maqrizi. *al-Mawa'iz,* vol. 1, pp. 104–105; Casanova. "Foustat," p. 224.
90   al-Maqrizi. *al-Mawa'iz,* vol. 1, p. 476.
91   Casanova. "Foustat," p. 224.
92   Ehrenkreutz, pp. 101–102.
93   al-Maqrizi. *al-Mawa'iz,* vol. 1, pp. 104–105.
94   Ibid.
95   Casanova. "Foustat," pp. 82–85.
96   Ibn Duqmaq, vol. 4, p. 96.

Appendix A
Glossary

abra', granaries
'alim, pl. *'ulama'*, religious scholar, member of the religious establishment
bab, door, gate
balad, city
birka, pond
burj, pl. *abraj*, tower
bustan, pl. *basatin*, garden
dar, pl. *dur*, mansion, palace
darb, road, lane, alley
da'wa, invocation
dihliz, pl. *dahaliz*, vestibule, gallery
diwan, pl. *dawawin*, administrative division
faqih, pl. *fuqaha'*, legist, expert on *fiqh*
feddan, 4,200.833 square meters
fiqh, jurisprudence
fisqiya, fountain
funduq, pl. *fanadiq*, caravanserai, inn
hammam, pl. *hammamat*, bath
hara, pl. *harat*, quarter (of city)
hawd, trough, cistern
hikr, pl. *ahkar*, monopolized land
hubs, religious endowment
'imara, building
iqta', assignment of land, revenue in exchange for government service,
   usually military
iwan, pl. *iwanat*, recessed audience hall, entered from courtyard
jabal, outcrop, mountain
jami', pl. *jawami'*, congregational (Friday) mosque
jawsaq, pl. *jawasiq*, villa, palace
jazira, island
jihad, religious war
jisr, pl. *jusur*, bridge, levy; also refers to boat bridge crossing Nile at southern
   tip of al-Roda
kawm, pl. *akwam*, rubble mound
khalij, pl. *khuljan*, canal
khan, pl. *khanat*, caravanserai, storage and sleeping facilities for traveling
   merchants
khandaq, trench

khanqah, pl. *khawaniq*, monastery for dervishes
kharab, ruins
kharaj, land tax
khitta, pl. *khitat*, quarter (of city)
khutba, Muslim Friday sermon
madhhab, pl. *madhahib*, one of four major schools of orthodox Islamic law
madrasa, pl. *madaris*, religious school—usually subscribing to one or more
    of the four *madhahib* of orthodox Islam
maks, pl. *mukus*, non-canonical taxes
manzara, pl. *manazir*, pavilion
manzil, pl. *manazil*, rest house
maristan, hospital
mashhad, pl. *mashahid*, shrine, martyrium
masjid, pl. *masajid*, general term for mosque
masbak, pl. *masabik*, foundry
maslak, pl. *masalik*, way, road
midan, pl. *mayadin*, open square, playing field
mihrab, niche in mosque indicating direction of Mecca
minbar, pulpit in mosque
muhtasib, municipal agent, variously in charge of weights, measures, police,
    and general morals
musalla, oratory
na'ib, deputy
qa'a, audience hall
qadi, pl. *qudah*, religious judge
qa'id, military commandant
qal'a, citadel
qantara, pl. *qanatir*, bridge, arch
qasaba, city center, main thoroughfare
qasr, pl. *qusur*, palace
qaysariya, pl. *qayasir*, roofed marketplace
qibla, direction towards Mecca
qit'a, section of land
qubba, dome, tomb
rab', pl. *rubu'*, combination residential and commercial building—probably
    two-story
ribat, pl. *ribatat*, inn for travelers, hospice (for sufis or the poor)
sabil, public fountain
sahib, leader, administrator
saliba, cross, cross street
sana'a, pl. *sana'at*, dockyard, naval arsenal
saqiya, pl. *sawaqi*, water scoops, water wheel
shari', pl. *shawari'*, main street, thoroughfare
sharif, pl. *ashraf*, descendant of the Prophet

shuna, pl. *shuwan*, storehouse, granary

shurta, police

sirdab, basement

suq, pl. *aswaq*, market

suwayqa, pl. *suwayqat*, small market

ustadar, major domo

wakala (*dar al-*), brokerage house, occasionally a customs house

wakil, manager

wali, municipal and/or provincial administrator

waqf, pl. *awqaf*, religious endowment

zahir, pl. *zawahir*, outskirts, periphery (of city)

zariba, enclosure

zawiya, pl. *zawaya*, small mosque or *madrasa*, section of larger mosque used for teaching

ziyada, extension (to a mosque)

zuqaq, pl. *aziqqa*, lane, alley

Appendix B
Fatimid and Ayyubid Rulers of Egypt

Fatimids

297/909	'Ubaydallah al-Mahdi
322/934	al-Qa'im
334/946	al-Mansur
341/953	al-Mu'izz
365/975	al-'Aziz
386/996	al-Hakim
411/1021	al-Zahir
427/1036	al-Mustansir
487/1094	al-Musta'li
495/1101	al-Amir
524/1130	interregnum; rule by al-Hafiz as regent but not yet as caliph
525/1131	al-Hafiz
544/1149	al-Zafir
549/1154	al-Fa'iz
555–67/1160–71	al-'Adid

Ayyubids

564/1169	al-Malik al-Nasir I Salah al-Din (Saladin)
589/1193	al-Malik al-'Aziz 'Imad al-Din
595/1198	al-Malik al-Mansur Nasir al-Din
596/1200	al-Malik al-'Adil I Sayf al-Din
615/1218	al-Malik al-Kamil I Nasir al-Din
635/1238	al-Malik al-'Adil II Sayf al-Din
637/1240	al-Malik al-Salih Najm al-Din Ayyub
647/1249	al-Malik al-Mu'azzam Turan-Shah
648–50/1250–52	al-Malik al-Ashraf II Muzaffar al-Din

Source: Bosworth, C.E. *The Islamic Dynasties*, Edinburgh: 1967, pp. 46, 59.

Appendix C
List of Numbered Sites

Map 1

1. Hammam Ibn Abi Damm
2. Hammam al-Dari
3. Hammam Ibn Qarqa
4. Hammam al-Sultan
5. Hammam al-Juyushi
6. Hammam al-Sabat
7. Hammam Tatar
8. Hammam al-Kuwayk
9. Hammam Khushayba
10. Hammam al-Rasasi
11. Hammam al-Qadi
12. Hammam Tughrik (A)
13. Hammam Tughrik (B)
14. Hammam 'Ujayna
15. Hammam al-Fadil
16. Hammam al-Sufiya
17. Hammam Kurji
18. Hammam Lu'lu'
19. Hammam Qaffasin
20. Hammam al-Juwayni
21. Hammam Ibn 'Abbud
22. Hammam al-Sayyida al-'Amma (A)
23. Hammam al-Sayyida al-'Amma (B)
24. Hammam al-Sultan
25. Hammam Ibn 'Alkan
26. al-Madrasa al-Qutbiya
27. Jami' al-Mu'ayyad Shaykh
28. Mashhad al-Husayn
29. al-Madrasa al-Suyufiya
30. al-Madrasa al-'Ashuriya
31. al-Madrasa al-Fadiliya
32. al-Madrasa al-Sahibiya
33. al-Madrasa al-Uzkushiya
34. al-Madrasa al-Sayfiya
35. al-Madrasa al-Ghaznawiya
36. al-Madrasa al-Masruriya
37. al-Madrasa al-Sharifiya

38. Dar al Hadith of al-Malik al-Kamil
39. al-Madrasa al-Sirmiya
40. al-Madrasa al-Fakhriya
41. al-Madrasa al-Salihiya
42. al-Madrasa al-Qutbiya
43. Jami' al-Azhar
44. Jami' al-Hakim
45. *Masjid* of Fakhr al-Din ibn Qizil
46. al-Khanqah al-Salahiya
47. *Ribat* of Safi al-Din ibn Shukr
48. Suq al-Shawwaiyin
49. Suwayqat al-Sahib
50. Suq al-Shamma'in
51. Suq Bab al-Zuhuma
52. Suq al-Muhayriyin
53. Suq al-Bunduqaniyin
54. Suq Harat Barjawan
55. Suq Bab al-Futuh
56. Suq al-Silah
57. Suwayqat Amir al-Juyush
58. Suq al-Mahamiziyin
59. Suq al-Sharabishiyin
60. Suq Bayn al-Qasrayn
61. Suwayqat al-Balashun
62. Suq al-Jamalun al-Saghir
63. Suwayqat al-Mas'udi
64. al-Sagha
65. Farriers
66. Qaysariyat Ibn Quraysh
67. Qaysariyat Ibn Abi Usama
68. Qaysariyat Ibn Yahya
69. *Qaysariya* (unnamed)
70. Qaysariyat Ibn al-Sharb
71. Qaysariyat Ibn al-Fadil
72. Qaysariyat Ibn Jaharkas
73. Qaysariyat Ibn al-Fa'izi
74. Khan Mankuwirish
75. Khan Sabil
76. Khan Masrur (A)
77. Khan Masrur (B)
78. Madrasat al-Ghuri
79. *Rab'* of al-Malik al-Kamil
80. Dar al-Wizara
81. Khizanat al-Bunud

82. Habs al-Ma'una
83. Khizanat Shama'il
84. Qasr al-Hijaziya
85. Qasr Awlad al-Shaykh
86. *Dar* of al-Qadi al-Fadil

Map 2

87. Mosque of al-Salih Tala'i'
88. Qantarat Bab al-Kharq
89. Qantarat al-Muski
90. Hawd Ibn Hanas

Map 3

91. Dar al-Mulk
92. Dar al-Tamr
93. Granaries at Fam al-Khalij
94. *Shuwan*
95. Rab' al-'Adil
96. Funduq al-Karim (smaller)
97. Funduq al-Karim (larger)
98. Qaysariyat al-Salih
99. Qaysariyat Ibn al-Arsufi (larger)
100. Qaysariyat Ibn al-Arsufi (smaller)
101. al-Madrasa al-Taqawiya
102. Funduq al-Nakhla
103. Tomb of Fakhr al-Farisi
104. Bab Misr
105. Hammam al-Ka'ki
106. Hammam al-Sayyida
107. *Hammam* at al-Mamsusa
108. Madrasat Ibn al-Arsufi
109. Madrasat al-'Adil
110. Madrasat Ibn Rashiq
111. Jami' al-Miqyas
112. Tomb of Ibn Tha'lib
113. Tomb of the Abbasid Caliphs
114. Tomb of Shajarat al-Durr

Bibliography

'Abd al-Latif al-Baghdadi. *Relation de l'Egypte*. DeSacy transl. Paris: 1810.

Abu Salih al-Armani. *The Churches and Monasteries of Egypt*. Evetts and Butler ed. Oxford: 1895.

Abu Shamah. *Kitab al-rawdatayn*. Vol. 1. Cairo: 1871.

Bahgat, Aly Bey and Albert Gabriel. *Fouilles d'al-Foustât*. Paris: 1921. *Album de photographies*. Cairo: 1928.

Benjamin of Tudela. *The Itinerary of Benjamin of Tudela*. Asher transl. 2 vols. London: 1840. Adler edition, London: 1907

Berchem, Max van. "Matériaux pour un Corpus Inscriptionem Arabicarum, part 1: Egypte." *Mémoires de la Mission Archéologique Française au Caire*. Vol. 19.

Cahen, Claude. "Ayyubids" in *The Encylopaedia of Islam*. 2d ed. Vol. 1. Leiden: 1960.

Casanova, Paul. "Les derniers Fatimides." *Mémoires de la Mission Archéologique Française au Caire*. Vol. 6, fasc. 3.

_____. "Essai de reconstitution topographique de la ville d'al-Foustat ou Misr." *Mémoires de la Mission Archéologique Française au Caire*. Vol. 35, fasc. 1–3. Cairo: 1913–1919.

_____. "Histoire et description de la citadelle du Caire." *Mémoires de la Mission Archéologique Française au Caire*. Vol. 6, fasc. 4–5. Cairo: 1894–1897.

Clerget, Marcel. *Le Caire* (2 vols.). Cairo: 1934.

Creswell, K. A. C. *The Muslim Architecture of Egypt*. Vol. 1. Oxford: 1952; Vol. 2. Oxford: 1959.

Description de l'Egypte. Paris: 1820–1830.

Ehrenkreutz, Andrew S. *Saladin*. Albany: 1972.

History of the Patriarchs of the Egyptian Church. Vol. 3, parts 2–3; vol. 4, parts 1–2. Cairo: 1970–1974.

Humphreys, R. Stephen. *From Saladin to the Mongols: the Ayyubids of Damascus, 1193–1260*. Albany: 1977.

Ibn Duqmaq. *Al-Intisar*. Vols. 4–5. Cairo: 1893.

Ibn Hawqal, Abu al-Qasim. *Configuration de la terre*. Kramers and Wiet transl. 2 vols. Paris: 1964.

Ibn Jubayr. *Rihlat Ibn Jubayr*. Beirut: 1964.

_____. *The Travels of Ibn Jubayr*. Broadhurst transl. London: 1952.

_____. *Voyages.* Gaudefroy-Demombynes transl. (4 vols.). Paris: 1949.

Ibn Khallikan, Shams al-Din. *Ibn Khallikan's Biographical Dictionary.* De Slane transl. (4 vols.). Paris and London: 1843–1871.

Ibn Muyassar. *Al-Muntaqa min Akhbar Misr.* Cairo: 1981.

Ibn Sa'id al-Maghribi, 'Ali ibn Musa. *Nujum al-zahira fi hula hadrat al-Qahira.* Nassar ed. Cairo: 1970.

Ibn Wasil. *Mufarrij al-kurub.* Shayyal ed. (5 vols.). Cairo: 1953–1977.

al-Idrisi, Muhammad. *Geographie.* Jaubert transl. Paris: 1836–1840.

Kubiak, Wladislaw. "The Burning of Misr al-Fustat in 1168. A Reconsideration of Historical Evidence." *Africana Bulletin.* 25 (1976): 51–64.

Labib, Subhi Y. "Karimi" in *The Encyclopaedia of Islam.* 2d ed. Vol. 4. Leiden: 1978.

Lapidus, Ira. "Ayyubid Religious Policy and the Development of the Schools of Law in Cairo." *Colloque internationale sur l'histoire du Caire.* Cairo. 27 March–5 April, 1969. Cairo: 1972. 272–86.

Lane–Poole, Stanley. *The Story of Cairo.* London: 1924.

Laoust, Henri. "Le Hanbalisme sous le califat de Baghdad." *Revue des études Islamiques.* (1959): 67–128.

al-Maqrizi, Ahmad ibn 'Ali. *Kitab al-mawa'iz wa-al-i'tibar (Khitat).* 2 vols. Cairo: 1853.

_____. *Kitab al-suluk.* Ziyadah ed. 2 vols. Cairo: 1934–42. Also Blochet transl. *Revue de l'Orient Latin* 8 (1900–1901): 165–212, 501–553; 9 (1902): 6–163, 466–530; 10 (1903–1904): 248–371;11 (1905–1908): 195–239.

_____. *Ittiaz al-hunafa'.* 3 vols. Cairo: 1947

Massignon, Louis. "La cité des morts au Caire." *Bulletin de l'Institut Français de l'Archéologie Orientale* 57 (1958): 25–79.

al-Mawardi. *Les statuts gouvernementaux.* Fagnan transl. Algiers: 1915.

al-Muqaddasi, Muhammad. *Ahsan al-taqasim.* De Goeje ed. Leiden: 1906.

Nasir-i Khusraw. *Sefer Nameh.* Schefer transl. Paris: 1881.

Pederson, J. "Masdjid" in *The Encyclopaedia of Islam.* 1st ed. vol. 3 (1936): 315–89.

al-Qalqashandi, Abu al-'Abbas Ahmad ibn 'Ali. *Subh al-a'sha.* Cairo: 1964.

Ravaisse, Paul. "Essai sur l'histoire et sur la topographie du Caire d'après Makrizi." *Mémoires de la Mission Archéologique Française au Caire,* vol.1, fasc. 3. 1881–1884.

Raymond, André. "La localisation des bains publics au Caire au quinzième siècle d'après les Ḥitat de Maqrizi." *Bulletin d'études Orientales* 30 (1978): 347–60.

_____. "Les porteurs d'eau." *Bulletin de l'Institut Français d'Archéologie Orientale* 57 (1958): 183–202.

Raymond, André and Gaston Wiet. *Les marchés du Caire.* Cairo: 1979.

Répertoire chronologique d'épigraphie Arabe. 16 vols. 1932–64.

Salmon, Georges. "Etudes sur la topographie du Caire."*Mémoires de l'Institut Français d'Archéologie Orientale* 7 (1902): 1–123.

Scanlon, George T. "Fustat Expedition: Preliminary Report 1964." *Journal of the American Research Center in Egypt* 4 (1965): 9ff.

_____. "Fustat Expeditions: Preliminary Report 1965." Part 1. *Journal of the American Research Center in Egypt* 5 (1966): 83–112. Part 2. *Journal of the American Research Center in Egypt* 6 (1967): 65–86.

Survey of Egypt. *Map of Cairo Showing Mohammadan Monuments.* 2 sheets. Cairo: 1949.

al-Suyuti, Jalal al-Din. *Husn al-muhadara.* 2 vols. 1967–1968.

Yaqut al-Rumi. *Jacut's Geographisches Woerterbuch.* Wustenfeld ed. 6 vols. Leipzig: 1866–1873.

Index